An
Anthology
Of Hope

Compiled by
CAMPBELL R. STEVEN

Warmest wishes

Campbell Steven

Grateful thanks are due to The John Jamieson Munro Charitable Trust and its administrators, also to The Drummond Trust, 3 Pitt Terrace, Stirling, for most generous help towards the publication of this book.

Published by Jamieson & Munro

British Library Cataloguing in Publication Data
Steven, Campbell, 1911 —
An Anthology of Hope,
Christian Life, Devotional Works No. 242

Printed by Sunprint, 38 Tay Street, Perth and
40 Craigs, Stirling. October, 1988.

3rd Reprint, September, 1993

To remember

HELEN MORRISON STEVEN

1916-1962

For John

Contents

			Page
Foreword			vii
Week	1.	Remembering	1
	2.	Desolation	8
	3.	The Furnace of Affliction	15
	4.	The Troubles of Others	22
	5.	Suffering	29
	6.	Darkness and Light	36
	7.	In All Things Thee to See	43
	8.	Hope in Dark Days	50
	9.	Resurrection	57
	10.	Consolation	64
	11.	The Place of Understanding	71
	12.	Plain Speaking	78
	13.	Indifference	85
	14.	Seeking and Finding	92
	15.	Advent	99
	16.	Christmas	106
	17.	Jesus	113
	18.	I Believe	120
	19.	Choice	127
	20.	Commitment (1)	134
	21.	Commitment (2)	141
	22.	Entering In	148
	23.	Taken Over	155
	24.	Holy Spirit	162
	25.	Love	169
	26.	Joy	176

Contents

			Page
Week 27.	Peace and Quiet		183
28.	Goodness		190
29.	Faith		197
30.	Humility		204
31.	Holy Week		211
32.	Easter		218
33.	Presence of Christ		225
34.	Quiet Time		232
35.	The Bible		239
36.	Prayer		246
37.	Prayers		253
38.	Healing		260
39.	Thanks		267
40.	Trust		274
41.	Strength for the Task		281
42.	Witnessing		288
43.	In His Service		295
44.	Courage		302
45.	Who Is My Neighbour?		309
46.	Action		316
47.	Giving		323
48.	Discipleship		330
49.	Self-giving		337
50.	Dedication		344
51.	Communion		351
52.	Blessing		358
Acknowledgements			365

Foreword

When a man loses a very dear wife, companion of many years of happiness, there seems to be only darkness. Ahead, with apparent finality, stretches nothing but bleak emptiness. Faith itself, imagined secure in its fastness, can come under bitter, demoralising attack.

Yet life goes on: stumblingly, uncertainly at first; then gradually shaped to new patterns as the ache slowly dulls. And then, unaccountably, in God's rich providence, another door can open, and light and happiness come flooding in once again.

This collection of fragments — many familiar, many obscure — was started at such a time of personal sadness. To begin with it was altogether haphazard and slow-growing, without underlying purpose. Gradually, however, as piece was added to piece, it came to suggest more and more emphatically a Christian anthology, to span, if possible, a full year. Carefully worked at, strictly selective, it could surely be made in due time into a memorial that would be truly fitting.

The years passed and I came to know the undeserved blessing of a second, wonderfully happy marriage. Meaning was given to the future; in fuller measure to memories of the past. Work on the anthology was inspired afresh; I was given invaluable encouragement when often enough there had seemed to be little light at the end of a very long tunnel. As it neared completion, the book had become a pilgrimage in faith, beginning in desolation and questioning, and leading up to a sure climax of certainty. To some extent it was personal, though inevitably there were numerous deviations as new quotations fused with new thoughts and were found suitable corners in the whole.

Now that it is indeed complete, all that is asked of the reader is to persevere beyond what may seem to be unpromising beginnings, and further on, to "think on these things" in some measure at least. How often we looked forward to this time when the book would be available for giving to friends enduring their own dark days of loneliness or discouragement! Hopefully, we believed, there would be many who might find in it new strength at those times when the lamp of faith was burning low.

One week in the anthology's progression might well have been entitled "Miracles". In it would have been included the story of how the book itself came eventually to be produced: a most generous grant from the Drummond Trust covering the high cost of the very many copyright permissions; a second miracle following, when the whole cost of the initial print run was promised through the remarkable, still hardly believable, generosity of the John Jamieson Munro Trust. It is impossible to thank adequately the trustees of these two bodies, who made the whole production possible when all was still doubt surrounding financial ways and means.

Foreword

There have been many helpers along the way, none more generous of time and sound advice in the very early days than the late Mr Jack Knox, of John Smith, Glasgow booksellers. Invaluable encouragement came too from Rev. John Birkbeck, of the erstwhile Drummond Press, Stirling, and later from Rev. Peter Bisset, warden of St. Ninian's Centre, Crieff. Members of the various house fellowships we have belonged to often heard extracts from the anthology read to them; as a result, a really helpful and immensely welcome interest was taken in the book's slow progress towards publication, never more enthusiastically than by my daughter Helen and our good friends Jim and Ann Shipway and Ken and Hilda Steel. In the all-important final stages of production, Mr Bill Lockhart, of Sun-Print, Perth, did more in bringing the whole thing to fruition than ever his kindly modesty would admit, and I am deeply grateful to him.

Finally, my sincere thanks to our son Kenneth for allowing me to include three of his poems and — more than I can say — to my wife Mais for sound advice, unfailing encouragement and always deep understanding as the months and years have gone by.

Campbell R. Steven
Aberfeldy, 1988

Remembering

Sunday

I have seen dawn and sunset on moors and windy hills
Coming in solemn beauty like slow old tunes of Spain:
I have seen the lady April bringing the daffodils,
Bringing the springing grass and the soft warm April rain.

I have heard the song of the blossoms and the old chant of the sea,
And seen strange lands from under the arched white sails of ships;
But the loveliest things of beauty God ever has showed to me,
Are her voice, and her hair, and eyes, and the dear red curve of
her lips.

John Masefield (1878-1967)

Remembering

Monday

Stepping down the hill with her fair companions,
Arm in arm, all against the raying West,
Boldly she sings, to the merry tune she marches,
Brave in her shape, and sweeter unpossessed.
Sweeter, for she is what my heart first awaking
Whispered the world was; morning light is she.
Love that so desires would fain keep her changeless;
Fain would fling the net, and fain have her free.

Hither she comes; she comes to me; she lingers,
Deepens her brown eyebrows, while in new surprise
High rise the lashes in wonder of a stranger;
Yet am I the light and living of her eyes.
Something friends have told her fills her heart to brimming,
Nets her in her blushes, and wounds her, and tames.
Sure of her haven, O like a dove alighting,
Arms up, she dropped: our souls were in our names.

George Meredith (1828-1909)

Remembering

The earth and the sea were a shadow, but over me opened
Heaven into uttermost heaven, and height into height
Boundless
With stars, with stars, with stars.

Laurence Binyon (1869-1943)

The skies were mine, and so were the sun and moon and stars, and all the World was mine; and I the only spectator and enjoyer of it.

Thomas Traherne (1637-1674)

Let purity of winds, ice-cold of river
Possess me,
Cool the ache that burns, yet burning,
Comes to no end.

Show me the hills, smoke blue and sun-tipped silver,
If only
Their far snows might claim the yearning,
Claim wearied thought.

Anon

Wednesday

Friendship

Oh, the comfort,
The inexpressible comfort,
Of feeling safe with a person;
Having neither to weigh thoughts nor measure words,
But pour them all out, just as they are —
Chaff and grain together,
Knowing that a faithful hand
Will take and sift them,
Keep what is worth keeping,
And then with the breath of kindness
Blow the rest away.

George Eliot (1819-1880)

Sun, and sky, and breeze, and solitary walks, and summer holidays, and the greenness of fields, and the delicious juices of meats and fishes, and society, and the cheerful glass, and candle-light, and fireside conversations, and innocent vanities, and jests, and irony itself — do these things go out with life?

Charles Lamb (1775-1834)

Remembering

If thou wilt ease thine heart
Of love and all its smart,
Then sleep, dear, sleep;
And not a sorrow
Hang any tear on your eyelashes;
Lie still and deep,
Sad soul, until the sea-wave washes
The rim o' the sun to-morrow,
In eastern sky.

But wilt thou cure thine heart
Of love and all its smart,
Then die, dear, die;
'Tis deeper, sweeter,
Than on a rose-bank to lie dreaming
With folded eye;
And there alone, amid the beaming
Of Love's stars, thou'lt meet her
In eastern sky.

Thomas Lovell Beddoes (1803-1849)

Remembering

Friday

If thou must love me, let it be for nought
Except for love's sake only. Do not say,
"I love her for her smile — her look — her way
Of speaking gently — for a trick of thought
That falls in well with mine, and certes brought
A sense of pleasant ease on such a day" —
For these things in themselves, Beloved, may
Be changed, or change for thee — and love, so wrought,
May be unwrought so. Neither love me for
Thine own dear pity's wiping my cheeks dry —
A creature might forget to weep, who bore
Thy comfort long, and lose thy love thereby!
But love me for love's sake, that evermore
Thou may'st love on, through love's eternity.

Elizabeth Barrett Browning (1806-1861)

Remembering

Remember me when I am gone away,
Gone far away into the silent land;
When you can no more hold me by the hand,
Nor I half turn to go, yet turning stay.
Remember me when no more day by day
You tell me of our future that you plann'd:
Only remember me; you understand
It will be late to counsel then or pray.
Yet if you should forget me for a while
And afterwards remember, do not grieve:
For if the darkness and corruption leave
A vestige of the thoughts that once I had,
Better by far you should forget and smile
Than that you should remember and be sad.

Christina Georgina Rossetti (1830-1894)

Desolation

Sunday

It darkens. I have lost the ford.
There is a change on all things made.
The rocks have evil faces, Lord,
And I am awfully afraid.

Hilaire Belloc (1870-1953)

I am alone.
You have taken me far, Lord; trusting, I followed you, and you
walked at my side,
And now, at night, in the middle of the desert, suddenly you have
disappeared.
I call, and you do not answer.
I search, and I do not find you . . .
Lord, it is dark.
Lord, are you here in my darkness?
Where are you, Lord?
Do you love me still?
Or have I wearied you?
Lord, answer,
Answer!

Michel Quoist

Desolation

. . . this soul hath been
Alone on a wide, wide sea:
So lonely 'twas, that God Himself
Scarce seemèd there to be.

Samuel Taylor Coleridge (1772-1834)

"When I'm alone" — the words tripped off his tongue
As though to be alone were nothing strange.
"When I was young," he said, "when I was young" . . .
I thought of age, and loneliness and change.
I thought how strange we grow when we're alone,
And how unlike the selves that meet and talk,
And blow the candle out, and say goodnight.
Alone . . . The word is life endured and known.
It is the stillness where our spirits walk
And all but inmost faith is overthrown.

Siegfried Sassoon (1886-1933)

Desolation

Tuesday

Desolate

From the sad eaves the drip-drop of the rain!
The water washing at the latchel door;
A slow step plashing by upon the moor;
A single bleat far from the famished fold;
The clicking of an embered hearth and cold;
The rainy Robin tic-tac at the pane.

"So as it is with thee
Is it with me,
So as it is and it used not to be,
With thee used not to be,
Nor me."
So singeth Robin on the willow tree,
The rainy Robin tic-tac at the pane.

Here in this breast all day
The fire is dim and low
Within I care not to stay,
Without I care not to go.

A sadness ever sings
Of unforgotten things,
And the bird of love is patting at the pane;
But the wintry water deepens at the door,
And a step is plashing by upon the moor
Into the dark upon the darkening moor,
And alas, alas, the drip-drop of the rain!

Sydney Dobell (1824-1874)

Desolation

Give sorrow words: the grief that does not speak
Whispers the o'er-fraught heart and bids it break.

William Shakespeare (1564-1616)

'O preacher, holy man, hear my heart weeping;
I long to stand and shout my protests:
Where is your power? and where is your message?
Where is the gospel of mercy and love?
Your words are nothingness! nothingness! nothingness!
We who have come to listen are betrayed.

Servant of God, I am bitter and desolate.
What do I care for perfection of phrase?
Cursed be your humour, your poise, your diction.
See how my soul turns to ashes within me.
You who have vowed to declare your Redeemer.
Give me the words that would save.'

Margaret Chaplin Anderson

Desolation

Thursday

It is useless, useless, said the Philosopher. Life is useless, all useless. You spend your life working, labouring, and what do you have to show for it? Generations come and generations go, but the world stays just the same. The sun still rises, and it still goes down, going wearily back to where it must start all over again. The wind blows south, the wind blows north — round and round and back again. Every river flows into the sea, but the sea is not yet full. The water returns to where the rivers began, and starts all over again. Everything leads to weariness — a weariness too great for words. Our eyes can never see enough to be satisfied; our ears can never hear enough. What has happened before will happen again. What has been done before will be done again. There is nothing new in the whole world. "Look," they say, "here is something new!" But no, it has all happened before, long before we were born. No one remembers what has happened in the past, and no one in days to come will remember what happens between now and then.

Ecclesiastes. I. 2-11
(Good News Bible — Today's English Version)

Desolation

From 'Markings' by Dag Hammarskjöld:
The road,
You shall follow it.
The fun,
You shall forget it.
The cup,
You shall empty it.
The pain,
You shall conceal it.
The truth,
You shall be told it.
The end,
You shall endure it.

Tired
And lonely,
So tired
The heart aches.
Meltwater trickles
Down the rocks,
The fingers are numb,
The knees tremble.
It is now,
Now, that you must not give in.
On the path of the others
Are resting places,
Places in the sun
Where they can meet.
But this
Is your path,
And it is now,
Now, that you must not fail.
Weep
If you can,
Weep,
But do not complain.
The way chose you —
And you must be thankful.

Desolation

Saturday

Dark and cold we may be, but this
Is no winter now. The frozen misery
Of centuries breaks, cracks, begins to move,
The thunder is the thunder of the floes,
The thaw, the flood, the upstart Spring.
Thank God our time is now when wrong
Comes up to face us everywhere,
Never to leave us till we take
The longest stride of soul men ever took.
Affairs are now soul size.
The enterprise
Is exploration into God.

Christopher Fry

The cry of man's anguish went up to God,
Lord, take away pain!
The shadow that darkens the world Thou hast made,
The close-coiling chain
That strangles the heart, the burden that weighs
On the wings that would soar.
Lord, take away pain from the world Thou hast made,
That it love Thee more!

Then answered the Lord to the cry of His world:
Shall I take away pain,
And with it the power of the soul to endure,
Made strong by the strain?
Shall I take away pity, that knits heart to heart,
And sacrifice high?
Will you lose all your heroes, that lift from the fire
White brows to the sky?
Shall I take away love that redeems with a price,
And smiles at the loss?
Can ye spare from your lives, that would climb unto mine,
The Christ on His Cross?

C. L. Drawbridge

14

The Furnace of Affliction

Behold, I have refined thee, but not with silver;
I have chosen thee in the furnace of affliction.

Isaiah. XLVIII. 10

"O God, my words are cold:
The frosted frond of fern or feathery palm
Wrought on the whitened pane —
They are as near to fire as these my words;
Oh that they were as flames!" Thus did I cry,
And thus God answered me: "Thou shalt have words,
But at this cost, that thou must first be burnt,
Burnt by red embers from a secret fire,
Scorched by fierce heats and withering winds that sweep
Through all thy being, carrying thee afar
From old delights. Doth not the ardent fire
Consume the mountain's heart before the flow
Of fervent lava? Wouldst thou easefully,
As from cool, pleasant fountains, flow in fire?
Say, can thy heart endure or can thy hands be strong
In the day that I shall deal with thee?

"For first the iron must enter thine own soul,
And wound and brand it, scarring awful lines
Indelibly upon it, and a hand
Resistless in a tender terribleness
Must throughly purge it, fashioning its pain
To power that leaps in fire.
Not otherwise, and by no lighter touch,
Are fire-words wrought."

Amy Carmichael of Dohnavur (1867-1951)

15

The Furnace of Affliction

Monday

Cancer Ward

"Behold us, conscripts in a nameless army,
Serving a sentence that has no repeal,
Held in the bondage of our flesh turned traitor —
Dumb mouths and shadowed eyes that cry 'unclean'.
We have not sinned more than the rest of you
Who walk untouched among us and in fear
To soil your hands with our alive corruption,
Whom no Christ touches to make whole again,
For whom no God shows pity; and no man
Dares lay our freedom at his conscience' door."

"Oh poor brave withered army, fighting still
Against your peace for life that is no life;
We strive to serve you more or less with patience,
Our small compassion blunted by long habit,
Try to forgive us the humiliations
That day by day we must inflict on you;
And understand that though we see but darkly
We still salute in you the uncorrupted
Spirit that shines beyond the dissolution:
In every bed a lantern in the shambles."

Mary Dickinson
('Nursing Mirror')

The Furnace of Affliction

He cannot heal who has not suffered much,
For only sorrow, sorrow understands.
They will not come for healing at our touch
Who have not seen the scars upon our hands.

Edwin McNeill Poteat

Ask any minister of wide and deep and varied experience of dealing with human nature who are the people who have made him feel more near to God, and he will unhesitatingly reply that they were, almost without exception, people who had suffered. They were people who had so learned to handle suffering that it brought them nearer to God. More than that, all of them, whatever the nature of their suffering, would bear unanimous witness to this, that they learned the secret from One whom Job never knew, in whom God made His Own still more wonderful response than that given to Job. He spoke this time, not out of the whirlwind, but with the still, small voice of a new-born child. He took the problem of suffering, raised it to the nth power, outlined it against the darkness of human sin and despair on a Cross to which He was nailed, and taught us to see there, as nowhere else in the Universe, that God still knows what He is doing, even when life seems one hideous muddle of utter wrong and injustice, and that even when God gives every evidence of being callously unheeding, or gratuitously cruel, the wonderful truth is still that God is Love.

R. Leonard Small

The Furnace of Affliction

Wednesday

Why in the world would it possibly be God's will to deny a Christian's request for healing? In some ways, this whole book is about that very thing. The pages of Scripture teem with good things that can come from suffering. Pain and discomfort get our minds off the temporary things of this world and force us to think about God. They drive us to pull His Word off the shelf far more than usual and to pay more attention when we do. Trials knock us off our proud pedestals and get us relying on God. Then we learn to know God better, for when we have to depend on someone to get us through each hour, we really get to know them. . . . Sometimes sickness serves as God's chastiser to wake us from our sin. This proves to us that He loves us, for every good father disciplines his children. Sometimes God uses suffering to help us relate to others who are suffering. And the list could go on. If nothing else, the fact that while Jesus was on earth God matured Him through suffering should tell us something. It should make us ask ourselves the question, "Should I expect anything less?"

I sometimes shudder to think where I would be today if I had not broken my neck. I couldn't see at first why God would possibly allow it, but I sure do now. He has gotten so much more glory through my paralysis than through my health! And believe me, you'll never know how rich that makes me feel. If God chooses to heal you in answer to your prayers, that's great. Thank Him for it. But if He chooses not to, thank Him anyway. You can be sure He has His reasons.

Do you remember the book that fell off my desk several chapters ago? Well, I still can't pick it up. It sure would be nice to have the use of my hands again so I could reach it. But the wish is fading. For my paralysis has drawn me close to God and given a spiritual healing which I wouldn't trade for a hundred active years on my feet.

Joni Eareckson

The Furnace of Affliction

A discussion on 'The Problem of Pain' between Malcolm Muggeridge and Archbishop Anthony Bloom of the Russian Orthodox Church.

Bloom: . . . If you give more thought to it, you come to the conclusion that if good and evil never met, that is, if there was never suffering inflicted on the innocent by evil in general, or by an evil person in particular, there would be two parallel lines, the one of utter damnation, and the other one of salvation. But the law of life as we see it in nature, in human relationships, is that whenever one is evil someone who is innocent will suffer. One has drunk before he drove his car, and this child has been killed. I have been irresponsible before I performed an operation, and I have overlooked something of importance, and so on. This meeting point between the sufferer and the one who inflicts suffering is a point of crucial importance. It is the crossroads, it's also a cross, a real crucifixion at times. And the moment you suffer either great suffering or trivial suffering at the hand of someone and can forgive, you manifest really divine power.

Muggeridge: You could apply that then to collective events. You could say the Nazis burnt up and killed six million Jews, the Stalinists killed three million peasants, and so on, and the fact of this, our wickedness resulting in this suffering, can purge the wickedness? Have I got that right?

Bloom: Yes, I think I can give you an example, taken from a concentration camp, a prayer left on a sheet of wrapping paper, which in substance says: 'O Lord remember not only the men of goodwill but also the men of ill will. But do not remember all the suffering they have inflicted on us, remember the fruits we have gathered, thanks to this suffering — our comradeship, our loyalty, our humility, the courage, the generosity, the greatness of heart which has grown out of this, and when they come to judgement, let all the fruits which we have borne be their forgiveness.'

Muggeridge: Therefore suffering is not a horrible thing necessarily? But a necessary thing, and sometimes an ennobling and elevating thing — is that right?

Bloom: I think it is ennobling and I think it is creative, but it may be nonsense if you do not see meaning or put meaning into it. The mere fact of suffering does not make you a martyr.

Malcolm Muggeridge

The Furnace of Affliction

Friday

I walked a mile with pleasure,
She chatted all the way,
But I am none the wiser
For all she had to say.

I walked a mile with sorrow
And ne'er a word said she,
But, oh, the things I learned from her,
When sorrow walked with me.

Robert B. Hamilton

Great truths are greatly won. Not found by chance,
Nor wafted on the breath of summer dream,
But grasped in the great struggle of the soul,
Hard buffeting with adverse wind and stream.

Grasped in the day of conflict, fear and grief,
When the strong hand of God, put forth in might,
Ploughs up the subsoil of the stagnant heart,
And brings the imprisoned truth-seed to the light.

Wrung from the troubled spirit in hard hours
Of weakness, solitude, perchance of pain,
Truth springs, like harvest, from the well-ploughed field,
And the soul feels it has not wept in vain.

Horatius Bonar (1808-89)

The Furnace of Affliction

A Factory of Peace

I watched her in the loud and shadowy lanes
Of life; and every face that passed her by
Grew calmly restful, smiling quietly,
As though she gave, for all their griefs and pains,
Largesse of comfort, soft as summer rains,
And balsam tinctured with tranquillity.
Yet in her own eyes dwelt an agony.
'Oh, halcyon soul!' I cried, 'what sorrow reigns
In that calm heart which knows such ways to heal?'
She said — 'Where balms are made for human uses,
Great furnace fires, and wheel on grinding wheel
Must crush and purify the crude herb juices,
And in some hearts the conflict cannot cease;
They are the sick world's factories of peace.'

Mary Webb (1881-1927)

What matters most of all is not what happens to us but how we respond. This alone determines whether temptation and trial erodes our trust or deepens our faith, fills us with self-pity or broadens our sympathy, turns us into cynics or saints.

The Soldier's Armoury
Sunday, August 30th, 1970

The Troubles of Others

Sunday

To the Christian suffering is real, and neighbours are to be loved. The Christian is not an isolated, existential, unrelated observer, but he must be deeply involved with his neighbour and his need. The Bible commands a separation from worldliness, but not from needy men and women in the world.

Many Christians are ignorant of the degree of need. Some statistics from the city of Birmingham indicate that around the average evangelical church there are 2,000 houses, with 10,000 people who could walk to the church within ten or fifteen minutes. You can reckon that there are:

500 households needing a neighbourly hand of friendship;
20 unmarried mothers;
100 elderly, housebound people, living alone;
10 discharged prisoners;
100 deprived children;
10 homeless;
100 broken marriages;
20 families in debt trouble;
100 juvenile delinquents who have been before the courts in the last three years;
80 persons in hospital;
80 alcoholics.

As we have opportunity, let us do good to all men, and especially to those who are of the household of faith (Gal. 6:10).

Michael Griffiths

The Troubles of Others

Lord, I can't sleep; I have got up out of bed to pray.
It is night outside, and the wind blows and the rain falls,
And the lights of the city, signs of the living, pierce the darkness. . . .
They were bothering me when I was trying to sleep.

I know that in one single room thirteen crowded people are breathing on one
   another.
I know a mother who hooks the table and the chairs to the ceiling to make
   room for mattresses.
I know that rats come out to eat the crusts and bite the babies.
I know a father who gets up to stretch oil-cloth above the rain-soaked bed of
   his four children.
I know a mother who stays up all night as there is room for only one bed, and
   the two children are sick.
I know a drunken father who vomits on the child sleeping beside him.
I know a big boy who runs away alone into the night because he can't stand it
   any more.
I know that some men fight for the women as there are three couples in the
   same attic.
I know a wife who avoids her husband as there is no room for another baby at
   home.
I know a child who is quietly dying, soon to join his four little brothers above.
I know . . .
I know hundreds of others — yet I was going to sleep peacefully between my
   clean-white sheets.

I wish I didn't know, Lord. I wish it were not true . . .
I've seen too much, I've listened too much, I've counted too much, and,
   Lord, these ruthless figures have robbed me forever of my innocent
   tranquillity.

So much the better, son . . . ask forgiveness for yourself and for others
   tonight. And tomorrow, fight with all your strength, for it hurts your
   Father to see that once more there is no room for his son at the inn.

Michel Quoist

The Troubles of Others

Tuesday

Loneliness

"Some elderly people in Manchester are so desperately lonely that they join a bus queue for the sake of companionship, not to catch a bus," Mr. Alec Dickson, founder of Voluntary Service Overseas, said at a conference on Saturday in Manchester.

'Glasgow Herald' 28th June, 1965

Miss Paley, aged sixty-seven, lived in a one-room tenement flat. It was a large airless room with dismal orange-brown wallpaper peeling off in huge strips. Two or three mats, ingrained with dirt, covered the floor. There was an old iron bedstead propped up in the middle by two strips of wood and on this was a heap of grey and brown blankets. Miss Paley wore a pair of stockings, extensively patched and tied around her knees, and ramshackle navy-blue skirt and slip. Her skin had the whiteness of someone who rarely went out and she was very shy of her appearance, particularly the open sores on her face. She said she suffered from blood poisoning, but had not seen her doctor since the war. (This was confirmed by the doctor.) She was the only child of parents who had been street traders and who had died when she was young, in the 1880s. 'I was with my aunt until I was nearly forty. She was eighty-five when she died. I had cousins in the street but they were my aunt's children. In the war they got scattered. They all had families to bring up and I haven't met them since the war.' Persistent questioning failed to reveal a single relative with whom she had any contact. She did not go to the cinema, to a club, or to church, and had no radio. She spent Christmas on her own and had never had a holiday away from home. She sometimes made conversation with her neighbours in the street but because of her appearance did not go into their homes or they into hers. She had only one friend, a young woman who 'used to live in the street where I lived', and they visited one another about once a week. At one point she said she went to bed about 8 p.m. and got up between 10 and 11 the next day. I also found she had an hour or two in bed in the afternoons.

Peter Townsend

The Troubles of Others

Always the children . . .

A boy, his ribs stark, his belly swollen, his thin arms brittle as charred wood, sitting by the dead or dying body of his mother in the dry grass of Africa . . . The eyes of a girl with trachoma, weeping into the futile night of blindness . . . Another with tuberculosis, one of millions, her eyes dull from weakness, her mouth too slack to hold its spittle . . . And other millions elsewhere — a shilling booklet will give you all the facts . . . the misery and shadows of a world in want, the slow murder of our brothers and sisters, the unspectacular death of children.

O God! Always the children!

So let's all have another slice or three, Jack, spread it on nice and thick and juicy, and pour us all another drink while you're at it — for there are the snack-bars and cafés and restaurants and tea-shops and food-stores and confectioners and bakers and supermarkets and public houses, and we can go on eating and drinking and laying up treasure to our heart's content, can't we? And if you turn on the television, or put another half-dozen on the record-player and set the switch to automatic play, well, there'll be no need to bother *too* much about the grain which *could* have made bread being made into booze, will there? Nor about the land which could have grown potatoes being given over to tobacco . . . No need to hear the whimpering (funny, how that word keeps cropping up), no need to let the children squatting naked in the gutter outside put you off your food — go on, draw the curtains, that way you don't have to see them at all.

No, there's no sense knocking yourself out over things you can't do all that much about, is there? Not much fun always looking on the black side, is there? You get morbid . . .

So all right, agreed, there's no magnificence when trachoma and tuberculosis dull the eyes; no music where lepers rot; no beauty in smallpox, no escape from such life except in death — and there's the Son of God dying it, *there* all the time, in this haunted landscape of the mind.

Father, forgive us, we know what it is we do.

G. W. Target

The Troubles of Others

Thursday

Drugs

I shall never be the same, as a result of the scene I witnessed in the next few moments. The preparation of the fix had taken some little time. By now each teenager, including Shorty, was pushing and struggling to shoot up first. The sickest was allowed to drill before the others, and Shorty suddenly went into a seizure of shaking and retching and moaning, I suppose so that he could be first. With starving eyes the four youngsters watched one of the boys pour heroin from the little cellophane bag into the cap cooker. Not one grain was wasted.

"Hurry up," they all screamed, low, into his ear.

With shaking hands the boy lit two matches under the cooker and boiled the contents. The other addict took off his belt and applied a tourniquet to Shorty's arm. The other addicts were now getting very agitated. They stood by gritting their teeth and clenching their fists to keep from grabbing the loaded needle from Shorty's hand. Tears were streaming down their cheeks, they were cursing under their breath and biting their lips.

And then, one by one, there was that final puncture that was so exhilarating: needle against extended vein.

I have never felt so close to hell. The kids drifted off into a kind of euphoria. For a long, long time I listened to their foolish gossip and rambling . . . I left the apartment. When I went back to try to help them again, Tammy and Shorty had disappeared. All their gear was gone. Nobody knew where they were. Nor did anybody seem to care.

David Wilkerson

The Troubles of Others

Apartheid

It was Holy Saturday in Sophiatown: the busiest day in the year for any priest who has charge of a parish as lively as that of Christ the King. For, in order that Easter and the Lord's Resurrection shall be the most glorious and triumphant day in the calendar, there is much to be done in preparation. So on this Saturday morning I was not too pleased when there strode into my office — and evidently angry — the young manager of the one and only milk-bar in Sophiatown: an ex-service man who had begun a few months back an experiment — a European in an African township running an American-style soda fountain. "It's Jacob . . ." he began. "Father, I'm damn' well going to do something about this . . . it's a bloody shame . . . Father, you've got to help me."

On Maundy Thursday night at Jeppe station, Jacob Ledwaba had been arrested for being out after the curfew and without his pass. On Saturday morning he came home. He told his wife he had been kicked in the stomach in the cells and that he was in such pain that he couldn't go to work. Would she go and tell the boss and explain? It was this that brought the manager of the milk-bar to my office at the Mission on Holy Saturday morning.

Jacob was taken to hospital and died of a bladder injury, leaving a widow and a month-old baby. We brought a case against the police, and in evidence produced affidavits concerning the nature of the injury from the two doctors who had attended Jacob. We also had the services of an eminent Q.C. The verdict (long after Jacob's body had been laid in the cemetery: long after any fresh medical evidence could possibly come to light) was that he had died of congenital syphilis. The magistrate added a rider to his verdict to the effect that the police had been shamefully misrepresented in this case, and that there was no evidence whatever inculpating them.

So Jacob died, in the first place because he had forgotten to carry his pass. In the second because, Good Friday being a public holiday in South Africa, he had spent twenty-four hours in the police cells in Jeppe . . . It will only be a few years more till the day when Jacob's son, too, must carry a pass. I only hope and pray he will not be so careless as his father was, and forget it one evening when he goes to visit his friends. It can be very costly to forget your pass.

Trevor Huddleston

The Troubles of Others

Saturday

We read in the Gospel of St. Luke "Jesus entered a certain village." I want to take you to a certain village where you, like the Lord Jesus Christ, are confronted with people suffering from leprosy. And this certain village is in the jungle area of North Sumatra, in Indonesia. . . .

It is something I will never forget. I have seen deformity in many, many countries. I have been confronted by thousands of people who suffer from leprosy, but I have never seen so much deformity as in this certain village. Jesus was confronted by ten leprosy sufferers. In this village there were 460 of them. Jesus heard a cry from afar off, "Jesus, Master, have mercy on us."

Not one word was uttered by any of the 460 inmates of this village. I wonder if you have seen people with no life in their faces? I wonder if you have seen something that is expressionless, that conveys nothing to you other than hopelessness? A gaze that is not even looking at you, that seems to go past you? This, and I don't have to exaggerate, was in the faces of all those people. Not one smile, not one word of welcome, nothing.

I walked over to one woman who was blind and had a six weeks old baby in her arms. She had no hands. She couldn't walk, there were no feet. She was the mother of that tiny baby, and as I spoke there was no response. Then I saw, on the perimeter of this ring of sufferers, a young girl. She could not have been more than 17 years of age. I walked over to her. I couldn't see any marks of leprosy until I took her hands and noticed the first signs of nerve involvement in one of them. I looked at her feet, no bandages, and I just turned the left foot over; I won't describe it to you.

As I looked at this young life amongst these people with such deformity, I thought "What hope? What hope for people so far from a hospital, forgotten by society, forgotten by all except One — the Lord Jesus Christ?" "Jesus, Master, have mercy on us!" To whom would that cry come today? Who can answer it?

W. R. McKeown, Secretary for Australia,
the Leprosy Mission.

Suffering

Sunday

Yet man is born unto trouble, as the sparks fly upward.

Job. V.7

Not until the loom is silent,
and the shuttles cease to fly,
Will God unroll the canvas,
and explain the reason why;
How the dark threads are as needful
in the weaver's skilful hand,
As the threads of gold and silver,
in the pattern he has planned.

I never knew, till the sufferings of Christ abounded in me, how near God could come to man; I never knew how rich His mercies could be, how intimate His sympathy, how inspiring His comfort.

James Denney (1856-1917)

"There cannot be a God of love," men say, "because if there was, and he looked upon the world, his heart would break." The Church points to the Cross and says, "It did break."

"It is God who made the world," men say. "It is he who should bear the load." The Church points to the Cross and says, "He did bear it."

William Temple (1881-1944)

29

Suffering

Monday

Love of self is a stolen love.
It was destined for others, they needed it to live, to thrive, and I
have diverted it.
So the love of self creates human suffering,
So the love of men for themselves creates human misery,
All the miseries of men, all the sufferings of men:

The suffering of the boy whose mother has slapped him without
cause, and that of the man whose boss has reprimanded him in
front of the other workers;
The suffering of the ugly girl neglected at a dance, and that of the
woman whose husband doesn't kiss her any more;
The suffering of the child left at home because he's a nuisance,
and that of the grandfather made fun of because he's too old;
The suffering of the worried man who hasn't been able to confide
in any one, and that of the troubled adolescent whose worries
have been ridiculed;
The suffering of the desperate man who jumps into the canal, and
that of the criminal who is going to be executed;
The suffering of the unemployed man who wants to work, and
that of the worker who ruins his health for a ridiculous wage;
The suffering of the father who has to pile his family into a single
room next to an empty house, and that of the mother whose
children are hungry while the remains of someone's party are
thrown into the dustbin;
The suffering of one who dies alone, while his family, in the
adjoining room, wait for his death, drinking coffee.
All sufferings.
All injustices, bitternesses, humiliations, griefs, hates, despairs,
All sufferings are an unappeased hunger,
A hunger for love.
So men have built, slowly, selfishness by selfishness, a disfigured
world that crushes them;
So men on earth spend their time feeding their self-love, while
around them others with outstretched arms die of hunger.
They have squandered love.
I have squandered your Love, Lord.

Michel Quoist

Suffering

I shall always remember a day in early May 1945. All through the war I had felt the burden of its suffering, although at a distance. But on that May morning, with the Victory bells about to join their glad chorus, my mother received a letter from the War Office, terse and business-like, to say that my brother had been killed in action in North-West Europe.

Now I knew something of the cost of war in personal terms. Now I knew personally the pain of sudden bereavement. And now the problem of human suffering became all at once more pointed and more urgent . . .

Beyond doubt there is a great deal of human suffering in the world. As a random example, let me quote you certain items in a recent working day of mine.

In the morning I conducted the funeral service of a young mother. Twenty-five years old, she left three children under school age. Her husband, on Merchant Navy service, had been on a Far-East trip and had not seen his wife for over a year. When news of her sudden and serious illness reached him he flew home at once from Hong Kong — but she died the day before he reached her.

In the afternoon I visited some sick people and I mention three particularly. One was a young woman in a maternity hospital. It was her first baby but it had lived only a few minutes. Another was a woman, with two teenage children, who was dying slowly and painfully of cancer. The third was an older woman, so severely crippled by arthritis that the future held no promise except the hospital bed in which she lay in constant pain.

My evening included a call from a man who wanted to share with me the shattering news that his wife, in her thirties and with three school-age children, had an inoperable cancer and must soon die.

These items did not belong to an extraordinary day. They were part of a fairly ordinary day, a day which just because it was not unusual underlines Job's declaration that man is born to trouble.

James Martin

Suffering

Wednesday

Patient

As though heaven supplied her breath
The tube disappeared, outwards, gasping
We polished the smooth and smiling floors beneath her
Left the outrage of her dying, a nightingale
Whose sylvan sonnets gleam upon the seas
While forests dawn-dipped mourn and melt to dust
She was grief, a sea of wheat without a reaper
Muffled in the starched efficiency of the veiled lie
The shallow white, that is merely beneath
A darkness unspeakable.

Kenneth C. Steven

Sermon in the Hospital

Such long weakness and such wearing pain
As has no end in view, that makes of life
One weary avenue of darkened days;
The bitter darkness growing darker still,
Which none can share or soothe, which sunders us
From all desire, or hope, or stir of change,
Or service of our Master in the world.
Or fellowship with all the faces round
Of passing pains and pleasures — while our pain
Passeth not, nor will pass; and only this
Remains for us to look for — more of pain,
And doubt if we can bear it to the end.

Hold fast His hand,
Though the nails pierce thine too! Take only care
Lest one drop of the sacramental wine
Be spilled, of that which ever shall unite
Thee, soul and body, to thy living Lord.

Ugo Bassi (1801-1849)

Suffering

Parable: the Long Silence

At the end of time there were billions of people scattered on a great plain before God's throne. Most shrank back from the brilliant light before them. But some groups near the front talked heatedly, not with cringing shame, but with belligerence.

"Can God judge us? How can He know suffering?" snapped a pert young brunette. She ripped open a sleeve to reveal a tattooed number from a concentration camp. "We endured terror . . . beatings . . . torture . . . death!" In another group a negro boy lowered his collar, showing an ugly rope burn: "Lynched for no crime except being black!" In another crowd, a pregnant schoolgirl with sullen eyes: "Why should I suffer? It wasn't my fault."

Far out across the plain were hundreds of such groups. Each had a complaint against God for the evil and suffering He permitted in the world. How lucky He was to live in heaven where all was sweet and light, where there was no weeping or fear, no hunger or hatred. What did He know of all that man had been forced to endure? For God lives a pretty sheltered life, they said.

So each of these groups sent forth their leader, chosen because he had suffered the most — a Jew, a negro, a person from Hiroshima, a horribly deformed arthritic, a thalidomide child. In the centre of the plain they consulted each other. At last they were ready to present their case. It was rather clever: before God could be qualified to be their judge, He must endure what they had endured; He should be sentenced to live on earth as man! Let Him be born a Jew. Let the legitimacy of His birth be doubted. Give Him work so difficult that His family will think Him out of His mind when He tries to do it. Let Him be betrayed by His closest friends. Let Him face false charges, be tried by a prejudiced jury and convicted by a cowardly judge. Let Him be tortured. Let Him see what it means to be terribly alone. Then let Him die — so that there can be no doubt He died. Let there be a great host of witnesses to verify it.

As each leader announced his part of the sentence, loud murmurs of approval went up from the great throng. When the last had finished there was a long silence. No one uttered another word. No one moved. For suddenly all knew that *God had already served His sentence.*

Suffering

Friday

Man's main concern with the dark fact of suffering is not to find an explanation: it is to find a victory. It is not to elaborate a theory: it is to lay hold upon a power. Even if you possessed the answer to the riddle, even if you had it written down to the last detail and could say, "There is the full and final explanation of the problem of pain," that would not be enough, would it? For the pain itself would still have to be borne. That, in the last resort, is the real demand of the human spirit — not the explaining of this thing, but grace and help to bear it. And that is why God gave us Christ.

Open your New Testament. On every page of it you see the living God coming towards you, and holding out in His hands — not a ready-made answer to the vexed questions of the mind, but something better and diviner far — a liberating, reinforcing power for the soul! And this is why all the other beams of light converge at length upon a cross. Towering out of the dark it stands — God's everlasting answer to the quest of all the world.

See how the cross transforms the age-long mystery. What does it tell about the fact of suffering? . . . God is in it with you, and you are in it with God — that is the message of the cross on the mystery of suffering. And that message means victory. There was victory at the cross for Christ: and God wants you to know that there can be victory at every cross for you.

"But what has all this to do with me?" you ask. ´ "Christ may have conquered in the day of trouble, but my battle has still to be fought — and what help is there in Calvary for me?"

Surely the answer is clear. If evil at its overwhelming worst has already been met and mastered, as in Jesus Christ it has; if God has got His hands on this baffling mystery of suffering in its direst, most defiant form, and turned its most awful triumph into uttermost, irrevocable defeat — if that in fact has happened, and on that scale, are you to say it cannot happen on the infinitely lesser scale of your own life by union with Christ through faith?

That is the only answer to the mystery of suffering: and the answer is a question — Will you let God in to reign? The answer is not a theory. It is a life. It is a dedicated spirit, a fully surrendered soul. That is the one finally valid answer. May God make that answer ours!

James S. Stewart

Suffering

He led me by the way of pain,
A barren and a starless place;
(I didn't know His eyes were wet,
He would not let me see His face).
He left me like a frightened child,
Unshielded in a night of storm,
(How should I dream He was so near?
The wind-swept darkness hid His form).
But when the clouds were driven back,
And dawn was breaking into day,
I knew Whose feet had walked with mine,
I saw the footprints all the way.

George Goodman

From the confusion of the world with its passing values,
O God, we turn to Thee;
from our despair to Thy hope,
from our sin to Thy forgiveness,
from our loneliness to Thy companionship,
from our sadness to Thy joy.

Help us to realise that we matter to Thee,
and that when we trust in Thee, we may know the peace
which the world cannot give,
which the world cannot take away.

But we are in contact with many people who are lacking in joy.
Help us to care for them —
those who have lost someone dear to them;
those who are having a hard time at work, or out of it;
those who have tension and difficulty at home;
those whose hopes have been shattered;
those who have many acquaintances, but few friends;
those who are often misunderstood;
those who feel out of things —
may they realise Thy care, and may they see it even through our
lives.

In Jesus' Name . . . Amen.

Alex. M. Gunn

Darkness and Light

Sunday
Just Please Yourself

It isn't easy now to get advice.
Not just because it isn't wanted:
*People can't be told what's **best***
*When there's no certainty about what's **good:***
When everything is just a matter of opinion —
Hers as good as his,
Or yours as mine.

It isn't easy now to know you're right.
Of course the new morality absolves us all
From being wrong. There is no 'Absolute.'
You look within; and if you think you like
What you see there — Okay!
No business but your own —
And maybe hers, if she agrees.

But to escape the guilt of being wrong
You have to sacrifice the peace of being right.

It isn't easy now to be at peace
With man, or God, or even with yourself.
The mocking fashion makes us fear
Not to conform, while high-class salesmanship
Flatters our immaturity into believing
We are quite important people if we buy
This thing, or do our shopping in that place.
But even when you do conform,
You're still aware you're being subtly gulled —
Pleasing what they are pleased to call 'yourself,'
But not the you that's You;
Not pleasing God — that doesn't matter now;
Not even pleasing others, for they too
Are in the dark, and watch you, questioning
(From eyes droop-lidded, casually, of course)
As you watch them, to see what goes.

It isn't easy now to know,
Since most experience is still to come, it seems
And all the lessons of the past
Irrelevant;
Tradition, doctrine, history, law —
All square.
So you have got to find out
For yourself . . .
. . . It isn't easy . . .

Norman M. Bowman

Darkness and Light

Monday

1931

In the entrance hall of Broadcasting House there is a Latin inscription. Translated, the words read:

This temple of the arts and muses is dedicated to Almighty God by the first governors of broadcasting in the year 1931, Sir John Reith being director-general. It is their prayer that good seed sown may bring forth a good harvest, that all things hostile to peace or purity may be banished from this house, and that the people inclining their ear to whatsoever things are beautiful and honest and of good report, may tread the paths of wisdom and righteousness.

1973

The slide to permissiveness, which is gathering momentum every day, is not a spontaneous popular move, but a non-popular move engineered by people who are, in the widest sense, nihilists. They make it their business to undermine popularly accepted taboos: they attack our sensibilities, blunting them with a constant bombardment of violence, sadism and sex: they deride our values, and ridicule the voice of conscience which, however weak, is a moral regulator in all but the already depraved. Their front men are clever, talented, but totally lacking in wisdom or responsibility. It was Kenneth Tynan who, like a smutty schoolboy responding to a dare, first used in television the commonest of the so-called four letter words, and because he's a well-known public figure in the cultural scene, he thereby weakened popular objection to public obscenity — even, to the more gullible, giving it a spurious cachet. And let no one try to condone his offence as a modern equivalent of Bernard Shaw's 'bloody' which was merely a non-U word, regarded as swearing but with no obscene connotation, and innocently funny when dropped into a stuffed-shirt conversation. Assiduous manipulation through drama, accustoming us to progressively stronger doses of horror and violence, perversion and cruelty, until we cease to be shocked by them, is part of the overall anti-authority, anti-establishment, moral-anarchic campaign to debauch us which is being waged with growing intensity and increasing success.

Moultrie R. Kelsall (1901-1980)

Darkness and Light

Tuesday
Daily Paper, Friday, 12th March, 1982

Three years after fleeing the Communist régime in Vietnam as a refugee with the boat people, Mr N. is so terrified of youths on his London estate that he says: "If I had known things would be like this I would have been afraid to come." He does not want his name published for fear of reprisals by white teenagers who have already attacked him and his baby daughter. His wife is afraid to go out.

Mr N., aged 25, is a fisherman from South Vietnam. He decided on escape for his family, helped to steal a fishing boat and put to sea with 50 others. After 10 days they were picked up by a British ship and landed in Japan. Mr N. spent two happy years in Japan waiting to come to England. He arrived seven months ago.

His family have been attacked twice. Walking past a fish-and-chip shop with his baby daughter, he saw a gang of youths inside, aged 17 to 19, using a cigarette lighter to set on fire the hair of two teenage Vietnamese girls. The gang ran out and one youth seized a cardboard box and smashed it over the head of Mr N.'s child. On the second occasion he was rushed, in broad daylight, by a gang of youths armed with sticks who started beating him.

Attacks on the estate, where gangs of children aged 11 to 14 roam wild, are not confined to the Vietnamese. Muggings, vandalism and burglaries are common. But the Vietnamese are especially vulnerable and many tend to accept harassment as the lot of the refugee.

Time is cluttered with the wreckage of communities which surrendered to hatred and violence. For the salvation of our nation and the salvation of mankind, we must follow another way. . . . To our most bitter opponents we say: "We shall match your capacity to inflict suffering by our capacity to endure suffering. We shall meet your physical force with soul force. Do to us what you will, and we shall continue to love you. . . . Throw us in jail, and we shall still love you. Send your hooded perpetrators of violence into our community at the midnight hour and beat us and leave us half dead, and we shall still love you. But be ye assured that we will wear you down by our capacity to suffer. . . ." Love is the most durable power in the world.

Martin Luther King (1929-1968)

Darkness and Light

Wednesday

Ethiopia

I stood and stared . . . I felt nothing . . . I couldn't cry . . . I couldn't speak . . . and I felt inadequate and helpless. Never in my life had I seen anything like it. People unable to stand, unable to walk, lying in mud and filth; unable even to lift the food to their lips; people covered in torn, dirty rags; people crawling with fleas and lice; people with limbs like sticks; people with no homes, no possessions; people with malaria, dysentery, typhoid; people without hope — people suffering.

For a week I toured the famine area, I visited the camps, the orphanages, the clinics. I went out into the villages and flew over the drought-stricken areas and for a week I didn't want to talk about it. Then I cried . . . I cried as I've never cried before.

Sarah Marrow

Britain

We opted for the à la carte and I began with prawn cocktail while my companion enjoyed a generous portion of parma ham and melon. For the more adventurous there were fried frogs' legs (£2.90), escargots (£3.35), or turtle soup with sherry. Almost all tastes were catered for in the impressive choice of main course which included pasta, veal, chicken, steak and fish dishes. Scampi Thermidor at £6.95 was tempting, but I decided on the similarly priced Beef Stroganoff which was excellent. My partner ordered Tournedos of Beef Chasseur (£7.35), accompanied by cauliflower mornay and sauté potatoes. While the potatoes looked somewhat limp, the rest was highly praised and the portions necessitated a pause before contemplating dessert.

Tables were packed so tightly in the large dining room that passage of the sweet trolley was impossible and we were denied a look at the selection of gateau, cheesecake and other delights on offer. Relying on the waiter's description, however, I ordered profiteroles and cream with a few fresh strawberries added; fresh fruit salad and cream sufficed for my companion.

Monthly Magazine

Darkness and Light

Thursday

Brazil

About 50,000 teenage girls, some of them only 12 years old, are reported to be illegally exploited as prostitutes in towns of North-east Brazil.

The girls usually began work between the ages of 12 and 14 and by 20 they were considered too old by the brothel-keepers, said Mr Benjamin Whitaker, British vice-chairman of the United Nations Sub-commission on the Prevention of Discrimination and Protection of Minorities.

He was speaking to a meeting in Geneva of the sub-commission, who were discussing child exploitation. Quoting Oxfam evidence, he said the girls received only 10 cruzeiros (about 16p) per client but had to pay brothel rents of 60 cruzeiros per day.

Prostitution was illegal in Brazil, but the girls continued to be exploited in vice zones of towns because the law could not prevail against vested interests and police corruption, he said.

Daily paper, 25th August, 1979

Britain

A nation's youth is its greatest asset. We are poor guardians if we do not ensure their inalienable right to childhood, to mystery, to dreams, to tenderness and to love; if we do not realise that by ceasing to provide authority we may also cease to care; if we do not conscientiously maintain the foundations without which the young cannot build anew; if we do not tell them that there is a third way, neither reactionary nor libertarian, which still waits to be explored; and if we do not offer them the riches of our Christian heritage.

Mary Whitehouse

Darkness and Light

Friday

Daily paper, Thursday, March 11th, 1982

The Cabinet are expected to approve the purchase of the Trident II missile this morning at a cost of anything up to £11 billion over the next two decades. Mr John Nott, Defence Secretary, will make a statement soon afterwards putting the case for the advanced D5 missile instead of the Trident I project which was given the go-ahead in July 1980. . . . The D5 has a range of 6,000 miles and can carry more than a dozen "silo-busting" warheads. It would probably be installed in four or five submarines, to be built at Barrow-in-Furness. . . . Mr Nott has been preparing a publicity campaign to follow his announcement. He is a firm believer in a first-strike capability for Britain, despite the claims that it significantly increases the risk of war.

Father Eternal, Ruler of Creation,
Spirit of Life, which moved ere form was made,
Through the thick darkness covering every nation,
Light to man's blindness, O be thou our aid!
Thy kingdom come, O Lord, thy will be done.

Races and peoples, lo! we stand divided,
And, sharing not our griefs, no joy can share;
By wars and tumults Love is mocked, derided,
His conquering cross no kingdom wills to bear;
Thy kingdom come, O Lord, thy will be done.

Envious of heart, blind-eyed, with tongues confounded,
Nation by nation still goes unforgiven;
In wrath and fear, by jealousies surrounded,
Building proud towers which shall not reach to heaven.
Thy kingdom come, O Lord, thy will be done.

Lust of possession worketh desolations;
There is no meekness in the sons of earth.
Led by no star, the rulers of the nations
Still fail to bring us to the blissful birth.
Thy kingdom come, O Lord, thy will be done.

How shall we love thee, holy, hidden Being,
If we love not the world which thou hast made?
O, give us brother-love, for better seeing
Thy Word made flesh and in a manger laid.
Thy kingdom come, O Lord, thy will be done.

Laurence Housman (1865-1959)

41

Darkness and Light

Saturday
Parable: the Little Lifesaving Station

On a dangerous sea-coast where shipwrecks often occur there was once a crude little lifesaving station. The building was just a hut and there was only one boat, but the few devoted members, with no thought for themselves, went out day and night tirelessly searching for the lost. Many lives were saved, so that the little station became famous. Some of those who were rescued and others in the surrounding area, wanted to support the work, so new boats were bought and new crews trained. The little lifesaving station grew.

Some of the members were unhappy that the building was so crude and poorly equipped. They felt that a more comfortable place should be provided, so they replaced the emergency cots with beds and put better furniture in the enlarged building. The station became a popular gathering place for its members; they decorated it beautifully and furnished it exquisitely for use as a sort of club. Fewer members were now interested in going to sea on lifesaving missions, so they hired lifeboat crews to do this work. The lifesaving motif still prevailed in the decoration and there was a liturgical lifeboat in the room where club initiations were held.

About this time a large ship was wrecked and the hired crew brought in boatloads of cold, wet and half-drowned people. They were dirty and sick, and some had black skin and some yellow. The beautiful new club was in chaos. So the property committee immediately had a shower house built outside where victims of shipwreck could be cleaned up before coming inside. At the next meeting there was a split in the club membership. Most members wanted to stop the lifesaving activities as being unpleasant and a hindrance to the normal social life of the club. Some insisted upon lifesaving as their primary purpose and pointed out that they were still called a lifesaving station, but they were finally voted down and told that if they wanted to save lives, they could begin their own lifesaving station down the coast. They did.

As time passed, however, the new station experienced the same changes. It evolved into a club and yet another station was founded. History continued to repeat itself, and if you visit that sea-coast today, you will find a number of exclusive clubs along it. Shipwrecks are still frequent, but most of the people drown.

In All Things Thee to See

Seek him that maketh the seven stars and Orion, and turneth the shadow of death into the morning.

Amos V.8

God is to be found and seen, not through an illimitable vacancy between Himself and the spirit of man, but in and through all things that stir men to love. He is to be seen in the light of a cottage window as well as in the sun or the stars. . . . God is revealed to us in the known, not hidden in the unknown; and we have to find Him where we are.

Arthur Clutton-Brock (1868-1924)

Teach me, my God and King,
In all things Thee to see;
And what I do in anything,
To do it as for Thee!

A man that looks on glass,
On it may stay his eye;
Or if he pleaseth, through it pass,
And then the heaven espy.

All may of Thee partake;
Nothing can be so mean,
Which with this tincture, 'for Thy sake',
Will not grow bright and clean.

A servant with this clause
Makes drudgery divine:
Who sweeps a room, as for Thy laws,
Makes that and the action fine.

This is the famous stone
That turneth all to gold;
For that which God doth touch and own
Cannot for less be told.

George Herbert (1593-1632)

In All Things Thee to See

Monday

And in everything, as we know, the Spirit co-operates for good with those who love God and are called according to his purpose.

Romans VIII. 28. (N.E.B.)

Joseph

And it came to pass, when Joseph was come unto his brethren, that they stript Joseph out of his coat, his coat of many colours; and they took him, and cast him into a pit: and the pit was empty, and there was no water in it. And they sat down to eat bread: and they lifted up their eyes and looked, and, behold, a company of Ishmeelites came from Gilead with their camels bearing spicery and balm and myrrh, going to carry it down to Egypt.

And Judah said to his brethren, What profit is it if we slay our brother, and conceal his blood? Come, and let us sell him to the Ishmeelites, and let not our hand be upon him; for he is our brother and our flesh. And his brethren were content. Then there passed by Midianites merchantmen; and they drew and lifted up Joseph out of the pit, and sold Joseph to the Ishmeelites for twenty pieces of silver: and they brought Joseph into Egypt.

*   *   *   *   *

Then Joseph could not refrain himself before all them that stood by him; and he cried, Cause every man to go out from me. And there stood no man with him, while Joseph made himself known unto his brethren.

And he wept aloud: and the Egyptians and the house of Pharaoh heard. And Joseph said unto his brethren, Come near to me, I pray you. And they came near. And he said, I am Joseph your brother, whom ye sold into Egypt. Now therefore be not grieved, nor angry with yourselves, that ye sold me hither: for God did send me before you to preserve life. For these two years hath the famine been in the land: and yet there are five years, in the which there shall neither be earing nor harvest. And God sent me before you to preserve you a posterity in the earth, and to save your lives by a great deliverance. So now it was not you that sent me hither, but God.

Genesis XXXVII. 23-28. XLV. 1-8

In All Things Thee to See

Tuesday

Whither shall I go from thy spirit? or whither shall I flee from thy presence? If I ascend up into heaven, thou art there: if I make my bed in hell, behold thou art there. If I take the wings of the morning, and dwell in the uttermost parts of the sea; even there shall thy hand lead me, and thy right hand shall hold me.

Psalm CXXXIX. 7-10

Martin Rinkart

In the bitter Thirty Years War (1618-48), the tide of battle ebbed and flowed across Central Europe and by the time it was stayed, the country was in ruins. When peace eventually brought the anarchy to an end, four-fifths of the population had perished, an even greater proportion of the wealth of the country was destroyed, and the land was virtually a desert.

Martin Rinkart was born, the son of a cooper, in Eilenburg, Saxony, in 1586. In 1617 he became archdeacon there and remained there for the rest of his life. During the war the town was crowded with refugees; pestilence broke out among them, and as the only clergyman left, Rinkart had to bury 4,480 people. He is said to have often read the funeral service over as many as forty persons in a day. Rinkart also impoverished himself and incurred crushing liabilities to secure food for the starving people. Worn out by his toils and anxieties, he died in the year following the peace.

Almost half-way through the war, in the midst of his darkest trials, Rinkart composed a hymn that wells up in gratitude, one in which the writer can still see the hand of God. It is now the German *Te Deum,* sung on all occasions of national thanksgiving. It begins "Nun danket alle Gott."

Now thank we all our God
With heart and hands and voices,
Who wondrous things hath done,
In whom His world rejoices —

In All Things Thee to See

Wednesday

I will bring the blind by a way that they knew not; I will lead them in paths that they have not known: I will make darkness light before them, and crooked things straight. These things will I do unto them, and not forsake them.

Isaiah XLII. 16

William Cowper

William Cowper, who lived from 1731 to 1800, suffered all his life from severe fits of depression and melancholy. After one particularly grievous attack of mental distress he resolved to do away with himself. He gave his coachman orders to drive him from his home at Olney to the River Ouse. The night, however, was very dark, the driver missed the way and Cowper found himself back at his own house. By then the clouds of his depression had lifted and, in thanks to God for his deliverance, he wrote the following hymn:

God moves in a mysterious way,
His wonders to perform;
He plants His footsteps in the sea,
And rides upon the storm.

Deep in unfathomable mines
Of never-failing skill
He treasures up His bright designs,
And works His sovereign will.

Ye fearful saints, fresh courage take;
The clouds ye so much dread
Are big with mercy, and shall break
In blessings on your head.

Blind unbelief is sure to err,
And scan His work in vain;
God is His own interpreter,
And He will make it plain.

In All Things Thee to See

Thursday

The Lord's goodness surrounds us at every moment, I walk through it almost with difficulty, as through thick grass and flowers.

R. W. Barbour. (1854-1891)

Helen Keller

Helen Keller was born in Alabama on June 27, 1880, a perfectly healthy and normal child. At the age of eighteen months she was stricken with a severe illness which left her deaf and blind; as a result of the deafness she soon became dumb also. For five years she remained imprisoned. Then, through Dr. Alexander Graham Bell, to whom her father appealed because he knew Dr. Bell's interest in the deaf, a deliverer was sent to her in the person of a 22-year-old graduate by the name of Anne Mansfield Sullivan. From the day of Miss Sullivan's arrival on March 2, 1887, the story of Miss Keller's life reads like a fairy tale. Within a month the teacher had presented the gift of language to her little pupil, in itself almost miraculous. . . . What Helen Keller achieved later, despite her deafness and her blindness, is a story of almost unbelievable courage. In her own writings she was to say:

"My autobiography is not a great work. Whatever value is in it is there not because I have any skill as a writer, nor because there are any thrilling incidents in it, but because God has dealt with me as with a son, and chastened me, and muffled His beams that He might lead me in the path of aid to the deaf and blind. He has made me the mouth of such as cannot speak, and my blindness others' sight, and let me be hands and feet to the maimed and helpless. And because I could not do this alone, being imprisoned in a great darkness and silence, it was necessary that another should liberate me. That other is Anne Sullivan, my guardian angel. . . . Slowly, slowly, out of my weakness and helplessness she has built up my life. . . . As she opened the locked gates of my being my heart leapt with gladness and my feet felt the thrill of the chanting sea. Happiness flooded my being as the sun overflows the earth, and I stretched out my hands in quest of life."

In All Things Thee to See

Friday

For my thoughts are not your thoughts, neither are your ways my ways, saith the Lord. For as the heavens are higher than the earth, so are my ways higher than your ways, and my thoughts than your thoughts.

Isaiah LV. 8-9

Dr. Barnardo

While he was still a medical student, Thomas Barnardo devoted an immense amount of his time to doing all he could to help the homeless, destitute boys of the East End of London.

'It is not surprising that his medical studies began to suffer seriously. Many of his advisers urged him to give himself wholly to the service of waif children, among whom he was becoming known all over the metropolis as a friend and comrade. But he felt himself bound by the choice he had made long before, to go as a medical missionary to China. Moreover, he dared not contemplate the constant and heavy expense which rescue work among destitute children would necessarily involve.

'One day, after much prayer, he was led to concentrate on the words of Psalm 32. v.8: "I will instruct thee and teach thee in the way thou shalt go; I will guide thee with mine eye." It seemed to him that this was all he wanted as a promise.

'It was only a few days after that experience that the young medical student received an amazing letter: the writer would provide £1,000 for the furtherance of the Doctor's work of child rescue if he felt able, for the time being at all events, to give up the thought of going to China, and would remain in England and establish in East London a Home for Waif and Stray Children. No other condition was attached! . . .

'And so were founded the institutions known all over the world as "Dr. Barnardo's Homes". "I did not choose this path", he declared emphatically. "My Father called me. The work which I have been permitted to carry on has, from the first, afforded a remarkable example of the reality of God's guiding hand in the affairs of life".'

A. E. Williams

In All Things Thee to See

Saturday

I am forced, good Father, to seek Thee daily, and Thou offerest Thyself daily to be found: whensoever I seek, I find Thee, in my house, in the fields, in the temple, and in the highway. Whatsoever I do, Thou art with me; whether I eat or drink, whether I write or work, go to ride, read, meditate, or pray, Thou art ever with me; wheresoever I am, or whatsoever I do, I feel some measure of Thy mercies and love. If I be oppressed, Thou defendest me; if I be envied, Thou guardest me; if I hunger, Thou feedest me; whatsoever I want Thou givest me. O continue this Thy loving-kindness towards me for ever, that all the world may see Thy power, Thy mercy, and Thy love, wherein Thou hast not failed me, and even my enemies shall see that Thy mercies endure forever.

John Norden (1548-1625)

To be with God there is no need to be continually in church. We may make an oratory of our heart in which to retire from time to time, and with him hold humble and loving converse. Everyone can converse closely with God. Lift up your heart to him, even at your meals, or when you are in company. You need not cry very loud, he is nearer to us than we think. Accustom yourself to beg his grace, to offer him your heart from time to time throughout the day's business, even every moment if you can. The time of business does not with me differ from the time of prayer. And in the noise and clatter of my kitchen, while several people are calling for different things at the same time, I possess God in as great tranquillity as if I were upon my knees at the Blessed Sacrament.

Brother Lawrence (1610-1691)

Hope in Dark Days

Sunday

Thou art my help and my deliverer; make no tarrying, O my God. — Thou art my hiding place; thou shalt compass me about with songs of deliverance.

Psalm XL. 17
Psalm XXXII. 7

A shower fell in the night and now dark clouds drift across the sky, occasionally sprinkling a fine film of rain.

I stand under an apple-tree in blossom and I breathe. Not only the apple-tree but the grass round it glistens with moisture; words cannot describe the sweet fragrance that pervades the air. Inhaling as deeply as I can, the aroma invades my whole being; I breathe with my eyes open, I breathe with my eyes closed — I cannot say which gives me the greater pleasure.

This, I believe, is the single most precious freedom that prison takes away from us: the freedom to breathe freely, as I now can. No food on earth, no wine, not even a woman's kiss is sweeter to me than this air steeped in the fragrance of flowers, of moisture and freshness.

No matter that this is only a tiny garden, hemmed in by five-storey houses like cages in a zoo. I cease to hear the motorcycles backfiring, the radios whining, the burble of loudspeakers. As long as there is fresh air to breathe under an apple-tree after a shower, we may survive a little longer.

Alexander Solzhenitsyn

Hope in Dark Days

Why are ye fearful, O ye of little faith?

God is our refuge and strength, a very present help in trouble. Therefore will not we fear, though the earth be removed, and though the mountains be carried into the midst of the sea; though the waters thereof roar and be troubled, though the mountains shake with the swelling thereof. The Lord of hosts is with us; the God of Jacob is our refuge.

Matthew VIII. 26
Psalm XLVI. 1-3, 11

The prayer which is answered to-day may seem to be unanswered to-morrow; the promises once so gloriously fulfilled may cease to be a reality to us; the spiritual blessing which was at one time such a joy may be utterly lost; and nothing of all we once trusted to and rested on may be left us, but the hungry and longing memory of it all. But when all else is gone God is still left. Nothing changes Him. He is the same yesterday, to-day, and forever, and in Him is no variableness, neither shadow of turning. And the soul that finds its joy in Him alone can suffer no wavering.

It is grand to trust in the promises, but it is grander still to trust in the Promiser. The promises may be misunderstood or misapplied, and at the moment when we are leaning all our weight upon them they may seem utterly to fail us. But no one ever trusted in the Promiser and was confounded.

The God who is behind His promises, and is infinitely greater than His promises, can never fail us in any emergency, and the soul that is stayed on Him cannot know anything but perfect peace.

Hannah Pearsall Smith (1832-1911)

Anxiety does not empty tomorrow of its sorrows — only today of its strength.

C. H. Spurgeon (1834-1892)

Hope in Dark Days

Tuesday

Hear my cry, O God; attend unto my prayer. From the end of the earth will I cry unto thee, when my heart is overwhelmed: lead me to the rock that is higher than I. For thou hast been a shelter for me, and a strong tower from the enemy. I will abide in thy tabernacle for ever: I will trust in the covert of thy wings.

Psalm LXI. 1-4

Workman of God! O lose not heart,
But learn what God is like,
And, in the darkest battle-field,
Thou shalt know where to strike.

Thrice blest is he to whom is given
The instinct that can tell
That God is on the field when He
Is most invisible.

He hides Himself so wondrously,
As though there were no God;
He is least seen when all the powers
Of ill are most abroad.

Ah! God is other than we think;
His ways are far above,
Far beyond reason's height, and reached
Only by childlike love.

Then learn to scorn the praise of men
And learn to lose with God;
For Jesus won the world through shame,
And beckons thee His road.

For right is right, since God is God,
And right the day must win;
To doubt would be disloyalty,
To falter would be sin.

Frederick William Faber (1814-63)

Hope in Dark Days

Go forward fearlessly.
Do not think about the Red Sea that lies ahead.
Be very sure that when you come to it the waters will part and you
will pass over to your promised land of freedom.

"God Calling" (A Devotional Diary)
Ed. A. J. Russell

Freedom's Crowning Hour

You that have faith to look with fearless eyes
Beyond the tragedy of a world at strife
And trust that out of night and death shall rise
The dawn of ampler life:

Rejoice, whatever anguish rend your heart,
That God has given you, for a priceless dower,
To live in these great times and have your part
In Freedom's crowning hour;

That you may tell your sons who see the light
High in the heaven, their heritage to take:
"I saw the powers of Darkness put to flight!
I saw the morning break!"

Owen Seaman (1861-1936)

Hope in Dark Days

Thursday

Don't throw away your trust now — it carries with it a rich reward in the world to come. . . . Faith means putting our full confidence in the things we hope for, it means being certain of things we cannot see.

This doesn't mean, of course, that we have only a hope of future joys — we can be full of joy here and now even in our trials and troubles. Taken in the right spirit these very things will give us patient endurance; this in turn will develop a mature character, and a character of this sort produces a steady hope, a hope that will never disappoint us.

Hebrews. X.35, XI.1. (Phillips)
Romans. V.3-4. (Phillips)

Has God been here? The one who made the world?
The lonely Man who walked awhile with men
Along the road, and blessed, and healed, and fed —
Was he then God?

'Why be concerned?' they ask. 'He did his work,
Like other men he came and went away:
And we, in turn, are travelling on; today
Is ours as his was then. Live in your day
And play the man, nor fret yourself of Christ
Or God; let each be free to find himself,
Evolve, achieve, the best he can . . . how could
A man be God?'

The question is but part of it; like lead
It settles in the heart. We pray, we cry,
My soul and I, we want to know; a world of men
Must know, tired men confused upon the road . . .
Is this man God?

My soul, look up! Our cry is answered from
The very Throne. Draw nigh with joy, sheer joy,
For now it shall be known from star to clod
That Christ is God.

And here we stand; nor would we boast or say
We found the road or learned the way — ah, no!
He heard the cry, he heard and answered, 'Yes,
My Son is God.'

A. E. Mitchell (1877-1964)

Hope in Dark Days

Friday

Although the fig tree shall not blossom, neither shall fruit be in the vines; the labour of the olive shall fail, and the fields shall yield no meat; the flock shall be cut off from the fold, and there shall be no herd in the stalls: yet will I rejoice in the Lord, I will joy in the God of my salvation. The Lord God is my strength, and he will make my feet like hinds' feet, and he will make me to walk upon mine high places.

Habakkuk. III. 17-19

Say not, 'The struggle nought availeth;
The labour and the wounds are vain;
The enemy faints not nor faileth,
And as things have been they remain.'

If hopes were dupes, fears may be liars;
It may be, in yon smoke concealed,
Your comrades chase even now the fliers,
And, but for you, possess the field.

For while the tired waves, vainly breaking,
Seem here no painful inch to gain,
Far back, through creeks and inlets making,
Comes silent, flooding in, the main.

And not by eastern windows only,
When daylight comes, comes in the light;
In front the sun climbs slow, how slowly;
But westward, look! the land is bright.

Arthur Hugh Clough (1819-1861)

Hope in Dark Days

Saturday

There was once a flood called Calvary. And all the bitterness and ugliness, all the shame and sorrow of life, entered into that flood, and came beating around the brave soul of Jesus, sweeping Him down at last to the barbarity and infamy of the death of the cross. 'What can God have been doing?' we want to ask. 'Was He asleep? Or on a journey? Or was He dead?' No! The Lord was sitting as King at the flood, that surging flood of Calvary; and out of that grim cross He has brought the salvation of the world. Tell me — if God did that with the cross of Jesus, do you think your cross can be too difficult for Him to deal with, and to transfigure? He can make it shine with glory.

Do you believe it? My friend, here is surely the final victory of faith — to be able to say, 'The Lord God omnipotent reigneth,' to cry it aloud, not only when life is kind and tender and smiling, and the time of the singing of birds is come and the flowers appear on the earth, but even more when the night is dark, and you are far from home, and the proud waters are going over your soul; to cry it then, not weakly nor diffidently nor uncertainly, but vehemently and passionately and with the ring of faith in every syllable of it — 'The Lord God omnipotent reigneth. Hallelujah!'

This is the Lord God who has come again to the gate of your life and mine today. This is the Lord God who claims the right to reign, and from whose patient, haunting pursuit we can never in this world get free. Behold, He stands at the door, and knocks. While the sands of time are running out and the hurrying days mould our destiny, He stands at the door and knocks. Tenderer than the kiss of a little child, mightier than the flashing lightnings of Heaven, He stands at the door and knocks. What will our answer be? 'You, out there at the door, you who have been haunting and troubling me all these years — begone, and leave me in peace!' Is that it? Or is it not rather this? 'Blessed and glorious Lord Almighty, dear loving Christ of God — come! Come now. My life is yours. See here is the throne. Oh, Christ, take your power — and reign!'

James S. Stewart

56

Resurrection

And, behold, two of them went that same day to a village called Emmaus, which was from Jerusalem about threescore furlongs. And they talked together of all these things which had happened. And it came to pass, that, while they communed together and reasoned, Jesus himself drew near, and went with them. But their eyes were holden that they should not know him.

And he said unto them, What manner of communications are these that ye have one to another, as ye walk, and are sad? And one of them, whose name was Cleopas, answering said unto him, Art thou only a stranger in Jerusalem, and hast not known the things which are come to pass there in these days? And he said unto them, What things?

And they said unto him, Concerning Jesus of Nazareth, which was a prophet mighty in deed and word before God and all the people: And how the chief priests and our rulers delivered him to be condemned to death, and have crucified him. . . .

And they drew nigh unto the village, whither they went: and he made as though he would have gone further. But they constrained him, saying, Abide with us: for it is toward evening, and the day is far spent. And he went in to tarry with them.

And it came to pass, as he sat at meat with them, he took bread, and blessed it, and brake, and gave to them. And their eyes were opened, and they knew him; and he vanished out of their sight.

And they said one to another, Did not our heart burn within us, while he talked with us by the way, and while he opened to us the scriptures? And they rose up the same hour, and returned to Jerusalem, and found the eleven gathered together, and them that were with them, Saying, The Lord is risen indeed, and hath appeared to Simon.

And they told what things were done in the way and how he was known of them in breaking of bread.

Luke. XXIV. 13-20; 28-35

Resurrection

Monday

Now if this is what we proclaim, that Christ was raised from the dead, how can some of you say there is no resurrection of the dead? If there be no resurrection, then Christ was not raised; and if Christ was not raised, then our gospel is null and void, and so is your faith; and we turn out to be lying witnesses for God, because we bore witness that he raised Christ to life, whereas, if the dead are not raised, it follows that Christ was not raised; and if Christ was not raised, your faith has nothing in it and you are still in your old state of sin. It follows also that those who have died within Christ's fellowship are utterly lost. If it is for this life only that Christ has given us hope, we of all men are most to be pitied.

But the truth is, Christ was raised to life — the firstfruits of the harvest of the dead. For since it was a man who brought death into the world, a man also brought resurrection of the dead. As in Adam all men die, so in Christ all will be brought to life.

I Corinthians XV. 12-22. (N.E.B.)

We know ourselves now to be on the way not to death, but to life. We know that death is not the end, but the beginning of life. We know ourselves to be not the children of a moment, but the pilgrims of eternity. And life has a new value, because it is on the way not to extinction and obliteration, but to consummation and completion.

So left to ourselves, we are bound to live a life in which the inevitable veils of humanity conceal God from us; but in Jesus Christ the veils are removed, and we see God face to face, knowing him as he is, rejoicing in our new-found friendship with him, triumphant in the power in which our weakness becomes his strength, certain that after life here there is a still greater life, both for us and for those whom we love.

William Barclay, (1907-1978)

Resurrection

It has been my lot in life to have to stand by many death-beds, and to be called in to dying men and women almost as a routine in my profession. Yet I am increasingly convinced that their spirits never die at all. I am sure that there is no real death. Death is no argument against, but rather for, life. Eternal life is the complement of all my unsatisfied ideals.

Wilfred Grenfell (1865-1940)

If death be just a last long sleep,
Then death were good, men say;
Yet say it knowing naught of sleep
Save light at dawn of day.

For sleep's a blank — a nothingness,
A thing we cannot know;
We can but taste the streams of life
That from its fountain flow.

When day puts off her gorgeous robes,
And darkness veils our sight,
Lest we should see her beauty laid
Upon the couch of night,

We crave for sleep because we hold
A memory of morn,
The rush of life renewed, that with
The birth of day is born.

So weary souls that crave for death,
As sweet and dreamless sleep,
As night when men may cease to war,
And women cease to weep,

Are longing still for life — more life,
Their souls not yet sufficed,
Cry out for God's eternal streams;
They crave not death — but Christ.

G. A. Studdert Kennedy (1883-1929)

Resurrection

Wednesday

What is excellent,
As God lives, is permanent;
Hearts are dust, hearts' loves remain;
Heart's love will meet again.

Ralph Waldo Emerson (1803-82)

All experiences of love and beauty, much as we may enjoy and appreciate them in this transitory life, are not rooted here at all. We should save ourselves a lot of disillusionment and heartbreak if we reminded ourselves constantly that here we have "no continuing city". The world is rich with all kinds of wonders and beauties, but we only doom ourselves to disappointment if we think that the stuff of this world is permanent; its change and decay are inevitable. The rich variety of transitory beauty is no more than a reflection or a foretaste of the real and the permanent. Something surely of this thought is included in Christ's words, "lay up for yourselves treasures in Heaven, where neither moth nor rust doth corrupt, and where thieves do not break through nor steal."

J. B. Phillips (1906-1982)

Resurrection

We walk by faith as strangers here;
but Christ shall call us home.

Paraphrase 61

I always thought I should love to grow old, and I find it is even more delightful than I thought. It is so delicious to be done with things, and to feel no need any longer to concern myself much about earthly affairs. I seem on the verge of a most delightful journey to a place of unknown joys and pleasures, and things here seem of so little importance compared to things there, that they have lost most of their interest for me.

I cannot describe the sort of done-with-the-world feeling I have. It is not that I feel as if I was going to die at all, but simply that the world seems to me nothing but a passage way to the real life beyond; and passage ways are very unimportant places. It is of very little account what sort of things they contain, or how they are furnished. One just hurries through them to get to the place beyond.

My wants seem to be gradually narrowing down, my personal wants, I mean, and I often think I could be quite content in the poor-house! I do not know whether this is piety or old age, or a little of each mixed together, but honestly the world and our life in it does seem of too little account to be worth making the least fuss over, when one has such a magnificent prospect close at hand ahead of one; and I am tremendously content to let one activity after another go, and to await quietly and happily the opening of the door at the end of the passage way, that will let me in to my real abiding place. So you may think of me as happy and contented, surrounded with unnumbered blessings.

Hannah Pearsall Smith (1832-1911)

Resurrection

Friday

Eye hath not seen, nor ear heard, neither have entered into the heart of man, the things which God hath prepared for them that love him.

I Corinthians II. 9

Still, still with Thee, when purple morning breaketh,
When the bird waketh, and the shadows flee;
Fairer than morning, lovelier than daylight,
Dawns the sweet consciousness, I am with Thee.

Alone with Thee, amid the mystic shadows,
The solemn hush of nature newly born;
Alone with Thee in breathless adoration,
In the calm dew and freshness of the morn.

As in the dawning, o'er the waveless ocean,
The image of the morning star doth rest;
So in this stillness, Thou beholdest only
Thine image in the waters of my breast.

Still, still with Thee! As to each newborn morning
A fresh and solemn splendour still is given;
So does this blessed consciousness, awaking,
Breathe each day nearness unto Thee and heaven.

When sinks the soul, subdued by toil to slumber,
Its closing eye looks up to Thee in prayer;
Sweet the repose beneath Thy wings o'ershading,
But sweeter still, to wake and find Thee there.

So shall it be at last, in that bright morning,
When the soul waketh, and life's shadows flee;
O in that hour, fairer than daylight dawning,
Shall rise the glorious thought — I am with Thee!

Harriet Beecher Stowe (1811-1896)

Resurrection

If these be fair, O what is Heaven!

Henry Vaughan (1622-1695)

And thus have you a Gate, in the prospect even of this world,
  whereby you may see into God's Kingdom.
Rich Diamond and Pearl and Gold
In evry Place was seen;
Rare Splendors, Yellow, Blew, Red, White and Green,
Mine Eys did evry where behold.
Great Wonders clothd with Glory did appear,
Amazement was my Bliss.
That and my Wealth was evry where:
No Joy to this!

Thomas Traherne (1637-1674)

Sunrise

Morning awakes sublime; glad earth and sky
Smile in the splendour of the day begun.
O'er the broad earth's illumined canopy,
Shade of its Maker's majesty, the sun
Gleams in its living light from cloud to cloud;
Streaks of all colours beautifully run
As if before heaven's gate there hung a shroud
To hide its grand magnificence. O heaven,
Where entrance e'en to thought is disallowed,
To view the glory that this scene is giving
What may blind reason not expect to see,
When in immortal worlds the soul is living
Eternal as its maker, and as free
To taste the unknowns of eternity?

John Clare (1793-1864)

Consolation

Sunday

When shall I come unto the healing waters?
Lifting my heart, I cry to Thee my prayer.
Spirit of peace, my Comforter and Healer,
In whom my springs are found, let my soul meet Thee there.

Albert Orsborn

Is any thing too hard for the Lord?

Commit thy way unto the Lord; trust also in him; and he shall bring it to pass.

Hast thou not known? Hast thou not heard, that the everlasting God, the Lord, the Creator of the ends of the earth, fainteth not, neither is weary? There is no searching of his understanding.

He giveth power to the faint; and to them that have no might he increaseth strength.

Even the youths shall faint and be weary, and the young men shall utterly fall:

But they that wait upon the Lord shall renew their strength; they shall mount up with wings as eagles; they shall run, and not be weary; and they shall walk, and not faint.

Genesis XVIII. 14
Psalms XXXVII. 5
Isaiah XL. 28-31

Consolation

Are you standing at Wit's End Corner, Christian with troubled brow?
Are you thinking of what is before you and all you are bearing now?
Does all the world seem against you and you in the battle alone?
Remember at Wit's End Corner is just where God's power is shown.

There is no sorrow, Lord, too light
To bring in prayer to Thee;
There is no anxious care too slight
To wake Thy sympathy.

Thou who hast trod the thorny road,
Wilt share each small distress;
The love which bore the greater load
Will not refuse the less.

There is no secret sigh we breathe
But meets Thine ear divine;
And every cross grows light beneath
The shadow, Lord, of Thine.

Life's ills without, sin's strife within,
The heart would overflow,
But for that love which died for sin,
That love which wept with woe.

Jane Crewdson (1809-63)

Consolation

Tuesday

'I love and love not: Lord, it breaks my heart
To love and not to love.
Thou veiled within Thy glory, gone apart
Into Thy shrine which is above,
Dost Thou not love me, Lord, or care
For this mine ill?'

'I love thee here or there,
I will accept thy broken heart — lie still.'

'Lord, it was well with me in time gone by
That cometh not again,
When I was fresh and cheerful, who but I?
I fresh, I cheerful: worn with pain
Now, out of sight and out of heart;
O Lord, how long?'

'I watch thee as thou art,
I will accept thy fainting heart — be strong.'

'Lie still, be strong, today: but, Lord, tomorrow,
What of tomorrow, Lord?
Shall there be rest from toil, be truce from sorrow,
Be living green upon the sward,
Now but a barren grave to me,
Be joy for sorrow?'

'Did I not die for thee?
Do I not live for thee? Leave me tomorrow.'

Christina Georgina Rossetti (1830-94)

Consolation

Be still, my soul: the Lord is on thy side;
Bear patiently the cross of grief or pain;
Leave to thy God to order and provide;
In every change He faithful will remain.
Be still, my soul: thy best, thy heavenly Friend
Through thorny ways leads to a joyful end.

Be still, my soul: thy God doth undertake
To guide the future as He has the past.
Thy hope, thy confidence let nothing shake;
All now mysterious shall be bright at last.
Be still, my soul: the waves and winds still know
His voice who ruled them while He dwelt below.

Be still, my soul: when dearest friends depart,
And all is darkened in the vale of tears,
Then shalt thou better know His love, His heart,
Who comes to soothe thy sorrow and thy fears.
Be still, my soul: thy Jesus can repay,
From His own fulness, all He takes away.

Be still, my soul: the hour is hastening on
When we shall be forever with the Lord,
When disappointment, grief, and fear are gone,
Sorrow forgot, love's purest joys restored.
Be still, my soul: when change and tears are past,
All safe and blessed we shall meet at last.

Katharina von Schlegel (1697- ?)
tr. by Jane Laurie Borthwick (1813-97)

Consolation

Thursday

God hath not promised skies ever blue,
Flower-strewn pathways all our lives through;
God hath not promised sun without rain,
Joy without sorrow, peace without pain.

But God hath promised strength for the day,
Rest for the labour, light for the way,
Grace for the trials, help from above,
Unfailing sympathy, undying Love.

A. J. Flint

Small were my faith should it weakly falter,
Now that the roses have ceased to blow;
Frail were the trust that now should alter,
Doubting His love when the storm-clouds grow.
If I trust Him once I must trust Him ever,
And His way is best, though I stand or fall,
Through wind or storm He will leave me never,
For He sends all.

Hannah Pearsall Smith (1832-1911)

Consolation

I dare say there are a good many of us who would confess that we have had hours when the peace of God was a reality, and then we have lost it again. Perhaps for days or months on end we possessed it: and then, disappointingly, it vanished from our grasp. Well, even our defeats can be of value, even our breakdowns of serenity can teach us something. This vital lesson they can teach us — that the peace of God is not something to be captured once for all: it is something requiring to be recaptured all over again every day. It is achieved, not by one big, spectacular resolution, but by a daily re-surrender of life to God, an ever renewed grip of the only Hand that can hold us upright and keep us safe.

This . . . is the ultimate secret — not fine resolutions, but contact with a dynamic, radiant Personality; not laborious efforts at self-improvement, but the transfiguring influence of a friendship with the noblest, strongest, and most understanding Friend in all the world. If only we would start each day with Jesus, reaching out from the dust and darkness of this low earth to clasp the hand of our Friend, the ever-old, ever-new miracle would happen once again, and our restless hearts find rest and healing in the invincible peace of God.

James S. Stewart

Consolation

Saturday

The heartfelt gratitude I have for this life in a wheelchair could only have come from God and His Word. They helped me piece together some of the puzzle which was so confusing. It took some seeking and studying. But today as I look back, I am convinced that the whole ordeal of my paralysis was inspired by His love. I wasn't a rat in a maze. I wasn't the brunt of some cruel divine joke. God had reasons behind my suffering, and learning some of them has made all the difference in the world. He has reasons for your suffering, too.

Joni Eareckson

O Love that wilt not let me go,
I rest my weary soul in Thee:
I give Thee back the life I owe,
That in Thine ocean depths its flow
May richer, fuller be.

O Light that followest all my way,
I yield my flickering torch to Thee:
My heart restores its borrowed ray,
That in Thy sunshine's blaze its day
May brighter, fairer be.

O Joy that seekest me through pain,
I cannot close my heart to Thee:
I trace the rainbow through the rain,
And feel the promise is not vain,
That morn shall tearless be.

O Cross that liftest up my head,
I dare not ask to fly from Thee:
I lay in dust life's glory dead,
And from the ground there blossoms red
Life that shall endless be.

George Matheson (1842-1906)

The Place of Understanding

The fool hath said in his heart, there is no God.

Psalm XIV 1

But where shall wisdom be found? And where is the place of understanding? Man knoweth not the price thereof; neither is it found in the land of the living. The depth saith, It is not in me: and the sea saith, It is not with me.

It cannot be gotten for gold, neither shall silver be weighed for the price thereof. It cannot be valued with the gold of Ophir, with the precious onyx, or the sapphire. The gold and the crystal cannot equal it: and the exchange of it shall not be for jewels of fine gold.

No mention shall be made of coral, or of pearls: for the price of wisdom is above rubies. The topaz of Ethiopia shall not equal it, neither shall it be valued with pure gold.

Whence then cometh wisdom? and where is the place of understanding? Seeing it is hid from the eyes of all living, and kept close from the fowls of the air.

Destruction and death say, We have heard the fame thereof with our ears. God understandeth the way thereof, and he knoweth the place thereof. For he looketh to the ends of the earth, and seeth under the whole heaven; to make the weight for the winds; and he weigheth the waters by measure.

When he made a decree for the rain, and a way for the lightning of the thunder: Then did he see it, and declare it; he prepared it, yea, and searched it out.

And unto man he said, Behold, the fear of the Lord, that is wisdom; and to depart from evil is understanding.

Job XXVIII 12-28

The Place of Understanding

Monday

Only darkness, year after year. No one could make him see. And then came Jesus, "Jesus of Nazareth passeth by." I hear the agony in the cry — "Lord, that I may receive my sight." And at once the man saw the blue sky and green trees and people and the brown, dusty, Jericho road, and — the Master's face.

Lord, how complacently I have treated this wondrous gift of physical sight! I can see the faces of my dear ones, and trees and flowers and mountains and seas; dawn's mystery and sunset's sacrament, moonlight on water and the night sky ablaze with stars. More importantly still, I can see to read. Forgive me. Make me more thankful. End my pitiful grumbling and fretful worry.

Yet I, too, must pray — "Lord, that I may receive my sight."

Let me see the world through Thy compassionate eyes. Let me see my brother's need. Let me see the lovely qualities in difficult and unattractive people. Let me see the sacred personalities of my dear ones and those whom I touch every day and so easily take for granted. Let me view, as persons dear to Thee, the shop girl, the bus conductor, the policeman and postman, the charwoman and the whore; rich man, poor man, beggar-man, thief. All are *persons* dear to Thee and immortal souls within Thy ken. Let me see all children as Thine, especially the unprivileged, and sick and unhappy. Let me see the foreigner as my neighbour and the enemy as Thy child.

Let me see Thy way with the nations and Thy will for the world. Let me detect the marks of Thy purposes and the trend of Thy plan. Let me see that prayer *is* answered, that men *are* guided, that hopes *are* fulfilled. Let me see right through the blinding things that are seen, to the unseen.

Let me see Thy way for me today.
Lord, that I may receive my sight!

Leslie D. Weatherhead (1893-1976)

The Place of Understanding

One thing I know, that, whereas I was blind, now I see.

John IX 25

I went out one afternoon for a walk alone. I was in the empty unthinking state in which one saunters along country lanes, simply yielding oneself to the casual sights around which give a town-bred lad with country yearnings such intense delight. Suddenly I became conscious of the presence of someone else. I cannot describe it, but I felt that I had as direct perception of the being of God all round about me as I have of you when we are together. It was no longer a matter of inference, it was an immediate act of spiritual (or whatever adjective you like to employ) apprehension. It came unsought, absolutely unexpectedly. I remember the wonderful transfiguration of the far-off woods and hills as they seemed to blend in the infinite being with which I was thus brought into relation. This experience did not last long. But it sufficed to change all my feeling. I had not found God because I had never looked for him. But he had found me.

Joseph Estlin Carpenter (1844-1927)

Sitting in my cell, I had a vision of our century in which the soul and spirit of man were going through a decisive test. Not only social systems but religions and philosophies were passing through the fires of a terrestrial purgatory. The fate of millions of human beings in centuries to come depended on the triumph or defeat of positive, eternal values, and on every man's capacity to understand and to defend them.

Silviu Craciunas.

The Place of Understanding

Wednesday

Never has a generation been called upon to experience more intense suffering, trouble, heartache, and despair than ours. Paralysing fear, benumbing pain, devastating war, tragic death, intellectual pessimism — all because man in his pride refuses to turn to God! We are reminded of the words of Jesus, who said: "Man shall not live by bread alone." Man is so constituted that he cannot subsist without God. Material prosperity alone will not suffice. We must have God. To penetrate space, to land on the moon or on Mars, as thrilling and as exciting as that may be, will not satisfy man's inner hunger. He must have God! To have more leisure time, to live in split-level homes, to drive high-powered cars, to watch colour television — these are not the answer. Man must have God!

At the end of his life Buddha said: "I am still searching for truth." This statement could be made by countless thousands of scientists, philosophers, and religious leaders throughout all history. However, Jesus Christ made the astounding claim: "I am the truth." He is the embodiment of all truth. The only answer to man's search is found in Him.

Billy Graham

The Christian ideal has not been tried and found wanting. It has been found difficult and left untried.

G. K. Chesterton (1874-1936)

The Place of Understanding

I increasingly see us in our human condition as manacled and in a dark cell. The chains are our mortal hopes and desires; the dark cell is our ego, in whose obscurity and tiny dimensions we are confined. Christ tells us how to escape, striking off the chains of desire, and putting a window in the dark cell through which we may joyously survey the wide vistas of eternity and the bright radiance of God's universal love. No view of life, as I am well aware, could be more diametrically opposed to the prevailing one today, especially as purveyed in our mass-communication media, dedicated as they are to the counter-proposition, that we *can* live by bread alone, and the more the better. Yet I am more convinced than I am in my own existence that the view of life Christ came into the world to preach, and died to sanctify, remains as true and as valid as ever, and that all who care to, young and old, healthy and infirm, wise and foolish, with or without 'A' or 'O' levels, may live thereby, finding in our troubled, confused world, as in all other circumstances and at all other times, an enlightenment and a serenity not otherwise attainable. Even though, as may very well prove the case, our civilisation like others before it soon finally flickers out, and institutional Christianity with it, the light Christ shed shines as brightly as ever for those who seek an escape from darkness. The truths he spoke will answer their dilemmas and assuage their fears, bringing hope to the hopeless, zest to the despairing and love to the loveless, precisely as happened two thousand years ago and through all the intervening centuries.

Malcolm Muggeridge

The Place of Understanding

Friday

Miracle on the River Kwai

I, too, sought an opportunity to put my experience to work. I had seen at first hand the cruelty of a totalitarian regime. I knew something of suffering and what it meant to look death in the face. I knew the depths to which men could sink and the heights to which they could rise. I could speak knowledgeably of despair, but also of hope; of hatred, but also of love; of man without God, but also of man sustained by God. I knew the power of the demonic, and I knew the greater power of the Holy Spirit. . . .

In my time of decision, nature and reason were neutral. They did not speak to me of anything that made possible a significant understanding of myself and my fellow man. They did not show me the vision of the Infinitely Great. Jesus, however, had spoken to me, had convinced me of the love of God and had drawn me into a meaningful fellowship with other men as brothers. Because of him I had come to see the world in a new way as the creation of God — not purposeless but purposeful. He had opened me to life and life to me. . . .

As I journey with those of the Way I see that the victory over the impersonal, destructive and enslaving forces at work in the world has been given to mankind because of what Jesus has done. This is the good news for man: God, in Christ, has shared his suffering; for that is what God is like. He has not shunned the responsibility of freedom. He shares in the saddest and most painful experiences of His children, even that experience which seems to defeat us all, namely death.

He comes into our Death House to lead us through it.

Ernest Gordon

The Place of Understanding

For the rest, let the Gospels speak. Of what I have learnt from these documents in the course of my long task, I will say nothing now. Only this, that they bear the seal of the Son of Man and God, they are the Magna Charta of the human spirit. Were we to devote to their comprehension a little of the selfless enthusiasm that is now expended on the riddle of our physical surroundings, we should cease to say that Christianity is coming to an end — we might even feel that it had only just begun.

E. V. Rieu (1887-1972)

He was born in an obscure village, the child of a peasant woman.

He grew up in still another village, where he worked in a carpenter's shop till he was thirty. Then for three years he was an intinerant preacher.

He never wrote a book. He never held an office. He never had a family or owned a house. He didn't go to college. He never visited a big city. He never travelled two hundred miles from the place where he was born. He did none of the things one usually associates with greatness.

He had no credentials but himself.

He was only thirty-three when the tide of public opinion turned against him. His friends ran away. He was turned over to his enemies and went through the mockery of a trial. He was nailed to a cross between two thieves. While he was dying, his executioners gambled for his clothing, the only property he had on earth. When he was dead he was laid in a borrowed grave through the pity of a friend.

Nineteen centuries have come and gone, and today he is the central figure of the human race and the leader of mankind's progress. All the armies that ever marched, all the navies that ever sailed, all the parliaments that ever sat, all the kings that ever reigned, put together, have not affected the life of man on this earth as much as that ONE SOLITARY LIFE.

Anon

Plain Speaking

Sunday

Most of the current experts, analysts, historians, scientists, philosophers, and statesmen agree that man is sick. But the crucial question is: Are we beyond saving? Are we beyond hope? Some of our greatest minds privately agree that we have already passed the point of no return.

The people who ask these questions and express these forebodings are the experts, not the rank and file of the people. In a declining culture, one of its characteristics is that the ordinary people are unaware of what is happening. Only those who know and can read the signs of decadence are posing the questions that as yet have no answers. Mr Average Man is comfortable in his complacency. . . . He is not asking any questions, because his social benefits from the government give him a false security. This is his trouble and his tragedy. Modern man has become a spectator of world events, observing on his television screen without becoming involved. He watches the ominous events of our times pass before his eyes, while he sips his beer in a comfortable chair. He does not seem to realise what is happening to him. He does not understand that his world is on fire and that he is about to be burned with it.

Into this cacophony of the voices of doom comes the Word of God. The Bible says that it is *not* too late. I do not believe that we have passed the point of no return. I do not believe that all is black and hopeless. There is still time to return to the moral and spiritual principles that made the West great. There is still time for God to intervene. But there is coming a time when it will be too late, and we are rapidly approaching that time!

Billy Graham

Plain Speaking

Monday

The Church is not a Think-Group, whose role is to duplicate or supplement the intellectual efforts of others. It is an Action-Corps daring to offer simple solutions to complex problems through the creative use of self-sacrifice.

We are prone, alas, to forget this insight and offer to the world that which has cost us nothing. In the late 1950s when Britain was preparing to explode her first hydrogen bomb in the Pacific, the Churches yelled bloody murder, passed frenzied resolutions, protesting, deploring, expressing grave concern etc. etc., and delegations of ecclesiastical dignitaries and political pundits waited on the Prime Minister to threaten and plead. But it was a 60-year-old Unitarian who quietly withdrew his life savings, bought a little boat and sailed it into the centre of the Test Area as his personal protest. Of course it was idiotic, irresponsible, quixotic of him, but his action commanded a queer sort of respect because he was prepared to lay his life on the line for what he believed.

And we comfortable, well-fed, well-housed soldiers of Jesus, having made our big speeches and rolled the rhetoric around our tongues went to our beds the night the bomb went off, shaking our heads sadly at the turn of events and hoping that someone would listen next time. They didn't and they won't. For politicians understand this word game too. Resolutions and deputations don't frighten them. If anything gives them unease it is crazy little men who sail right into the heart of big issues in total disregard for their lives. Such men are dangerous. The rest of us could not be tamer.

Colin Morris

Plain Speaking

Tuesday

We are not here, after all, to fill empty pews with holy gimmicks. We are not here to restore the ancient parish church and keep the merry bells aringing in the steeple and the merry kettle aboiling on the gas-ring of the Woman's Guild. We are here to share God with the world. Our enemy is the power of death in the minds of the people, not the ravages of the death-watch beetle in the beams of the church. . . .

If we spent our faith listening to our neighbours instead of trying to make them come and listen to us on a Sunday. If we invested our faith in the translating of the Incarnation, the Crucifixion and the Resurrection into meaningful terms for our twentieth century society instead of in the heart-breaking struggle to raise enough money to install a new heating system and still have a modest balance to give to foreign missions.

If we believed in the Incarnation, would we be content with Christmas cards and lights on the tree in December, and 'I'm all right, Jack' in January when the bills come rolling in?

If we believed in the Sermon on the Mount on Sunday, would our slogan through the rest of the week still be 'Business is business'?

If we believed in the Crucifixion, would we continually hammer home the nails and thrust in the spear in a degrading struggle to keep up with the Joneses (agnostic, humanist, Anglican, Methodist, Congregational and all)?

If we believed in the Resurrection, would we still be afraid to see our church die that another might be born? If we believed in the love of God, would we perhaps understand the meaning of mission? If we understood the meaning of mission, would we discover the means of unity?

'If anyone wishes to be a follower of mine, he must leave self behind; he must take up his cross and come with me. Whoever cares for his own safety is lost; but if a man will let himself be lost for my sake, he will find his true self.'

If we believed that . . .

Stuart Jackman

Plain Speaking

Those who make religion their god will not have God for their religion.

Thomas Erskine of Linlathen
(1788-1870)

The Christians say that God has done miracles. The modern world, even when it believes in God, and even when it has seen the defencelessness of Nature, does not. It thinks God would not do that sort of thing. Have we any reason for supposing that the modern world is right? I agree that the sort of God conceived by the popular "religion" of our own times would almost certainly work no miracles. The question is whether that popular religion is at all likely to be true.

I call it "religion" advisedly. We who defend Christianity find ourselves constantly opposed not by the irreligion of our hearers but by their real religion. Speak about beauty, truth and goodness, or about a God who is simply the indwelling principle of these three, speak about a great spiritual force pervading all things, a common mind of which we are all parts, a pool of generalised spirituality to which we can all flow, and you will command friendly interest. But the temperature drops as soon as you mention a God who has purposes and performs particular actions, who does one thing and not another, a concrete, choosing, commanding, prohibiting God with a determinate character. People become embarrassed or angry. Such a conception seems to them primitive and crude and even irreverent. The popular "religion" excludes miracles because it excludes the "living God" of Christianity and believes instead in a kind of God who obviously would not do miracles, or indeed anything else. This popular "religion" may roughly be called Pantheism.

C. S. Lewis (1898-1963)

Plain Speaking

Thursday

If the Church is in peril today, it is not primarily because in certain important respects its structure is out-of-date or because it is overburdened with plant, or crippled by lack of finance. It is because too few of its members grasp what our profession of the Faith demands of us.

We may be prepared — up to a point — to help the poverty-stricken, the homeless, the under-privileged, the unfortunate. But in doing so, what are we doing more than others?

The real test for the Christian is when he comes up against the offensive, the ungrateful, the arrogant, the irresponsible, the downright bad. To love them and to give yourself for them and to them, this is where the blood, sweat and tears begin.

Horace Walker

The disturbing, uncomfortable truth is that Christians in the developed countries are living in comparative gross *affluence*. We have accepted a lifestyle which is so similar to that of the covetous world around us as to be indistinguishable from it. We may try, sometimes with high-sounding spiritual reasons, to justify the money we spend on ourselves, our homes, our food, our clothes, our possessions, our entertainment, our holidays, our children's education, and even our church buildings. We may talk about "trying to win our friends for Christ", about "nothing less than the best being good enough for God", or about "church buildings that must reflect the beauty and glory of our Creator"; yet, however we may describe it, we cannot escape from the fact that (in Jesus' parable of Dives and Lazarus) we are the rich man, clothed and fed in comfort, and also guilty of appalling negligence concerning the starving and sick man at our gate. Since all that we are and all that we possess belong to God, we must one day give account of our stewardship to him.

David Watson (1933-1984)

Plain Speaking

For if ye forgive men their trespasses, your heavenly Father will also forgive you: but if ye forgive not men their trespasses, neither will your Father forgive your trespasses.

Matthew VI 14-15

We prayed so that all bitterness could be taken from us and we could start the life for our people again without hatred. We know out of our own suffering that life cannot begin for the better except by us all forgiving one another. For if one does not forgive, one does not understand; and if one does not understand, one is afraid; and if one is afraid, one hates; and if one hates, one cannot love. And no new beginning on earth is possible without love, particularly in a world where men increasingly do not know how to love, but cannot even recognise it when it comes searching for them. The first step towards this love then must be forgiveness.

Laurens van der Post

(From a story of a group of people who had survived a massacre in South Africa.)

Plain Speaking

Saturday

Christian, up and smite them! I am all for dialogue with the Communists, Fascists, The Flat Earth Society, Old Uncle Tom Cobley and all. I would and do enjoy arguments with them; but on our (Christian) terms.

I am not prepared to start with doubts that Jesus Christ is the Son of God, any more than a Communist is prepared to argue on the assumption that the working-class are a collection of vagabonds who should be treated as slaves by all right-thinking people.

I have yet to learn that the early Christians before walking into the arena, made it clear that there was much to be said for the official Roman point of view. . . .

It is terribly unfashionable to say, "The world is in its present mess because the churches are half-empty. And until it gets its priorities right it is heading straight for Hell."

Mr Chad Varra once reduced a clever TV panel to disorganised and routed silence. "Oh, come, Mr Varra!" they taunted, "you're not going to tell us you have actually met the Devil?"

"I am certain," he replied, "that a little girl met the Devil face to face last Wednesday when she was raped and strangled and her body thrown into a wood."

If Christians would only smite the hosts of Midian with the weapons Our Master has furnished — and these include righteous anger — the results would be phenomenal.

Let us, just occasionally, stop apologising for our religion. . . . Let us not be frightened of the world. It has precious little to be proud of and at the moment it is scared stiff, for all its proud front.

Let it laugh its head off at us. For the extraordinary thing is that if we stand up and speak as Our Master bids us, the laugh comes off its face in double quick time.

A challenge issued by 'Commuter',
the Director of a Publishing Company

Indifference

And unto the angel of the church of the Laodiceans write; These things saith the Amen, the faithful and true witness, the beginning of the creation of God;

I know thy works, that thou art neither cold nor hot: I would thou wert cold or hot.

So then because thou art lukewarm, and neither cold nor hot, I will spue thee out of my mouth.

Because thou sayest, I am rich, and increased with goods, and have need of nothing; and knowest not that thou art wretched, and miserable, and poor, and blind, and naked:

I counsel thee to buy of me gold tried in the fire, that thou mayest be rich; and white raiment, that thou mayest be clothed, and that the shame of thy nakedness do not appear; and anoint thine eyes with eyesalve, that thou mayest see.

Revelation III 14-18

If part of our problem today be lack of great passions, intense beliefs, then how is the Holy Spirit an answer? Because of His power to revive man's emotional life. For in the first century or the twentieth, people have never been able to confront Jesus Christ face to face and remain coolly impassive. Something about Him kindles either a total devotion or provokes men to violent opposition. And Jesus Himself seems always to have preferred antagonism to apathy. For apathy is the symptom of a sick and dying spirit.

Catherine Marshall (1914-1983)

Indifference

Monday

He who can burn with enmity
can also burn with love of God,
but he who is coldly hostile
will always find the way closed.

Rabbi Yaakov Yitzhak of Lublin (d. 1815)

His earnest love, His infinite desires,
His living, endless, and devouring fires,
Do rage in thirst, and fervently require
A love 'tis strange it should desire.

We cold and careless are, and scarcely think
Upon the glorious spring whereat we drink,
Did He not love us we could be content:
We wretches are indifferent.

'Tis death, my soul, to be indifferent;
Set forth thyself unto thy whole extent,
And all the glory of His passion prize,
Who for thee lives, who for thee dies.

Thomas Traherne (1637-1674)

Indifference

The forces positively opposed to Christianity are smaller, probably, in this country than anywhere else in the world. Hostility is negligible, by comparison with indifference; but whereas hostility hammers, indifference rusts, and the latter may be the quicker cause of the metal giving way under strain.

'The Times',
Monday, May 2nd, 1938

The great causes of God and humanity are not defeated by the hot assaults of the Devil, but by the slow, crushing, glacier-like mass of thousands and thousands of indifferent nobodies. God's causes are never destroyed by being blown up, but by being sat upon. It is not the violent and anarchical whom we have to fear in the war for human progress, but the slow, the staid, the respectable; and the danger of these lies in their real scepticism. Though it would abhor articulately confessing that God does nothing, it virtually means so by refusing to share manifest opportunities for serving Him.

George Adam Smith (1856-1942)

Indifference

Wednesday

When Jesus came to Golgotha they hanged Him on a tree,
They drove great nails through hands and feet, and made a
  Calvary;
They crowned Him with a crown of thorns, red were His wounds
  and deep,
For those were crude and cruel days, and human flesh was cheap.

When Jesus came to Birmingham they simply passed Him by,
They never hurt a hair of Him, they only let Him die;
For men had grown more tender, and they would not give Him
  pain,
They only just passed down the street, and left Him in the rain.

Still Jesus cried, "Forgive them, for they know not what they do,"
And still it rained the wintry rain that drenched Him through and
  through;
The crowds went home and left the streets without a soul to see,
And Jesus crouched against a wall and cried for Calvary.

G. A. Studdert Kennedy (1883-1929)

Indifference

Is it Nothing to You?
We were playing on the green together,
My sweetheart and I —
O! so heedless in the gay June weather
When the word went forth that we must die.
O! so merrily the balls of amber
And of ivory toss'd we to the sky,
While the word went forth in the King's chamber
That we both must die.

O! so idly straying thro' the pleasaunce
Pluck'd we here and there
Fruit and bud, while in the royal presence
The King's son was casting from his hair
Glory of the wreathen gold that crown'd it,
And, ungirdling all his garments fair,
Flinging by the jewell'd clasp that bound it,
With his feet made bare.

Down the myrtled stairway of the palace,
Ashes on his head,
Came he, thro' the rose and citron alleys,
In rough sark of sackcloth habited,
And in the hempen halter — O! we jested
Lightly, and we laugh'd as he was led
To the torture, while the bloom we breasted
Where the grapes grew red.

O! so sweet the birds, when he was dying,
Piped to her and me —
Is no room this glad June day for sighing —
He is dead, and she and I go free!
When the sun shall set on all our pleasure
We will mourn him — What, so you decree
We are heartless? Nay, but in what measure
Do you more than we?

May Probyn

89

Indifference

Friday

"I shall be in agony till the end of time," God says.
I shall be crucified till the end of time.
My sons the Christians don't seem to realize it.
I am scourged, buffeted, stretched out,crucified; I die
in front of them and they don't know it,
they see nothing, they are blind.
They are not true Christians, or they would not go on
living while I am dying.

Lord, I don't understand; it is not possible; you exaggerate.
I would defend you if you were attacked.
I would be at your side if you were dying.
Lord, I love you! . . .

Yes, son, it is you.
You, and your brothers, for
several blows are needed to drive in a nail,
several lashes are needed to furrow a shoulder,
several thorns are needed to make a crown,
and you belong to the humanity that all together condemns me.

It matters not whether you are among those who hit or
among those who watch, among those who perform or
among those who let it happen.
You are guilty, actors and spectators.
But above all, son, don't be one of those who are asleep,
one of those who can still fall asleep . . . in peace. Sleep!
Sleep is terrible!
"Can you not watch one hour with me?"

Michel Quoist

Indifference

I was hungry and you blamed it on the Communists;
I was hungry and you circled the moon;
I was hungry and you told me to wait;
I was hungry and you set up a commission;
I was hungry and you said, "So were my ancestors";
I was hungry and you said, "We don't hire over 35s";
I was hungry and you said, "God helps those . . .";
I was hungry and you told me I shouldn't be;
I was hungry and you told me machines do that work now;
I was hungry and you had defence bills to pay;
I was hungry and you said, "The poor are always with us".

Lord, when did we see You hungry?

God — let me be aware!
Stab my soul fiercely with other's pain.
Let me walk seeing horror and stain.
Let my hands, groping, find other hands.
Give me the heart that divines, understands,
Give me the courage, wounded, to fight,
Flood me with knowledge, drench me with light.
Please keep me eager just to do my share.
God — let me be aware!

Miriam Teichner

Seeking and Finding

Sunday

Then Job answered and said . . .

Oh that I knew where I might find him! That I might come even to his seat! I would order my cause before him, and fill my mouth with arguments. I would know the words which he would answer me, and understand what he would say unto me . . .

Behold, I go forward, but he is not there; and backward, but I cannot perceive him:

On the left hand, where he doth work, but I cannot behold him: he hideth himself on the right hand, that I cannot see him: but he knoweth the way that I take: when he hath tried me, I shall come forth as gold.

Job XXIII. 1, 3-5, 8-10

Whilst I was speaking thus, and my heart was driven to and fro with every wind, time still slipped away, and I was slow in being converted to my Lord; from day to day I deferred to live in thee, but I deferred not to die daily in myself. While I thus desired a happy life, I yet feared to seek it in its true abode, and I fled from it while yet I sought it. . . .

To thee be praise, to thee be glory, O thou fountain of Mercies. I grew the more miserable, and thou camest nearer to me. Thy right hand was ready even now to take me out of the mire and cleanse me from it, but I knew it not. Nor did anything recall me from that deep pit of carnal pleasure, save the fear of death and of thy future judgement which, for all the changing of my opinions, never departed from my heart. . . .

O crooked ways of mine! Woe be to my audacious soul, which hoped that, had it forsaken thee, it might find something else which was better. Though it turn and toss, upon the back and side and breast, it hath found all things hard; and that thou alone art Rest. And behold, thou art near at hand, thou deliverest us from our wretched errors, thou dost place us in thy right way, and dost comfort us, saying, "Run on, and I will carry you, I will conduct you to the end, and even there will I uphold you."

From the "Confessions" of St Augustine (353-430)

Seeking and Finding

There are times of loneliness and need and sorrow, when no human friend can enter into our heart, and when our whole nature cries out for the comfort and strength which it believes God can bring. No preacher who is really in touch with people, and who has achieved any skill in the art of reading faces, could look down from a pulpit without being deeply impressed by the kind of spiritual hunger which people's faces express. And if he is in sympathy at all he is bound to be deeply moved by the amazing courage of men and women. Many of them are carrying heavy burdens and going through the darkest valleys. Some are troubled as to how in the world they are going to make both ends meet. Some are in deep distress over husband or wife or child. Some are bearing a loneliness which is almost a physical pain. Yet, for the most part, men and women put on a bright face and bear their troubles in an uncomplaining silence; and only when they relax, as they do in church, can it be seen that some are almost at the end of their strength — tired in heart and brain and body, wondering if they will really get through another week, and almost desperate to find God. So much so that the preacher, if they only knew it, is almost as desperate, with a longing to give them the sense of God which has come to himself, which he knows would buoy up their spirits, steady their nerves, be a tonic to their minds, and send them forth with radiant face and renewed strength, feeling that because God was with them, nothing in heaven or earth or hell could down them. Yes, there is not the slightest doubt that we want God. We simply must have Him or break down.

But there is another side to the picture and we must be brave enough to face both sides of our conflict. Many of us want God much as we want a hot-water bottle at night — a little temporary comfort, which would just bring us through a trying hour and then could be pushed away by other things within the self. We cannot play fast and loose with God like that. . . . God must not be thought of as a beneficent fairy godmother, who, by the turning of a ring, can be brought to our aid to turn our dusty rubbish heaps into gold and our hovels into fairy palaces. Nor must we treat Him as a kind of Harrods . . . or bargain with Him as Jacob did. We must want Him with our whole mind, and want Him for His own sake, and not for what we can get out of Him.

Leslie D. Weatherhead (1893-1976)

Seeking and Finding

Finding God is really letting God find us; for our search for Him is simply surrender to His search for us. When the truth of this is clearly seen, prayer becomes real. There is no more talking into empty space, no more fumbling in the dark to lay hold on Him. We go into the secret place and there let every fine and ennobling influence which God is sending to us have free play. We let Him speak to us through our best thoughts, our clearest spiritual visions, our finest conscience. . . .

"I said, 'I will find God,' and forth I went
To seek Him in the clearness of the sky,
But over me stood unendurably
Only a pitiless, sapphire firmament
Ringing the world, blank splendour; yet intent
Still to find God, 'I will go seek,' said I,
'His way upon the waters,' and drew nigh
An ocean marge, weed-strewn and foam-besprent;
And the waves dashed on idle sand and stone,
And very vacant was the long, blue sea;
But in the evening as I sat alone,
My window open to the vanishing day,
Dear God! I could not choose but kneel and pray,
And it sufficed that I was found of Thee."

Harry Emerson Fosdick (1878-1969)
(Quoting Edward Dowden)

Seeking and Finding

Thursday

Console thyself, thou wouldst not seek Me,
if thou hadst not found Me.

Blaise Pascal (1623-1662)

I sought the Lord, and afterward I knew
He moved my soul to seek Him, seeking me;
It was not I that found, O Saviour true —
No, I was found by Thee.

Thou didst reach forth Thy hand and mine enfold;
I walked and sank not on the storm-vexed sea —
'Twas not so much that I on Thee took hold,
As Thou, dear Lord, on me.

I find, I walk, I love, but O the whole
Of love is but my answer, Lord, to Thee;
For Thou wast long beforehand with my soul,
Alway Thou lovedst me.

Anon

Seeking and Finding

The odd thing was that before God closed in on me, I was in fact offered what now appears a moment of wholly free choice. In a sense. I was going up Headington Hill on the top of a bus. I became aware that I was holding something at bay, or shutting something out. Or, if you like, that I was wearing some stiff clothing, like corsets, or even a suit of armour, as if I were a lobster. I felt myself being, there and then, given a free choice. I could open the door or keep it shut; I could unbuckle the armour or keep it on. The choice appeared to be momentous but it was also strangely unemotional. I was moved by no desires or fears. In a sense I was not moved by anything. I chose to open, to unbuckle, to loosen the rein. . . . Then came the repercussion on the imaginative level. I felt as if I were a man of snow at long last beginning to melt. The melting was starting in my back — drip-drip and presently trickle-trickle: I rather disliked the feeling. Total surrender, the absolute leap in the dark, were demanded. The demand was not even "All or nothing". I think that stage had been passed, on the bus-top when I unbuckled my armour and the snow-man started to melt. Now the demand was simply "All."

You must picture me alone in that room at Magdalen, night after night, feeling, whenever my mind lifted even for a second from my work, the steady, unrelenting approach of Him whom I so earnestly desired not to meet. That which I greatly feared had at last come upon me. In the Trinity Term of 1929 I gave in, and admitted that God was God, and knelt and prayed: perhaps, that night, the most dejected and reluctant convert in all England. I did not then see what is now the most shining and obvious thing; the Divine humility which will accept a convert even on such terms. The Prodigal Son at least walked home on his own feet. But who can duly adore that Love which will open the high gates to a prodigal who is brought in kicking, struggling, resentful, and darting his eyes in every direction for a chance of escape? The words *compelle intrare,* compel them to come in, have been so abused by wicked men that we shudder at them; but, properly understood, they plumb the depth of the Divine mercy. The hardness of God is kinder than the softness of men, and His compulsion is our liberation.

C. S. Lewis (1898-1963)

Seeking and Finding

Saturday

The Hound of Heaven

I fled Him, down the nights and down the days;
I fled Him, down the arches of the years;
I fled Him, down the labyrinthine ways
Of my own mind; and in the midst of tears
I hid from Him, and under running laughter.
Up vistaed hopes I sped;
And shot, precipitated,
Adown Titanic glooms or chasmed fears,
From those strong Feet that followed, followed after.
But with unhurrying chase,
And unperturbed pace,
Deliberate speed, majestic instancy,
They beat — and a Voice beat,
More instant than the Feet —
"All things betray thee, who betrayest Me."
I pleaded, outlaw-wise,
By many a hearted casement, curtained red,
Trellised with intertwining charities;
(For, though I knew His love Who followed,
Yet was I sore adread
Lest, having Him, I must have naught beside).

Now of that long pursuit
Comes on at hand the bruit;
That Voice is round me like a bursting sea.

"Whom wilt thou find to love ignoble thee,
Save Me, save only Me?
All which I took from thee I did but take,
Not for thy harms,
But just that thou might'st seek it in My arms.
All which thy child's mistake
Fancies as lost, I have stored for thee at home:
Rise, clasp My hand, and come!"
Halts by me that footfall:
Is my gloom, after all,
Shade of His hand, outstretched caressingly?
"Ah, fondest, blindest, weakest,
I am He Whom thou seekest!
Thou dravest love from thee, who dravest Me."

Francis Thompson (1859-1907)

Advent

And there shall come forth a rod out of the stem of Jesse, and a Branch shall grow out of his roots:

And the spirit of the Lord shall rest upon him, the spirit of wisdom and understanding, the spirit of counsel and might, the spirit of knowledge and of the fear of the Lord;

And shall make him of quick understanding in the fear of the Lord; and he shall not judge after the sight of his eyes, neither reprove after the hearing of his ears:

But with righteousness shall he judge the poor, and reprove with equity for the meek of the earth: and he shall smite the earth with the rod of his mouth, and with the breath of his lips shall he slay the wicked.

And righteousness shall be the girdle of his loins, and faithfulness the girdle of his reins.

The wolf also shall dwell with the lamb, and the leopard shall lie down with the kid; and the calf and the young lion and the fatling together; and a little child shall lead them. . . .

They shall not hurt nor destroy in all my holy mountain: for the earth shall be full of the knowledge of the Lord, as the waters cover the sea.

For unto us a child is born, unto us a son is given: and the government shall be upon his shoulder: and his name shall be called Wonderful, Counsellor, The mighty God, The everlasting Father, The Prince of Peace.

Of the increase of his government and peace there shall be no end, upon the throne of David, and upon his kingdom, to order it, and to establish it with judgement and with justice from henceforth even for ever. The zeal of the Lord of hosts will perform this.

Isaiah XI. 1-6, 9; IX 6, 7

Advent

Monday

Hark, the glad sound! The Saviour comes,
The Saviour promised long;
Let every heart exult with joy,
And every voice be song!

He comes, the prisoners to relieve,
In Satan's bondage held;
The gates of brass before him burst,
The iron fetters yield.

Our glad hosannas, Prince of Peace,
Thy welcome shall proclaim;
And heaven's exalted arches ring
With thy most honoured Name.

Scottish Paraphrases, 1781

God our Father, as Christmas time approaches we have a lot to get ready. There are presents to be bought and wrapped, greetings to be sent.

Never let us forget to prepare our own hearts for the time of your coming. What will be the good of all our activity if it crowds you out, or of our gifts and greetings unless our own lives are presentable to you and to other people?

Not that our trying to put a fair covering on ourselves would be any use. You know us too well for that. We can only ask that you will make the best of us. At least with your help we can see to it that other people receive the presents you have told us to deliver to them — gifts of love, and joy, and peace, and hope — food for the hungry, houses for the homeless, welcome for the despised.

God our Father, there is more to get ready than we realised, and time may be shorter than we think before we are called to account. May our praise now give new zest to our stewardship: for Jesus Christ's sake.

Caryl Micklem (Ed.)

Advent

He hath filled the hungry with good things; and the rich he hath sent empty away.

Luke I 53

Stock up for Christmas! Yuletide food hampers only £87.00 (£2.90 for 30 weeks) . . .
Pilchards in tomato juice . . . peeled prawns in brine . . . cream of chicken soup . . . four steakburgers with onions and gravy . . . pork luncheon meat . . . Christmas pudding . . . mincemeat with brandy . . . mandarin oranges in syrup . . . rum butter . . . chocolate eclairs . . . shortbread . . . beer and lemonade shandy . . .

Mail order catalogue

In developing countries one child in four dies before the age of five. The infant mortality rate there is ten times higher than in developed countries. And half of these deaths are related to inadequate diets. In 1974 UNICEF estimated that 210 million children under five in the world were malnourished. That means three malnourished children for every man, woman and child living in the U.K. and Australia! . . . World poverty is a hundred million mothers weeping because they cannot feed their children.

Ronald J. Sider

Advent

Wednesday

At Christmas we do know that there *is* another sense of values in which true worth lies. If the magic which possesses us at Christmas could only be made to last, how different the world picture would look. It is a world in which all men want peace — and prepare for war; a world in which there is plenty for all to eat, and yet where millions perish with hunger. In a world which might be as bright as a spring morning, our hates and fears and suspicions make a bitter winter, heartless and cold as death.

When the Christ-child draws our stubborn necks as low as His manger, and when His spirit really rules our hearts, only then can the New Age be born and the Christmas magic last for ever.

Leslie D. Weatherhead (1893-1976)

Men travel bravely by a thousand roads,
Some broad and lined with palaces, some steep
And hard and lonely, some that blindly twist
Through tangled jungles where there is no light;
And mostly they are travelled thoughtlessly.
But once a year an ancient question comes
To every traveller passing on his way,
A question that can stab and burn and bless:
"Is this the road that leads to Bethlehem?"

Source unknown

Advent

The darkest time in the year,
The poorest place in the town,
Cold, and a taste of fear,
Mary and Joseph alone,
What can we hope for here?

More light than we can learn,
More wealth than we can treasure,
More love than we can earn,
More peace than we can measure,
Because one child is born.

Christopher Fry.

Twelfth Night

No night could be darker than this night,
no cold so cold,
as the blood snaps like a wire,
and the heart's sap stills,
and the year seems defeated.

O never again, it seems, can green things run,
or sky birds fly,
or the grass exhale its humming breath
powdered with pimpernels,
from this dark lung of winter.

Yet here are lessons for the final mile
of pilgrim kings;
the mile still left when all have reached
their tether's end: that mile
where the Child lies hid.

For see, beneath the hand, the earth already
warms and glows;
for men with shepherd's eyes there are
signs in the dark, the turning stars,
the lamb's returning time.

Out of this utter death he's born again,
his birth our saviour;
from terror's equinox he climbs and grows,
drawing his finger's light across our blood —
the sun of heaven, and the son of God.

Laurie Lee

Advent

Friday
Night of Nights

Now it is night. But it is to become the greatest, most significant night of history. It is the night that will conquer darkness and bring in the day when there shall be night no more. It is the night when those who sit in darkness shall see a great light. It is the night that shall make eternal light, for it is the night when God shall bring into the world him who is the light of the world.

In the stable of the inn at Bethlehem, where the cattle are breathing softly in slumber, a virgin mother brings forth her child and lays him in a manger. Over the cave a bright star shines and an angelic chorus begins to sing. What a moment! What an hour! This is Emmanuel, God with us. It staggers our imagination to believe that God himself has become a man in the person of his Son.

The incarnation of Jesus Christ is not merely a doctrinal tenet about which theologians of different schools may hold differing views. It is a glorious reality, a wondrous fact apart from which there can be no salvation for sinful men. Who in the world that Rome ruled at the time could possibly believe that this little baby in a stable was the great God of creation come in the flesh? This child nestled in Mary's arms would be both God and man united in one person, never again to be separated. This is the glorious mystery of the incarnation. . . .

Who would dream that he is the King of kings and Lord of lords? Who would imagine in Rome that night that he would reach down the ages, overturning kingdoms and empires, changing the world; and that even today, two thousand years later, millions would be ready to die for him?

Billy Graham

O come, all ye faithful,
Joyful and triumphant,
O come ye, O come ye to Bethlehem;
Come and behold him
Born the King of angels;
O come, let us adore him,
O come, let us adore him,
O come, let us adore him, Christ the Lord.

Possibly by John Wade (c. 1711-1786)

Advent

Love came down at Christmas,
Love all lovely, Love Divine;
Love was born at Christmas,
Star and angels gave the sign.

Worship we the Godhead,
Love Incarnate, Love Divine;
Worship we our Jesus:
But wherewith for sacred sign?

Love shall be our token,
Love be yours and love be mine,
Love to God and all men,
Love for plea and gift and sign.

Christina Georgina Rossetti (1830-1894)

But art Thou come, dear Saviour? Hath Thy love
Thus made Thee stoop, and leave Thy throne above
The lofty heavens, and thus Thyself to dress
In dust to visit mortals? Could no less
A condescension serve? And after all,
The mean reception of a cratch and stall?
Dear Lord, I'll fetch Thee thence; I have a room.
'Tis poor, but 'tis my best, if Thou wilt come
Within so small a cell, where I would fain
Mine and the world's Redeemer entertain.
I mean my heart; 'tis sluttish, I confess,
And will not mend Thy lodging, Lord, unless
Thou send before Thy harbinger, I mean
Thy pure and purging grace, to make it clean
And sweep its nasty corners; then I'll try
To wash it also with a weeping eye;
And when 'tis swept and washed, I then will go
And, with Thy leave, I'll fetch some flowers that grow
In Thine own garden, faith and love to Thee;
With those I'll dress it up; and these shall be
My rosemary and bays; yet when my best
Is done, the room's not fit for such a guest,
But here's the cure; Thy presence, Lord, alone
Will make a stall a court, a cratch a throne.

Sir Matthew Hale (1609-1676), Lord Chief Justice of England

Christmas

Sunday

And it came to pass in those days, that there went out a decree from Caesar Augustus that all the world should be taxed. (And this taxing was first made when Cyrenius was governor of Syria). And all went to be taxed, every one into his own city.

And Joseph also went up from Galilee, out of the city of Nazareth, into Judaea, unto the city of David, which is called Bethlehem; (because he was of the house and lineage of David): To be taxed with Mary his espoused wife, being great with child.

And so it was that, while they were there, the days were accomplished that she should be delivered. And she brought forth her firstborn son, and wrapped him in swaddling clothes, and laid him in a manger; because there was no room for them in the inn.

And there were in the same country shepherds abiding in the field, keeping watch over their flock by night. And, lo, the angel of the Lord came upon them, and the glory of the Lord shone round about them: and they were sore afraid.

And the angel said unto them, Fear not: for, behold, I bring you good tidings of great joy, which shall be to all people. For unto you is born this day in the city of David a Saviour, which is Christ the Lord.

And this shall be a sign unto you; Ye shall find the babe wrapped in swaddling clothes, lying in a manger. And suddenly there was with the angel a multitude of the heavenly host praising God, and saying, Glory to God in the highest, and on earth peace, good will toward men.

And it came to pass, as the angels were gone way from them into heaven, the shepherds said one to another, Let us now go even unto Bethlehem, and see this thing which is come to pass, which the Lord hath made known unto us.

And they came with haste, and found Mary, and Joseph, and the babe lying in a manger. And when they had seen it, they made known abroad the saying which was told them concerning this child. And all they that heard it wondered at those things which were told them by the shepherds. But Mary kept all these things, and pondered them in her heart.

Luke II. 1-19

Christmas

A village unremarked for fame or beauty,
A simple carpenter, a girl unknown,
A donkey weary with its load, a stable
Where they could bed, untended and alone.

Hope was given birth within the shadows,
And Victory in swaddling clothes was dressed,
Grace was sweetly cradled in a manger,
And Love lay gentle on a mother's breast.

E. Ruth Glover

O little town of Bethlehem,
How still we see thee lie!
Above thy deep and dreamless sleep
The silent stars go by:
Yet in thy dark streets shineth
The everlasting Light;
The hopes and fears of all the years
Are met in thee tonight.

How silently, how silently,
The wondrous gift is given!
So God imparts to human hearts
The blessings of his heaven.
No ear may hear his coming;
But in this world of sin,
Where meek souls will receive him, still
The dear Christ enters in.

O Holy Child of Bethlehem,
Descend to us, we pray;
Cast out our sin, and enter in;
Be born in us today.
We hear the Christmas angels
The great glad tidings tell;
O come to us, abide with us,
Our Lord Immanuel.

Phillips Brooks (1835-93)

107

Christmas

Tuesday

Brightest and best of the sons of the morning,
Dawn on our darkness, and lend us thine aid;
Star of the east, the horizon adorning,
Guide where our infant Redeemer is laid.

Reginald Heber (1783-1826)

Born in a stable in Bethlehem,
Gently in manger laid,
Jesus the King of the human race,
Grant us Your holy peace.

Mary and Joseph watch o'er Him there,
Oxen and ass by their side;
Worship together the Holy Babe,
Saviour of all mankind.

Far from the East there came wise men three,
Bearing their gifts for a King,
Kneeling to Him who would save the world,
Jesus the Lord of all.

Though for our Saviour no room was found,
Son of the Highest of all,
Still, in our hearts there is room for You;
Come, with Your holy peace.

Kenneth C. Steven

Christmas

In the bleak mid-winter
Frosty wind made moan,
Earth stood hard as iron,
Water like a stone;
Snow had fallen, snow on snow,
Snow on snow,
In the bleak mid-winter,
Long ago.

Our God, heaven cannot hold him,
Nor earth sustain:
Heaven and earth shall flee away
When he comes to reign:
In the bleak mid-winter
A stable-place sufficed
The Lord God Almighty,
Jesus Christ.

Angels and archangels
May have gathered there,
Cherubim and seraphim
Throngèd the air;
But only his mother,
In her maiden bliss,
Worshipped the Belovèd
With a kiss.

What can I give him,
Poor as I am?
If I were a shepherd,
I would bring a lamb;
If I were a wise man,
I would do my part;
Yet what I can I give him —
Give my heart.

Christina Georgina Rossetti (1830-94)

Christmas

Thursday

"The Man Born to be King." First play: "Kings in Judaea."

Scene II (Bethlehem). The Tent of the Three Kings.

ANGEL: Caspar! Melchior! Balthazar!

CASPAR: (in his sleep): Who calls?

ANGEL: The warning of a dream, in a horror of great darkness.

MELCHIOR: (in his sleep): What is it? Oh, what is it?

ANGEL: A sword in the path on the road to Jerusalem.

BALTHAZAR: (waking): O me, it is gone! . . . Caspar!

CASPAR: Is that you, Melchior?

MELCHIOR: I thought it was you cried out.

BALTHAZAR: I had a dream.

CASPAR: And so had I.

MELCHIOR: And I.

CASPAR: I dreamed I was going by night to Jerusalem, but the wind blew out my lantern. So I reached up to heaven and plucked down the Star to serve for a candle. And behold! a great darkness. And I fell — down — down — and woke to the sound of a voice calling my name.

MELCHIOR: I too was going up to Jerusalem, when suddenly the earth gaped open before me. So I drew my sword, and crossed the chasm, walking on the narrow blade. But when I was over, I found the point of the sword plunged in the heart of Mary, and in my ears was the desolate cry of a child.

BALTHAZAR: I also was going up to Jerusalem, by a deep valley between mountain forests. And I heard the voice of Mary calling: "Come back, come back! My child is lost in the hills." And I searched long among the thorns, for I knew that I never could reach the city until I had found the Christ.

CASPAR: Brothers, I cannot think that these are idle dreams.

MELCHIOR: I believe that if we return to Jerusalem we shall find a sword in the path.

CASPAR: We have looked into the heart of Herod, and seen only a horror of great darkness.

MELCHIOR: To be plain with you, I deeply distrust his intentions.

BALTHAZAR: Do as you will, my brothers. But I will not return to Jerusalem.

CASPAR: Then we are all agreed. Ho, there, strike the tents. Make ready our horses . . . We will return to our own country another way.

Dorothy L. Sayers (1893-1957)

Christmas

Journey of the Magi

A cold coming we had of it,
Just the worst time of the year
For a journey, and such a long journey:
The ways deep and the weather sharp,
The very dead of winter.
And the camels galled, sore-footed, refractory,
Lying down in the melting snow.
There were times we regretted
The summer palaces on slopes, the terraces,
And the silken girls bringing sherbet.
Then the camel men cursing and grumbling
And running away, and wanting their liquor and women,
And the night-fires going out, and the lack of shelters,
And the cities hostile and the towns unfriendly
And the villages dirty and charging high prices:
A hard time we had of it.
At the end we preferred to travel all night,
Sleeping in snatches,
With the voices singing in our ears, saying
That this was all folly.

Then at dawn we came down to a temperate valley,
Wet, below the snow line, smelling of vegetation;
With a running stream and a water mill beating the darkness,
And three trees on the low sky,
And an old white horse galloped away in the meadow.
Then we came to a tavern with vine leaves over the lintel,
Six hands at an open door dicing for pieces of silver,
And feet kicking the empty wine-skins.
But there was no information, and so we continued
And arrived at evening, not a moment too soon
Finding the place; it was (you may say) satisfactory.

All this was a long time ago, I remember,
And I would do it again, but set down
This set down
This: were we led all that way for
Birth or Death? There was a Birth, certainly,
We had evidence and no doubt. I had seen birth and death,
But had thought they were different; this Birth was
Hard and bitter agony for us, like Death, our death.
We returned to our places, these kingdoms,
But no longer at ease here, in the old dispensation,
With an alien people clutching their gods.
I should be glad of another death.

T. S. Eliot (1888-1965)

111

Christmas

Saturday

Son of God

Did Mary know this was the Son of God,
The child she, in her innocence, had borne?
She knew. She'd said "Behold thy handmaid, Lord"
And to His will had given up her own.

Did Herod know this was the Son of God,
The babe whom, in his wrath, he sought to kill,
Or did he care, so long as he was left
To be the ruler of the country still?

The shepherds, did they know that this was He
By whom the whole created world was made?
Perhaps they did, for they all left their flocks
And reverently to him their homage paid.

And do we know this is the Son of God?
And have we given the gifts He longs to have —
The worship of a heart given o'er to Him,
The service of a life He died to save?

Margaret McCleary

Moonless darkness stands between.
Past, O Past, no more be seen!
But the Bethlehem star may lead me
To the sight of Him who freed me
From the self that I have been.
Make me pure, Lord: Thou art holy;
Make me meek, Lord: Thou wert lowly;
Now beginning, and alway:
Now begin, on Christmas day.

Gerard Manley Hopkins (1844-1889)

Jesus

I am the light of the world. . . . I am the way, the truth, and the life: no man cometh unto the Father, but by me. . . . I am the bread of life: he that cometh to me shall never hunger; and he that believeth on me shall never thirst. . . . I am with you alway, even unto the end of the world.

John IX 5
John XIV 6
John VI 35
Matthew XXVIII 20

Christianity is based on a life lived in places which still may be visited. We have the witness of pagan historians, Trajan, Pliny, Tacitus, Josephus. A life was begun at Bethlehem which changed other lives and is changing the face of the world, and would change ours if we would let His baby fingers pull down our stubborn necks as low as His manger and let His loving spirit fill our hearts. The critic may argue as he likes, and use the divisions of Christendom as the object of his easy scorn. But in one thing all Churches agree. A life was begun in Bethlehem which offers to all men the key to the problem of the art of living, an art all must seek to practise and He alone mastered. The records of that life have been subjected to the most rigid criticism and enquiry. The white light of nearly two thousand years of scholarship has beaten upon the records, and not only do they bear the scrutiny, but out of the pages leaps the figure of a living Man. Every age of criticism but releases Him more completely from the fetters in which He has been held down, and reveals Him the most knowable, lovable of all the sons of men; the Son of God who became the Son of Man that we, even we, might become the sons of God.

O come let us adore Him, Christ the Lord!

Leslie D. Weatherhead (1893-1976)

Jesus

Monday

Every book I read about Him helps me, but none satisfies me. None deals adequately with those awe-inspiring contrasts. The word humanity describes Him, but the word deity cannot be left out without doing injustice to the records. He is tender and compassionate; but He is violent and uncompromising. He could make a child feel at home on His knee; but He could make His powerful enemies quail before Him. He said that by Him men would be judged; but He was meek and lowly in heart. He said the most awful things about sin that have ever been spoken; but He said the kindest things to sinners that human ears have ever heard. He asks from me my all. Yet he gives Himself to me utterly. He is the most knowable Man who ever lived. Yet no one has ever explained Him. He asserts His authority at every turn. Yet He withdraws from the applauding crowds. His joyous comradeship raises scandal. Yet they call Him the Man of sorrows. He raises from the dead. Yet He deliberately chooses death. He has power such as none has ever had before or since. Yet He ever knocks and waits and listens before He passes the low lintel of the human life, awaiting the true love of the heart, the full allegiance of the will and concerned that no violence to our mental processes is ever demanded from us. He died two thousand years ago. Yet to thousands He is a greater reality than their dearest friend, without whom joy would pass away from life, and leave it cold and bleak and dead.

Leslie D. Weatherhead (1893-1976)

A Splinter

Irony nails you
The Carpenter
To a wooden cross.

K.C.S. 1986

Jesus

Look at some of those crushed, cowering lives without any self-respect left. Matthew, selling his birthright to the hated foreigner, loathed and despised. You, who can read faces, look at his hard eyes and cynical mouth. Jesus says, "Follow Me," and he comes. Saint Matthew! Why? How? How in the world? "*He* did it," says Matthew, "He showed me a new world and then brought me to it, and I was glad to die for Him at last." Mary Magdalene! Look at her! Seven devils, so they said. A woman of the pavement. A fallen woman, A dreadful creature. The lowest of the low. No teacher in this world has ever called to his band a woman like that, but Jesus called her and she came, and His divine, redeeming friendship changed her life. Ask her. "He did it," she says. "He did it. He lifted me up. And I would bathe His feet in my own blood if I could do Him a service."

And this is the refrain all down the years. "He did it. He did it." Mary Slessor couldn't cross Sauchiehall Street in Glasgow by herself, but she became a White Queen among savage tribes in the heart of a foul jungle. Ask her how! "He did it." John Wesley was an unkindled, conventional, prosy Church of England parson. But once enkindled, once really in the new world, that little man climbed on his horse and rode through England, his whole personality blazing like a flaming torch, and the dispassionate historian writes, "The man who saved England in the eighteenth century was John Wesley," but Wesley only says again and again, "He did it." "He did it." "He took away *my* sins, even *mine*, and saved me from the law of sin and death."

He can make you hate sin like hell. He can deliver you from it. It can all be true for you. He can give you an inward peace that nothing can break. He can make that grey face of yours light up with rapture. He can give you back your self-respect. He can help you to self-adjustment. He can put you on top of life instead of underneath it. He can steady your nerves. He can rid you of morbid self-interest and deliver you from fear. He can give you Life!

Leslie D. Weatherhead (1893-1976)

115

Jesus

Wednesday

I will therefore attempt to put into words some impressions of Jesus as a man which the study of all four Evangelists has left on my mind. . . .

Superimposed on all my previous impressions is one of power, tremendous power, utterly controlled. A strong wind swept through Palestine; but if it rooted up the rotten tree, it did not crush the injured reed. The eyes that carved a way for Jesus through a murderous crowd could also draw a tax-collector to abandon his profession. . . .

But there was little relaxation. He had his times of rest and prayer (if prayer was rest), but when in action he was ruthless to himself and well-nigh inexhaustible. Not quite; for the great reservoir of healing power within him was sometimes drained. Then he evaded the importunate crowds or fell into the sleep of exhaustion. On one occasion he slept through a storm at sea; yet the moment he was wakened he was in command. Sometimes too it seems that the power was not at his disposal. He was of two worlds and always mindful of his great commission; but there were hours of doubt and disappointent. He had his times of exultation, but moments of divine impatience too, when he was homesick for Heaven. He kept his eyes on Satan and he saw him fall like lightning from the sky; but Satan also had his eye on him. The passage from the Jordan to beyond the empty tomb was not an effortless and undisputed progress; and no man can conceive the force that went into the final victory.

E. V. Rieu (1887-1972)
Introduction to the Four Gospels

Jesus

H. G. Wells in his *Outline of History* writes:
'Perhaps the priests and the rulers and the rich men understood Him better than His followers . . . He was like some terrible moral huntsman digging mankind out of the snug burrows in which they had lived hitherto. In the white blaze of this Kingdom of His, there was to be no property, no privilege, no pride and precedence; no motive indeed and no reward but love. Is it any wonder that men were dazzled and blinded and cried out against Him? . . . Is it any wonder that the priests realised that between this man and themselves there was no choice but that He or priestcraft should perish? Is it any wonder that the Roman soldiers, confronted and amazed by something soaring over their comprehension and threatening all their disciplines, should take refuge in wild laughter, and crown Him with thorns and robe Him with purple and make a mock Caesar of Him? For to take Him seriously was to enter on a strange and alarming life, to abandon habits, to control instincts and impulses, to essay an incredible happiness . . . Is it any wonder that to this day this Galilean is too much for our small hearts?'

Wells' agnostic sting is in the tail, the last sentence . . . Christ can be accepted, He can be rejected — what He cannot be if a person is worth his salt, is ignored.

Facing Facts

Jesus

Friday

If we look at the Gospel story of the Passion as a whole and do not isolate the Cross from its context, one of the most impressive and revealing things in it is the air of strong deliberation and mastery which characterizes Jesus throughout those last days. He is so manifestly not in the least a straw on the stream of events. His enemies are not manipulating Him so much as He is manipulating them, not in any wrong way, but in the way in which God does lay hold of the wrath and sin of man and make them subserve His infinite purpose of love. To the end He could have escaped the Cross by the simple expedient of going somewhere else; but He did not do so. He deliberately directs His steps to it. There is an atmosphere of mastery all about Him as He steadfastly sets His face towards Jerusalem. Standing before the council, or before Pilate, there is no suggestion of fumbling or hesitancy. Nor on the other hand is there any suggestion of a merely excited and fanatical confidence. It is the other people who are excited, not He. And it is always the excited people who are the weak people. He says almost regally, 'No man taketh my life from me; I lay it down of myself.' He says — very plainly, quietly, with the direct steadiness of clear-sighted conviction — 'Hereafter ye shall see the Son of man seated at the right hand of power.' The hereafter refers to their seeing. He Himself sees now. He is conscious of being in a very real sense at the right hand of power now. He is with God now, the victory is His now.

H. H. Farmer (1892-1981)

118

Jesus

Jesus Rediscovered

And You — what do I know of You? A living presence in the world; the one who, of all the billions and billions and billions of our human family came most immediately from God and went most immediately to God, while remaining most humanly and intimately here among us, today, as yesterday and tomorrow; for all time. Did You live and die and rise from the dead as they say? Who knows, or for that matter, cares? History is for the dead, and You are alive. Similarly, all those churches raised and maintained in Your name, from the tiniest, weirdest conventicle to the great cathedrals rising so sublimely into the sky — they are for the dead, and must themselves die; are, indeed, dying fast. They belong to time, You to eternity. At the intersection of time and eternity — nailed there — You confront us; a perpetual reminder that, living, we die and dying, we live. An incarnation wonderful to contemplate; the light of the world indeed.

Fiat lux! Let there be light! So everything began at God's majestic command; so it might have continued till the end of time — history unending — except that You intervened, shining another light into the innermost recesses of the human will, where the ego reigns and reaches out in tentacles of dark desire. Having seen this other light, I turn to it, striving and growing towards it as plants do towards the sun. The light of love, abolishing the darkness of hate; the light of peace, abolishing the darkness of strife and confusion; the light of life, abolishing the darkness of death; the light of creativity, abolishing the darkness of destruction. Though, in terms of history, the darkness falls, blacking out us and our world, You have overcome history. You came as light into the world, that whoever believed in You should not remain in darkness. The promise stands for ever. Your light shines in the darkness, and the darkness has not overcome it. Nor ever will.

Malcolm Muggeridge

I Believe

Sunday

I believe in God
because I am a child of the age that asked life, 'Why?'
so I walked a road of honest reason, searching,
to find each answer pointing like light in his direction.
I needed a pathway
I reached for reality
I hungered to *live* —
and he was closer than I dreamed.

I believe in God.
Each day this world declares him;
his wisdom stamps each snowflake 'Made in Heaven'!
In the fresh chill of each new day
the air is alive with his closeness.
I feel his sky flare blue in praise above me,
watch a warm wind running ripples
as if he blows across a field;
grip the good earth
and feel its rich black river cry,
'He lives!'
How can I help but believe?

I believe in God
for I have watched the men who do not care to own him;
I've seen, with sickness, little lives wrapped up in foolish pride,
with faces marked for all the world to see their sin,
who
just as I did
ran from holy light
or tried to hide their selfish lives beneath a shell of right.

Oh, stand them by a man who walks with God — and see!
Yes,
I knew men who said there was no God;
but I listened as they died
and I knew that they had lied.

Say I am too young to be so sure,
but I am old enough to feel my age's agony,
its brokenness and barrenness,
to watch it waste with fear and war.
Yet I have seen from every tongue and tribe
like springing grain amid the sterile stone,
men come alive to live in love,
to share and care beneath Christ's cross . . .
. . . and if you saw their smiles you'd know why I believe in God.

William Alfred Pratney

I Believe

I believe in life. I believe that God has created nothing so wonderful, so completely miraculous as this human life. I believe He made it to be good, full, glad, enriching, useful and rewarding, and that we are here to make it so, for ourselves and as many others as we can. In a world bewilderingly full of rival theories, ideologies, even religions, I still maintain that Christ offers a quality of life unique in its fulness, and a quality of living of which we can rightly use the word 'everlasting'. I cannot imagine that a God as wise, as great, as loving as we see in Jesus Christ would, at the moment of our physical death, allow life to be blotted out as if it had never been and, as an act of gratuitous cruelty, break, totally and forever, hearts He has made to love as they can and do. . . .

To me it is crucially important what I can believe about this Jesus Christ. I say that as a minister. Suppose this Jesus is only a man like ourselves, a very good man, a man who had some brilliant ideas about God, the most totally loving man who ever lived — that and nothing more. Then what have I to say to a mother whose child has been killed in a road accident or has died of leukaemia, and who is wondering in her agony of mind and heart if there is a God at all, and if so what is he like? Is he callous, cruel, uncaring and unheeding, sitting up in heaven and letting things like that happen; or right in the centre of her agony, taking the hurt into his own heart? How am I to help a man who has been unfaithful to his wife, imperilled the family he really loves, and who, although his wife has freely forgiven him, cannot forgive himself? You see the enemies of Jesus objected to him saying to a crippled man "Your sins are forgiven" for only God could forgive sins. Were they not right, and how can the best of good men impart assurance of forgiveness?

For myself, just as a person, I only know that the God I see in Jesus Christ totally satisfies every demand of my mind and heart. If God is like that, then I can go on. I also know that this Jesus confronts and shames me as only God could do, and that he challenges and claims me as only God has any right to do. The very simplest form of creed of which there is the very earliest record in the story of the Church said merely this: "Jesus Christ is Lord." This I totally accept. It stands at the heart of what I believe.

R. Leonard Small.

I Believe

Tuesday

He is More

I cannot explain my faith in the manner
of the intellectual
or in terminology of the theologian,
for my faith is basically a simple thing
arising from the yearning
of a young girl's heart for
something better
something more than the disappointment
of continually missing the mark
the frustration of wanting to be best
but not knowing how to go about it
and the resultant burden of discontent.

When I heard of One
who understood my heart's distress
who really cared that I suffered so
I ran to Him with swift eagerness of youth.

Bewildered, my loved ones said
'She will grow out of it'.
But one does not grow out of Christ
one only grows up into Him.
'It won't last,' they predicted, but it has
and He is more precious today
than when I first believed.

You ask, 'Is He then all He claims to be?'
He is more! He is more!
In joy He has been the light of the morning
in trouble the clear shining after rain
in sorrow morning without clouds.
He has plumbed depths I never knew existed.
He has set goals for me
that I never dreamed possible.
He has put such meaning into life —
how can I help but believe?

Wendy Langton

I Believe

I'm not one of those who can point to one Damascus Road experience. I was born into a family where the Christian faith was known and honoured, where actually the afterglow of D. L. Moody still lingered after fifty years; and I heard the Gospel stories before I ever learned to read, and I sang the childhood hymns, as we all do; and then, of course, you go out into the world and all this comes under strain and stress. There is the mood of revolt, the reaction, the sense that anything traditional must be Victorian and bourgeois and dull and tame. But beyond that one comes to this — I'm speaking of my own experience now — this is what I came to eventually. It seemed to me that if you look at those who have discarded the unseen and the eternal from their thinking, you come to the conclusion that whoever may have found the secret of life, they have not.

Which makes sense and rationality, between you and me? Is it Christ's view, when He assures me that this life is spiritual and the training ground for immortality, or is it the sceptic — the Kingdom of God is a myth — we all die like dogs in the end? Which makes sense? One of them is mistaken. Christ or that sceptic, which? Now my soul said to me "Not Christ — He's not mistaken." . . .

I believe in this man Jesus because I've met Him in the Word of God. He claims for Himself such extraordinary things. A greater than Solomon is here, a greater than Jonah is here, a greater than Messiah is here. Now if one makes this kind of claim, either one must be some kind of pathological megalomaniac or else the thing is true — there's no third option. And the extraordinary thing is that whereas on the lips of anyone else these things would sound absolutely incredible, nevertheless on Jesus' lips they seem to me quite understandable. They come home to me in that sense.

Very Rev. Professor James S. Stewart,
in 'Why I Believe', a discussion of
personal Christian belief on B.B.C.
Scottish television, 1962-63.

I Believe

Thursday

Do you really look forward to every day, whatever the problems of that day may be? That is just one of the things that being a Christian means to me. If I had to say in one sentence what my experience of being a Christian is, it would be quite simply a continuous consciousness of the presence of Christ in my life.

I was brought up, as many others, in a church home, where church-going and Sunday school attendance were the natural order of the day. I followed the usual Anglican pattern, christening, confirmation, Holy Communion, Sunday school teaching, youth leadership, church council — but all, looking back, external things without inner conviction.

My "religion" was not part of me; it was something tacked on, to be put on and off as a cloak, as it were. But I thank God I was not left only with the problem. I was pointed to the answer, namely,

"There is life for a look at the Crucified One
There is life at this moment for thee;
Then look, sinner, look unto Him and be saved,
Unto Him who was nailed to the tree."

By His Grace I did just that — I looked and lived. Do not ask me how it works — I do not know. All I do know is that it does, and has lasted and grown over more than 20 years. I am not only a lawyer but a Northerner, and if this did not work out in practice I would not be writing this. But it does — in public life, in private life, in the office, in the family, wherever I am, whatever I am doing. Whether in the hurly burly of a public council meeting or whether in the solitude of my own car, Christ is more real to me than any other single thing — not because of any merit in me, but because by His Grace I have fulfilled the conditions — I have accepted Him as my Saviour and Lord and behold all things have become new.

J. Neville Knox,
Town Clerk of Harrogate

I Believe

Words, just words! I can hear you saying. Well, yes, words; but there's something else — a man, who was born and lived like us; whose presence and teaching have continued to shine for generation after generation, just as they did for his disciples and for all who knew and listened to him in Galilee all those centuries ago. A man who died, but who none the less, in some quite unique way, remained, and remains, alive. A man who offered us the mysterious prospect of dying in order to live; who turned all the world's values upside down, telling us that it was the weak, not the strong, who mattered, the simple, not the learned, who understood, the poor, not the rich, who were blessed. A man whose cross, on which he died in agony, became the symbol of the wildest, sweetest hopes ever to be entertained, and the inspiration of the noblest and most joyous lives ever to be lived.

And now? Well, all I can say is, as one ageing and singularly unimportant fellow-man, that I have conscientiously looked far and wide, inside and outside my own head and heart, and I have found nothing other than this man and his words which offer any answer to the dilemmas of this tragic, troubled time. If his light has gone out, then, as far as I am concerned, there is no light.

Malcolm Muggeridge
(The conclusion of a sermon delivered in the
chapel of Hertford College, Oxford, 3rd November, 1968)

I Believe

Saturday

A Confession of Faith for Today

*We believe in one world, full of riches meant for everyone to
enjoy;*
*We believe in one life, exciting and positive, harmonised with the
life of Jesus, growing into perfect happiness;*
We believe in one morality — love:
the holiness of sharing the joys and sorrows of others;
of deepening true Christian friendship,
*of co-operating to rid our world of poverty, injustice, ignorance
and fear;*
We believe in Jesus, who was the man for others,
whose life was given for others,
whose death has won for us the victory over all life's negatives,
whose power is freely available to all who accept the Holy Spirit;
We believe in the purposes of God
to unite all men and all things in Christ,
whose kingdom shall have no end.

Amen.

Jesus said unto him, If thou canst believe, all things are possible to him that believeth.

And straightway the father of the child cried out, and said with tears, Lord, I believe; help thou mine unbelief.

Mark IX 23-24

Choice

For this commandment which I command thee this day, it is not hidden from thee, neither is it far off.

It is not in heaven, that thou shouldest say, Who shall go up for us to heaven, and bring it unto us, that we may hear it, and do it?

Neither is it beyond the sea, that thou shouldest say, Who shall go over the sea for us, and bring it unto us, that we may hear it, and do it?

But the word is very nigh unto thee, in thy mouth, and in thy heart, that thou mayest do it. . . .

I have set before you life and death, blessing and cursing: therefore choose life, that both thou and thy seed may live: that thou mayest love the Lord thy God, and that thou mayest obey his voice, and that thou mayest cleave unto him: for he is thy life, and the length of thy days.

And Joshua said unto all the people: Now therefore fear the Lord, and serve him in sincerity and in truth: and put away the gods which your fathers served on the other side of the flood, and in Egypt; and serve ye the Lord.

And if it seem evil unto you to serve the Lord, choose you this day whom ye will serve: whether the gods which your fathers served that were on the other side of the flood, or the gods of the Amorites, in whose land ye dwell: but as for me and my house, we will serve the Lord.

Deuteronomy XXX 11-14, 19-20
Joshua XXIV 2, 14-15

Choice

Monday

Choose you this day . . . We will be that which we follow. It does not matter where we are or what work we are doing. What we follow, that we will become. Follow what is worthless, and we become worthless. Follow truth, love, righteousness, faithfulness, and we will become true, loving, right-living and faithful. Each one of us has a choice. For every day we live we become more and more like that which we choose to follow.

Amy Carmichael of Dohnavur (1867-1951)

'I'm ready to accept Jesus as a great moral teacher, but I don't accept His claim to be God.' That is the one thing we must not say. A man who was merely a man and said the sort of things Jesus said would not be a great moral teacher. He would either be a lunatic — on a level with the man who says he is a poached egg — or else he would be the Devil of Hell. You must make your choice. Either this man was, and is, the Son of God: or else a madman or something worse. You can shut Him up for a fool, you can spit at Him and kill Him as a demon; or you can fall at His feet and call Him Lord and God. But let us not come with any patronising nonsense about His being a great human teacher. He has not left that open to us. He did not intend to.

C. S. Lewis (1898-1963)

Choice

We seem then to have only two choices open to us. We have to choose between despair and faith. On the one hand there is the final defeat of the hopes by which alone we can live; on the other there is the looking forward to some kind of transcendent realisation of these hopes beyond the boundaries and possibilities of this present life. This is a conclusion which robust thinking cannot possibly escape. It is the conclusion which has been reached by all robust thinkers, Christians and unbelievers alike. I have no respect whatever for your timid mediating illusionists — 'the trembling throng whose sails were never to the tempest given;' but for those who have been brave enough to look the bleak prospect in the face without blinkers I entertain very high respect indeed. They may not be in possession of the true solution, but at least they permit themselves a clear-sighted view of the terms of the problem.

At the heart of the Christian faith there lies not only the negative conviction that the perfect kingdom can never be realised in this world, but also the positive conviction that it nevertheless is real and will be realised. This is what Jesus Christ came to preach. 'Now after that John was delivered up, Jesus came into Galilee, preaching the gospel of God, and saying, The time is fulfilled, and the kingdom of God is at hand: repent ye, and believe in the gospel.' Such is our summary of the first Christian sermon. 'For here we have no continuing city, but we seek one to come.' The pilgrimage to which I would invite you is a believing pilgrimage towards this Celestial City.

John Baillie (1886-1961)

It is one primal tenet of my belief that God gives us all, the stones to build our lives and we can do with them one of two things. We can build a high containing wall round our own happiness, to the shutting out of God and man, only to witness a garden becoming a desert and the soul within dying the death. Or else we can take the stones He puts into our hands and from them build a bridge into other less privileged lives, so that daily we pass over it on errands of love and mercy.

G. Johnstone Jeffrey (1881-1961)

Choice

Wednesday

Who Thou art I know not
But this much I know;
Thou hast set the Pleiades
In a silver row;

Thou hast sent the trackless winds
Loose upon their way,
Thou hast reared a colour wall
Twixt the night and day:

Thou hast made the flowers to bloom
And the stars to shine;
Hid rare gems of richest ore
In the tunnelled mine.

But chief of all Thy wondrous works,
Supreme of all Thy plan,
Thou hast put an upward reach
Into the heart of man.

Harry Kemp

To every man there openeth
A way and ways and a way.
And the high soul climbs the high way
And the low soul gropes the low
And in between on the misty flats
The rest drift to and fro.
But to every man there openeth
A high way and a low
And every man decideth the way his soul shall go.

John Oxenham (1852-1941)

Choice

For the which cause I also suffer these things: nevertheless I am not ashamed: for I know whom I have believed, and am persuaded that he is able to keep that which I have committed unto him against that day.

2 Timothy I 12

The Story of Janusz Korczak

As a specialist in children's complaints in Warsaw before the First World War and while still a young man, Dr Janusz Korczak had surrendered a wealthy practice to devote himself to the orphans of Poland. A first-rate child psychologist, he had written about children and he had also written for them. He had written plays, and had proved himself a successful editor and broadcaster.

A man with a rare understanding of the meaning of events, he had raised himself to the status of a prophet by foretelling many of the major events of the 'thirties and 'forties before they happened. When the Germans blitzed Poland into submission in 1939, the last voice of their own the people heard over the radio was that of Janusz Korczak. He went on speaking words of encouragement until the station was put out of action.

No man has shown greater courage than he did. In 1942 it was his fate to undertake what must be one of the most heartbreaking journeys in history. He was compelled to lead the two hundred children of his orphanage to the railway trucks waiting to take them to the gas chambers of Lubienka concentration camp. On reaching the siding, Korczak was offered his life. The Germans told him he could be of use to them. He refused the offer and so crowned a life of sacrifice with martyrdom, dying with his children.

H. Gresswell

Choice

Friday

The position was not, as I had been comfortably thinking all these months, merely a question of whether I was to accept the Messiah or not. It was a question of whether I was to accept Him — or *reject*. My God! There was a gap *behind* me, too. Perhaps the leap to acceptance was a horrifying gamble — but what of the leap to rejection? There might be no certainty that Christ was God — but, by God, there was no certainty that He was not. If I were to accept, I might and probably would face the thought through the years: 'Perhaps, after all, it's a lie; I've been had!' But if I were to reject, I would certainly face the haunting, terrible thought: 'Perhaps it's true — and I have *rejected my God!*'

This was not to be borne. I could not reject Jesus. There was only one thing to do, once I had seen the gap behind me. I turned away from it and flung myself over the gap *towards* Jesus.

Early on a damp English morning with spring in the air, I wrote in the Journal and to C. S. Lewis:

I *choose* to believe in the Father, Son, and Holy Ghost — in Christ, my Lord and my God. Christianity has the ring, the feel, of unique truth. Of essential truth. By it, life is made full instead of empty, meaningful instead of meaningless. Cosmos becomes beautiful at the Centre, instead of chillingly ugly beneath the lovely pathos of spring. But the emptiness, the meaninglessness, and the ugliness can only be seen, I think, when one has glimpsed the fullness, the meaning, and the beauty. It is when heaven and hell have *both* been glimpsed that going back is impossible. But to go on seemed impossible, also. A glimpse is not a vision. A choice was necessary: and there is no certainty. One can only choose a side. So I — I now choose my side: I choose beauty; I choose what I love. But choosing to believe *is* believing. It's all I can do: choose. I confess my doubts and ask my Lord Christ to enter my life. I do not *know* God is, I do but say: Be it unto me according to Thy will. I do not affirm that I am without doubt, I do but ask for help, having chosen, to overcome it. I do but say: Lord, I believe — help Thou mine unbelief.

Sheldon Vanauken

Choice

Light looked down and beheld Darkness.
'Thither will I go,' said Light.
Peace looked down and beheld War.
'Thither will I go,' said Peace.

Love looked down and beheld Hatred.
'Thither will I go,' said Love.
So came Light and shone.
So came Peace and gave rest.
So came Love and brought Life.
And the Word was made Flesh, and dwelt among us.

Laurence Housman (1865-1959)

I have to choose. I back the scent of life
Against its stink. That's what Faith works out at
Finally. I know not why the Evil,
I know not why the Good, both mysteries
Remain unsolved, and both insoluble. I know that both are there,
the battle set,
And I must fight on this side or on that.
I can't stand shiv'ring on the bank, I plunge
Head first. I bet my life on Beauty, Truth
And Love, not abstract but incarnate Truth,
Not Beauty's passing shadow but its self.
Its very self made flesh, Love realised.
I bet my life on Christ — Christ Crucified.
Behold your God! . . .   . . . I see
All history pass by, and through it all
Still shines that face, the Christ-Face, like a star
Which pierces drifting clouds, and tells the Truth. . . .
So through the clouds of Calvary — there shines
His face, and I believe that Evil dies,
And Good lives on, loves on, and conquers all —
All War must end in Peace. These clouds are lies.
They cannot last. The blue sky is the Truth.
For God is Love. Such is my Faith, and such
My reasons for it, and I find them strong
Enough. And you? You want to argue? Well,
I can't. It is a choice. I choose the Christ.

G. A. Studdert Kennedy (1883-1929)

133

Commitment (1)

Sunday

Behold, I stand at the door, and knock: if any man hear my voice, and open the door, I will come in to him, and will sup with him, and he with me.

If any man be in Christ, he is a new creature: old things are passed away; behold, all things are become new.

These things have I spoken unto you, that my joy might remain in you, and that your joy might be full.

Revelation III 20
2 Corinthians V 17
John XV 11

There is nothing so important for any man as that he should get right with God, that he should find the full, rich life which Christ alone offers, that he should enter into that new relationship which lasts through time into eternity. You may call it being born again, or being converted, or finding Christ, or accepting Christ; the final meaning is the same — here is a matter of life and death, more literally than any other we have to face.

R. Leonard Small

Commitment (1)

He who stands at the door has come with a gift, but we are so ready to think that He has come for a payment. The knock is a Saviour's knock, but we are so ready to think it a Taskmaster's. That is perhaps the greatest misunderstanding to which religion has been subject in every age. It is the common error of most pre-Christian and non-Christian forms of religion, and it is also the error which has done most to falsify and limit the true understanding of Christianity itself. We interpret the Divine summons merely as a demand for obedient service, and so we try to still the knocking by feverish action. We turn our religion into a code of good conduct, an ideal to be striven for, a law to be obeyed.

All these have indeed their own part to play within the Christian life. Law and commandment, good conduct and the quest of the ideal, hard work and loyal service must all be given due place; and to deny them place would be to fall into the error opposite to that which we are now considering. But their place is not at the root of the spiritual life. They are not of the root but of the fruit.

Christianity is, when fundamentally regarded, not a law but a gospel. It was as a gospel that it was preached from the very beginning. The word 'gospel' or (in its original Greek form) 'evangel' means good news; and good news is precisely what Christianity sets out to be. . . .

But something is expected of the man who hears good news, no less than of the man who is merely reminded of his debts and duties, though it is not the same thing that is expected. . . . It is not that I am expected to produce something out of myself, or to achieve something in my own strength, but that I am expected to allow Another to work His will with me. The demand is much more fundamentally a demand for surrender than a demand for effort. I am asked, not to assert my will, but to yield it.

John Baillie (1886-1961)

Commitment (1)

Tuesday

It daily becomes more apparent that God's respect for the freedom of our affections, thoughts and purposes is complete. It is part of that respect for our freedom that He never forces upon us His own gifts. He offers them, but unless we actively accept them, they remain ineffective as far as we are concerned. 'Behold, I stand at the door and knock' — that is always the relation of God our Redeemer to our souls. He has paid the whole price; he has suffered the atoning Death; yet still He waits till we open the door of our hearts to let in His love which will call our love out. He never breaks down that door. He stands and knocks. And this is true not only of His first demand for admission to the mansion of the soul; it is true also of every room within that mansion. There are many of us who have opened the front door to Him, but have only let Him into the corridors and staircases: all the rooms where we work or amuse ourselves are still closed against Him. There are still greater multitudes who have welcomed Him to some rooms, and hope that He will not ask what goes on behind the doors of others. But sooner or later He asks; and if we do not at once take Him to see, He leaves the room where we were so comfortable with Him, and stands knocking at the closed door. And then we can never again have the joy of His presence in the first room until we open the door at which He is now knocking. We can only have Him with us in the room that we choose for Him, if we really make Him free of all the house.

William Temple (1881-1944)

Commitment (1)

What, then, is the nature of that spiritual law of life under the direction of which, as he [Edward Wilson] saw it, man should order his life if he would truly live? It was his steadfast and unalterable conviction that for a man who has wrapped his will in God's will, put his life consciously in the stream of the divine life, freed his soul from all personal ambitions, taken his life on trust as a divine gift — that for such a man there is an over-ruling Providence which guards and guides him in every incident of his life, from the greatest to the least. He held that all annoyances, frustrations, disappointments, mishaps, discomforts, hardships, sorrows, pains and even final disaster itself, are simply God's ways of teaching us lessons that we could never else learn. That circumstances do not matter, are nothing; but that the response of the spirit that meets them is everything; that there is no situation in human life, however apparently adverse, nor any human relationship, however apparently uncongenial, that cannot be made, if God be in the heart, into a thing of perfect joy; that in order to attain this ultimate perfection, one must accept every experience and learn to love all persons; that the love particular should lead up to the love universal; that the worth of life is not to be measured by its results in achievement or success, but solely by the motive of one's heart and the effort of one's will; that the value of experience depends not so much upon its variety or duration as upon its intensity; and that by one single concentrated effort a brief life might attain a level that ages of ordinary development would fall short of, so that a man who lives his life thus 'having become perfect in a little while fulfils long years.'

'The Faith of Edward Wilson' —
George Seaver (1890-1976)

Commitment (1)

Thursday

Christianity is not a programme to be adopted. It is a life to be lived. . . .
The Christian commitment is not primarily commitment to a cause or an
institution or a creed; it is commitment to a person — to the person of Christ
Himself. "I know," says the Apostle Paul, "whom I have believed, and am
persuaded that He is able to keep what I have committed unto Him against
that day." Not "I know what," but "I know whom." It is not what I believe
that matters in the end of the day; it is in Whom I have put my trust; it is to
Whom I have committed my life.

The commitment for which Christ asks is one that involves the whole of
life. It means putting my past in His hands. It means putting my present in His
hands. It means putting my future in His hands.

It means that I leave Him to deal with my yesterdays as only He can. All I
have been and done, and all I have failed to be and do until now — the
influences for good or evil I have exercised, the words I have spoken, the
guilty silences of which I am only too painfully aware.

It means putting my today in His hands — all the relationships in which I
find myself involved; my home and family; my daily life and work in the
world; my leisure time interests and pursuits; my time, my talents, my means
— not deciding just what proportion of these will be His and what I will keep
for my own use, but laying all I am and have down at His feet, making it over
to Him for whatever He wants to do with it; making myself over to Him for
whatever He wants to do now with me. "They first gave their own selves to
the Lord."

It means putting all the tomorrows of my life in His hands — the question
of what I do with every day and every hour of the life which lies in front of
me.

D. P. Thomson (1896-1974)

Commitment (1)

But there must be a real giving up of the self. You must throw it away "blindly" so to speak. Christ will indeed give you a real personality: but you must not go to Him for the sake of that. As long as your own personality is what you are bothering about you are not going to Him at all. The very first step is to try to forget about the self altogether. Your real, new self (which is Christ's and also yours, and yours just because it is His) will not come as long as you are looking for it. It will come when you are looking for Him. Does that sound strange? The same principle holds, you know, for more everyday matters. Even in social life, you will never make a good impression on other people until you stop thinking about what sort of impression you are making. Even in literature and art, no man who bothers about originality will ever be original: whereas if you simply try to tell the truth (without caring twopence how often it has been told before) you will, nine times out of ten, become original without ever having noticed it. The principle runs through all life from top to bottom. Give up yourself, and you will find your real self. Lose your life and you will save it. Submit to death, death of your ambitions and favourite wishes every day and death of your whole body in the end: submit with every fibre of your being, and you will find eternal life. Keep back nothing. Nothing that you have not given away will ever be really yours. Nothing in you that has not died will ever be raised from the dead. Look for yourself, and you will find in the long run only hatred, loneliness, despair, rage, ruin and decay. But look for Christ and you will find Him, and with Him everything else thrown in.

C. S. Lewis (1898-1963)

Commitment (1)

Saturday

Christ says "Give me all. I don't want so much of your time and so much of your money and so much of your work: I want You. I have not come to torment your natural self, but to kill it. No half-measures are any good. I don't want to cut off a branch here and a branch there. I want to have the whole tree down. I don't want to drill the tooth, or crown it, or stop it, but to have it out. Hand over the whole natural self, all the desires which you think innocent as well as the ones you think wicked — the whole outfit. I will give you a new self instead. In fact, I will give you Myself: my own will shall become yours."

Both harder and easier than what we are all trying to do. You have noticed, I expect, that Christ Himself sometimes describes the Christian way as very hard, sometimes as very easy. He says, "Take up your Cross" — in other words, it is like going to be beaten to death in a concentration camp. Next minute He says, "My yoke is easy and my burden light." He means both. And one can just see why both are true. . . .

I find I must borrow yet another parable from George Macdonald. Imagine yourself as a living house. God comes in to rebuild that house. At first, perhaps, you can understand what He is doing. He is getting the drains right and stopping the leaks in the roof and so on: you knew that those jobs needed doing and so you are not surprised. But presently He starts knocking the house about in a way that hurts abominably and does not seem to make sense. What on earth is He up to? The explanation is that He is building quite a different house from the one you thought of — throwing out a new wing here, putting on an extra floor there, running up towers, making courtyards. You thought you were going to be made into a decent little cottage: but He is building a palace. He intends to come and live in it Himself.

C. S. Lewis (1898-1963)

Commitment (2)

For it is God Who is at work within you, giving you the will and the power to achieve His purpose.

Philippians II 13 (Phillips)

What is so often lacking in present-day Christians is an adequate sense of God within us. . . . The Christian religion is all too often reduced to a performance to please an external God, while to the early Christians it was plainly the invasion of their lives by a new quality of life — nothing less than the life of God Himself. I believe this lack of faith in God-within-us is largely unconscious, for while we should be the first to recognise that lack of faith on man's part inhibited even the powers of Christ Himself, yet I do not think we realise that this same lack of faith in Christ-within-us prevents the operation of His power, and our proper development as sons of God. There is far too much strenuous, even hysterical effort, and far too little quiet confidence in the Christ within us. Certainly Christians admit that they need the help of God in the tasks to which they are called, and certainly they seek it. But I have an uneasy feeling that many do not really believe that God Himself actually operates within their personalities. It is almost as though they visualise themselves like Christian in *Pilgrim's Progress,* as treading a dangerous and narrow path and winning the Celestial City only by the skin of their teeth. I doubt very much whether they see themselves as sons and daughters of the Most High, not merely receiving occasional help from God, but continually and without intermission indwelt by the living Spirit of God.

In the experience of St. Paul and his followers, the revolutionary thought — "that sacred mystery which up till now has been hidden in every age and generation" — is that God is no longer the external power and authority, but One who lives *in* them, transforming their thinking and feeling, renewing their minds, inspiring their hearts, and effectually preventing them from being conformed to this fleeting world. Such a conviction is indeed revolutionary, and we may well ask ourselves whether this revolution in thought has taken place effectually within each one of us; for so long as we do not really believe this truth in our heart of hearts, it remains a theological idea or a beautiful thought and has no noticeable effect upon our lives.

J. B. Phillips (1906-1982)

Commitment (2)

Monday

It is to Paul chiefly that we owe the thought (which is also found in John's first letter), that Christ Himself lives in men's hearts. No one could read with an open mind the Letters of the New Testament without seeing that people are being, sometimes suddenly and sometimes step by step, transformed. The reason for this, according to Paul, is an open secret. In the past, he says in effect, men have striven to please an external God; now God's great secret is plain. With the coming of the Good News, indeed it is part of the Good News, God is prepared to live within the personalities of those who use their faculty of faith towards Him. In Paul's writings we do not read of Jesus Christ as an Example Who lived and died some years before and Who must be followed and imitated. On the contrary, Paul's letters are ablaze with the idea that, if men will believe it, Christ is alive and powerful, ready to enter and transform the lives of even the most unlikely. This happens, he says, "by faith." But how rarely in present-day Christianity do we meet such a faith! Many Christians do not appear to have grasped this, one of the essentials of the Gospel. It is true that they believe in God, they pray to God and they try to follow the example of Christ. But, as far as one can tell, they have not begun to realise that Christ could be living and active at the very centre of their own personalities. And, of course, so long as they do not believe it, it is not true for them. For just as in the days of Christ's human life the divine power was inhibited or limited by the absence of faith, so His activity within the personality is limited where a man does not in his heart of hearts believe in it. If we modern Christians are steadfastly refusing to believe in this inward miracle, it is not surprising that our Christian life becomes a dreary drudge.

J. B. Phillips (1906-1982)

Commitment (2)

Life is a matter not of conforming to external rules but of being transformed from within.

This truth, which is mentioned again and again in the New Testament, seems to us too good to be true. We labour and strive and pray as though Christianity were a difficult *performance*. Theoretically we would agree with the notion of the "indwelling Christ," but most of us for most of the time act as though we did not. We have lost sight of the fact that Christ is *in us*, both willing and doing. Consequently we lack that joy, confidence and spontaneity which rightly belong to the sons of God. This does not, naturally, make our path smooth and free from trouble — neither Jesus nor Paul lived that kind of life. But it makes a whole world of difference when we believe that God, the whole unimaginable power, love and wisdom behind everything, is not merely on our side but actually at work in our hearts and minds. . . .

But how far removed from the idea of the New Testament are the insipid words of the hymn which says "he came sweet influence to impart, a gracious willing guest," and goes on to say, "and his that gentle voice we hear soft as the breath of even, that checks each fault, that calms each fear . . ." Anyone who has any experience at all of the living God knows that he is nothing at all like this somebody who tut-tuts politely at our failings and lays a soothing hand upon our anxious little heads. The God who lives in us if we allow him, is not necessarily always gentle: he can be wind and fire and a whole lot of other things. He can give us strength, but he can also show us our weakness! He will "increase our faith," but frequently not in the way we want or expect. He will show us, as we can bear it, more and more truth, but he will shatter our illusions without scruple, perhaps especially illusions about ourselves. He will give us moments of wonderful perception, but will also allow us to endure terrifying darkness. His dealings with us are not some optional religious game; he is in deadly earnest and he is intent on "bringing many sons to glory." He is indeed all goodness and light but he will show no more compunction towards the evil things that we have allowed to grow in our hearts than a human surgeon would to a malignant growth. The men of old were hardly exaggerating when they said, "Our God is a consuming fire."

J. B. Phillips (1906-1982)

Commitment (2)

Wednesday

Can we not say a willing "Yes" to our Lord?

It is a very simple transaction, and yet very real. The steps are but three: first, we must be convinced that the Scriptures teach this glorious indwelling of God; then we must surrender our whole selves to Him to be possessed by Him; and finally, we must believe that He *has* taken possession, and *is* dwelling in us. We must begin to reckon ourselves dead, and to reckon Christ as our only life. We must maintain this attitude of soul unwaveringly. It will help us to say, "I am crucified with Christ: nevertheless I live, yet not I, but Christ liveth in me," over and over, day and night, until it becomes the habitual breathing of our souls. We must put off our self-life by faith continually, and put on the life of Christ; and we must do this, not only by faith, but practically as well. We must continually put self to death in all the details of daily life, and must let Christ instead live and work in us. I mean we must never do the selfish thing, but always the Christ-like thing. We must let this become, by its constant repetition, the attitude of our whole being. And as surely as we do, we shall come at last to understand something of what it means to be made one with Christ as He and the Father are one. Christ left all to be joined to us; shall we not also leave all to be joined to Him, in this Divine union which transcends words, but for which our Lord prayed when He said, "Neither pray I for these alone, but for them also which shall believe on me through their word: that they all may be one; as thou, Father, art in me, and I in thee, that they also may be one in us."

Hannah Pearsall Smith (1832-1911)

Commitment (2)

Do not stint or measure your obedience or your service. Let your heart and your hand be as free to serve Him, as His heart and hand were to serve you. Let Him have all there is of you, body, soul, mind, spirit, time, talents, voice, everything. Lay your whole life open before Him, that He may control it. Say to Him each day, "Lord, enable me to regulate this day so as to please thee! Give me spiritual insight to discover what is thy will in all the relations of my life. Guide me as to my pursuits, my friendships, my reading, my dress, my Christian work." Do not let there be a day nor an hour in which you are not consciously doing His will, and following Him wholly. . . . Bring Christ thus into your life and into all its details, and a romance, far grander than the brightest days of youth could ever know, will thrill your soul, and nothing will seem hard or stern again.

Hannah Pearsall Smith (1832-1911)

Heaven above is softer blue,
Earth around is sweeter green;
Something lives in every hue,
Christless eyes have never seen.

George Wade Robinson (1838-77)

Commitment (2)

Friday

When Christians say the Christ-life is in them, they do not mean simply something mental or moral. When they speak of being 'in Christ' or of Christ being 'in them', this is not simply a way of saying that they are thinking about Christ or copying Him. They mean that Christ is actually operating through them; that the whole mass of Christians are the physical organism through which Christ acts — that we are His fingers and muscles, the cells of His body.

C. S. Lewis (1898-1963)

I know not why God's wondrous grace
To me has been made known;
Nor why — unworthy as I am —
He claimed me for His own.
> *But "I know whom I have believed; and am persuaded that He*
> *is able to keep that which I've committed unto Him against that*
> *day."*

I know not how this saving faith
To me He did impart;
Or how believing in His word
Wrought peace within my heart.
> *But "I know whom I have believed; and am persuaded that He*
> *is able to keep that which I've committed unto Him against that*
> *day."*

I know not what of good or ill
May be reserved for me —
Of weary ways or golden days
Before His face I see.
> *But "I know whom I have believed; and am persuaded that He*
> *is able to keep that which I've committed unto Him against that*
> *day."*

D. W. Whittle (1840-1901)

Commitment (2)

Let us open our lives to Him, by removing the barriers that habitually keep Him out. Let us turn ourselves over to Him, remembering that this is not the act of a day but the work of a lifetime. . . . For the giving of oneself to Christ is never finished, but always to be reaffirmed, with a new existential decision every morning and a fresh surrender every night, until one day death seals the offering and makes our commitment complete.

And if at this present time there is some new demand He is laying upon us, some sacrifice from which we shrink, some burnt-offering we are disinclined to make — shall we not remember the example, singled out by our Lord Himself as worthy of perpetual remembrance, of one who, possessing a lovely alabaster box of most precious ointment, did not hesitate when Jesus crossed her path to break it at His feet?

James S. Stewart

In Thee would we lose ourselves utterly; do in us what Thou wilt.

Jakob Boehme (1575-1624)

Entering In

Sunday
Opening the Door to Christ

This step is the beginning and nothing else will do instead. You can believe in Christ intellectually and admire Him. You can say your prayers to Him through the keyhole (as I did for many years); you can push coins at Him under the door; you can be moral, decent, upright and good; you can be religious and pious; you can have been baptised and confirmed; you can be deeply versed in the philosophy of religion; you can be a theological student and even an ordained minister — and still not have opened the door to Christ. There is no substitute for this.

John Stott

Whitsunday, 1961

I don't know Who — or what — put the question, I don't know when it was put. I don't even remember answering. But at some moment I did answer *Yes* to Someone — or Something — and from that hour I was certain that existence is meaningful and that, therefore, my life, in self-surrender, had a goal.

From that moment I have known what it means 'not to look back', and 'to take no thought for the morrow'.

Led by the Ariadne's thread of my answer through the labyrinth of Life, I came to a time and place where I realised that the Way leads to a triumph which is a catastrophe, and to a catastrophe which is a triumph, that the price for committing one's life would be reproach, and that the only elevation possible to man lies in the depths of humiliation. After that, the word 'courage' lost its meaning, since nothing could be taken from me.

As I continued along the Way, I learned, step by step, word by word, that behind every saying in the Gospels, stands *one* man and *one* man's experience. Also behind the prayer that the cup might pass from him and his promise to drink it. Also behind each of the words from the Cross.

Dag Hammarskjöld (1905-61)

Entering In

Tuesday

It was in my second year [at London Hospital and University], 1885, that, returning from an out-patient case one night, I turned into a large tent erected in a purlieu of Shadwell, the district to which I happened to have been called. It proved to be an evangelistic meeting of the then famous Moody and Sankey. It was so new to me that when a tedious prayer-bore began with a long oration, I started to leave. Suddenly the leader, whom I learned afterwards was D. L. Moody, called out to the audience, "Let us sing a hymn while our brother finishes his prayer." His practicality interested me, and I stayed the service out. When eventually I left, it was with a determination either to make religion a real effort to do as I thought Christ would do in my place as a doctor, or frankly abandon it. That could only have one issue while I still lived with a mother like mine. For she had always been my ideal of unselfish love. So I decided to make the attempt, and later went down to hear the brothers J. E. and C. T. Studd speak at some subsidiary meeting of the Moody campaign. They were natural athletes, and I felt that I could listen to them. I could not have listened to a sensuous-looking man, a man who was not master of his own body, any more than I could to a precentor who, coming to sing the prayers at college chapel dedication, I saw get drunk on sherry which he abstracted from the banquet table just before the service. Never shall I forget, at the meeting of the Studd brothers, the audience being asked to stand up if they intended to try and follow Christ. It appeared a very sensible question to me, but I was amazed how hard I found it to stand up. At last one boy, out of a hundred or more in sailor rig, from an industrial or reformatory ship on the Thames, suddenly rose. It seemed to me such a wonderfully courageous act — for I knew perfectly well what it would mean to him — that I immediately found myself on my feet, and went out feeling that I had crossed the Rubicon, and must do something to prove it.

Wilfred Grenfell (1865-1940)

Entering In

There seemed to be no hope, no ultimate purpose, any more. If there was a God, the people at the seminary had subtly hinted that I must have turned away from Him (or perhaps this was my imagination). At any rate I felt things closing in on me in the inner chamber of my life.

I used to walk down the streets, I remember, and suddenly would break out in a cold sweat. I thought I might be losing my mind. One day it was so bad that I got in my company car and took off on a field trip alone. As I was driving through the tall pine woods country of East Texas I suddenly pulled up beside the road and stopped. I remember sitting there in complete despair. I had always been an optimistic person, and had always had the feeling that there was 'one more bounce in the ball.' After a good night's sleep, or perhaps a couple of martinis and a good night's sleep, one could always start again tomorrow. But now there was no tomorrow in my situation. I was like a man on a great grey treadmill going no place, in a world that was made up of black, black clouds all around me.

As I sat there I began to weep like a little boy, which I suddenly realized I was inside. I looked up toward the sky. There was nothing I wanted to do with my life. And I said, 'God, if there's anything you want in this stinking soul, take it.'

This was almost ten years ago. But something came into my life that day which has never left. There wasn't any ringing of bells or flashing of lights or visions; but it was a deep intuitive realization of what it is God wants from a man, which I had never known before. And the peace which came with this understanding was not an experience in itself, but was rather a cessation of the conflict of a lifetime. I realized then that God does not want a man's money, nor does He primarily want his time. He wants your *will;* and if you give Him your will, He'll begin to show you life as you've never seen it before.

It *is* like being born again. Although I could not understand nor articulate for many months what had happened to me, I knew to the core of my soul that I had somehow made personal contact with the very Meaning of Life.

I started the car and turned toward home.

Keith Miller

Entering In

Thursday

At thirty Fulton Oursler was a self-styled agnostic. He believed in no absolutes of right and wrong, certainly not in anything approaching the supernatural. As he described himself, he was "genially loyal to ethical standards when they did not interfere with what I wanted to do. But I sneered at God as an elaborate self-deception and did all that I could to tear down the faith of those close to me."

Then trouble surrounded Fulton Oursler in all phases of his life. *Liberty* magazine went under, so he was out of a job. At the same time there were health and marriage difficulties. There came the day when he realised that he was absolutely helpless to do one thing for himself.

What happened then is vividly described by Oursler himself. On a blustery day with dark clouds lowering, the distraught man wandered down Fifth Avenue in New York City. He stopped in front of a church — self-conscious, filled with conflicting emotions, but knowing that unless he got help he had come to the end of the way. For the first time in years he ventured inside a church. "In ten minutes or less I may change my mind," he prayed. "I may scoff at this — and love error again. Pay no attention to me then. For this little time I am in right mind and heart. This is my best. Take it and forget the rest; and if You are really there, help me." . . .

Within two weeks Fulton Oursler's problems began to resolve. "Only chance would explain it to the unbelieving," he said later, "because nothing either I or anyone else did contrived the events. By what the rationalist would call a series of beautiful coincidences God literally took over my life, took it out of my hands."

The more impressive proof that God accepted Fulton Oursler's gift of his will that day is the massive contribution to the religious life of the nation that he made during the remainder of his life. His enthusiasms, his intensity, his insatiable love of a good story that had once poured into murder mysteries, plays and movie scripts he now dedicated to the building up of faith in others. Since that experience his work includes some eighteen books, an endless succession of articles and his column "Modern Parables", syndicated in about a hundred newspapers. When he was stricken with a heart attack on May 23, 1952, his *The Greatest Faith Ever Known* was interrupted in mid-sentence.

Catherine Marshall (1914-1983)

Entering In

Nothing in the world interested me except the incredible voyage of discovery on which I had set out. From time to time, also, Thile asked me if I had found a job. This was a more serious problem. Obviously until I had a job I couldn't even suggest to Thile the dream I had had so long for her and me. I set out job-hunting in earnest.

Before I found one, though, a fragile little event occurred that changed my life far more radically than the bullet that had torn through bone and muscle a year before. It was a stormy night in the dead of winter, 1950. I was in bed. The sleet blew across the polders as it can only blow in Holland in mid-January. I pulled the covers higher under my chin, knowing that outside the sleet was driving almost parallel to the ground. There were many voices in that wind. I heard Sister Patrice. "The monkey will never let go . . ." I heard the singing under the big tent. "Let My people go . . ."

What was it I was hanging on to? What was it that was hanging on to me? What was standing between me and freedom?

The rest of the house was asleep. I lay on my back with my hands under my head staring at the darkened ceiling and all at once, very quietly, I let go of my ego. With a new note in the wind yelling at me not to be a fool, I turned myself over to God — lock, stock and adventure. There wasn't much faith in my prayer. I just said, "Lord, if You will show me the way, I will follow You. Amen."

It was as simple as that.

Brother Andrew

Entering In

Saturday

For once there walked this earth a Man who had not where to lay His head. In nakedness and pain and desolation He tasted death for every man, and out of the last darkness cried "My God, My God, why hast Thou forsaken Me?" And God in everlasting mercy brought Christ through, and set Him on high, and shattered death with resurrection; so that today wherever the name of Jesus is called upon — even if it is only a half articulate cry, "Jesus, from Your cross have mercy!" — He is veritably present in the midst. This is not pious metaphor. It is sober fact.

You may have been having a difficult time in all conscience, and life may have hurt you sore. But do you not see that it is just there through the tender mercy of your God that the dayspring from on high has visited you? And the secret of weathering the storm in the day when the rain descends and the floods come and the winds blow and beat upon the house — the secret is not your tenacity and endurance: it is God's constancy, Christ's fidelity. Place your confidence there, and you build on the rock that nothing can move.

There was a night many years ago when one of Henry Drummond's great student meetings in Edinburgh was nearing its end, and Drummond was appealing for decisions. "I cannot guarantee," he said, "that the stars will shine brighter when you leave this hall tonight, or that when you wake tomorrow a new world will open before you. But I do guarantee that Christ will keep that which you have committed to Him." He will keep His promise, right on to the unknown end.

I should be a fool to stand here today and talk to you about religion, if I were not dead sure of that elemental fact. I know Whom I have believed. I know that His promise stands fast for ever.

James S. Stewart

Taken Over

There is not in the world a kind of life more sweet and more delightful than that of a continual walk with God; those only can comprehend it, who practise and experience it. Yet I do not advise you to do it from that motive, it is not pleasure that we ought to seek in this exercise; but let us do it from the motive of love, and because God would have us so walk.

Brother Lawrence (1610-1691)

To find Jesus means that I hate sin with a new hatred, that so far from being critical I want to worship, that while I hate myself I am not driven, as other historical figures drive me, into inferiority. I believe in myself, am delivered from myself, am admitted into a new kingdom of creative values, am delivered even from my priciples and resolutions and pledges and the other railings I have put up on the side of the road to keep myself straight. I find myself pushing the railings over. I am on the moors, laughing and running, throwing up my hat. I am free and life is intoxicating. I find the glory of the liberty of the sons of God. I am delivered from all the cares of selfhood into the free country of otherness, and I tend to become as impatient of railings and roads and signposts as a man who is in love with his wife would be impatient of written promises and pledges that he would stand by her always. Love is the country of freedom, and to find Christ is to be free from self and from every bond save love.

Leslie D. Weatherhead (1893-1976)

Taken Over

Monday

Life of my life, I shall ever try to keep my body pure, knowing that thy living touch is upon all my limbs.

I shall ever try to keep all untruths out from my thoughts, knowing that thou art that truth which has kindled the light of reason in my mind.

I shall ever try to drive all evils away from my heart and keep my love in flower, knowing that thou hast thy seat in the inmost shrine of my heart.

And it shall be my endeavour to reveal thee in my actions, knowing it is thy power gives me strength to act.

Rabindranath Tagore (1861-1941)

In your service of others you will feel, you will care, you will be hurt, you will have your heart broken. And it is doubtful if any of us can do anything at all until we have been very much hurt, and until our hearts have been very much broken. And that is because God's gift to us is the Glory of Christ crucified — being really sensitive to the pain and sorrow that does exist in so much of the world.

With this, a serenity that is deep in you — and because it's deep in you it brings to others peace and healing. "Peace I leave with you. My peace I give unto you." The life of a Christian ought to be like the ocean, with the surface constantly battered about by storms, but miles and miles below deep peace, unmoved tranquillity.

Michael Ramsey

Taken Over

When gently from my tight, clenched hands
God took of earthly things which I held dear,
Confused, his love I did not understand;
I grasped still more, lest more should disappear.

But yet in love he took until
To him alone I turned, for all else seemed
Unsteady, apt to fade; reluctant still,
I gave to him the things I precious deemed.

He took, but then he gladly gave
First of himself, his love, his joy, and rest;
Until it seemed the things which I had saved
Were worthless toys compared to heaven's best.

Then, while with willing, open hands
I held all earthly gifts for him to see
And take or give, apart from my demands,
He gave me back the things he took from me.

Elizabeth Skoglund

Taken Over

Wednesday

We see the figure of Jesus Christ, speaking to us of success, indeed, and of the victories of faith, but also of persecution. Jesus does not tell us that happiness is to be found in the satisfaction of our desires, but in a spirit of renunciation and poverty. He speaks of a narrow door, and says to us, "Whoever does not bear his own cross and come after me, cannot be my disciple." Then we follow him along the road he took when everything was stripped from him. In Gethsemane he met the horror of failure: his disciples deserting him, the triumph of his enemies — whom he had wished to save, and who were now to crucify him — the insults, the torture, the sensation of having been abandoned by God, and death.

Even for him, true God but also true man, this collapse is terrible. He says, "My soul is very sorrowful, even to death." Then he prays. He begs his Father to spare him. But, faced with God's awful silence, he adds, "My Father, if this cannot pass unless I drink it, thy will be done." The will of God: that is the key to our problem. God has a purpose, and it will be realized also through the failures we must face in obedience.

God has a purpose: the entire Bible proclaims this. What matters is that his plan should be understood and fulfilled. So, in the light of the Bible, the problem is shifted onto new ground. The question is no longer whether one is succeeding or failing but whether one is fulfilling God's purpose or not, whether one is adventuring with him or against him. It is, of course, always a joyful thing to succeed. But the joy is very deceptive if it comes from the satisfaction of an ambition that is contrary to the will of God. And of course failure is still very painful; but the pain is fruitful if it is part of God's purpose. A failure, within God's purpose, is no longer really a failure. Thus the Cross, the supreme failure, is at the same time the supreme triumph of God, since it is the accomplishment of his purpose of salvation. This is the true answer to the painful discovery that it is not possible to establish a clear frontier between success and failure. What is success and what is failure? The answer of the Bible is "What is the will of God? Are you obeying him?" What matters is to listen to him, to let ourselves be guided, to face up to the adventure to which he calls us, with all its risks. Life is an adventure directed by God.

Paul Tournier

Taken Over

"If we have put our earthly life in God's hands — that is to say, if we are ready to die today, as we should be — we can have absolutely no fear, no matter what happens. For I know that once having given myself to God, to be in His hand a mere tool on earth, a tool with which some good work may be done while I live — having once and for all done away with my own free-will and having put God's will in its place — I know that no power on earth can do me any harm till God's day comes. My trust is in God, so that it matters not what I do nor where I go."

Edward Wilson, of the Antarctic

What he did and whither he went, and the manner of his going, are matters which he did not foresee when he wrote these words, but they have passed into history.

George Seaver

As Captain Scott wrote in a last letter to Mrs Wilson when the three who had been to the South Pole — Scott, Wilson and Bowers — lay in their tent dying:

My dear Mrs Wilson,

If this letter reaches you, Bill and I will have gone out together. We are very near it now and I should like you to know how splendid he was at the end — everlastingly cheerful and ready to sacrifice himself for others. His eyes have a comfortable blue look of hope, and his mind is peaceful with the satisfaction of his faith in regarding himself as part of the great scheme of the Almighty. I can do no more to comfort you than to tell you that he died as he lived, a brave, true man — the best of comrades and the staunchest of friends.

My whole heart goes out to you in pity,

Yours,

R. Scott

Taken Over

Friday

When I stand at the judgment seat of Christ,
And He shows me His plan for me,
The plan of my life as it might have been
Had He had His way, and I see

How I blocked Him here, and I checked Him there,
And I would not yield my will —
Will there be grief in my Saviour's eyes,
Grief though He loves me still?

He would have me rich, and I stand there poor,
Stripped of all but His grace,
While memory runs like a hunted thing
Down the paths I cannot retrace.

Then my desolate heart will well-nigh break
With the tears I cannot shed;
I shall cover my face with my empty hands,
I shall bow my uncrowned head.

Lord of the years that are left to me,
I give them to Thy hand;
Take me, and break me, and mould me
To the pattern Thou hast planned.

Martha Snell Nicholson

Taken Over

Hold to Christ, and for the rest be totally uncommitted.

Herbert Butterfield (1900-1979)

Just as you received Christ, so go on living in Him — in simple faith.

With deep roots and firm foundations, may you be strong to grasp, with all God's people, what is the breadth and length and height and depth of the love of Christ, and to know it, though it is beyond knowledge. So may you attain to fullness of being, the fullness of God himself.

Now unto him that is able to do exceeding abundantly above all that we ask or think, according to the power that worketh in us, unto him be glory in the church by Christ Jesus throughout all ages, world without end.

Colossians II 6 (Phillips)
Ephesians III 18-19 (N.E.B.)
Ephesians III 20-21 (A.V.)

161

Holy Spirit

Sunday

If ye love me, keep my commandments.

And I will pray the Father, and he shall give you another Comforter, that he may abide with you for ever;

Even the Spirit of truth; whom the world cannot receive, because it seeth him not, neither knoweth him: but ye know him; for he dwelleth with you, and shall be in you.

I will not leave you comfortless: I will come to you.

John XIV 15-18

Then when the actual Day of Pentecost came they were all assembled together. Suddenly there was a sound from heaven like the rushing of a violent wind, and it filled the whole house where they were seated. Before their eyes appeared tongues like flames, which separated off and settled above the head of each one of them. They were all filled with the Holy Spirit and began to speak in different languages as the Spirit gave them power to proclaim His Message. . . .

Everyone was utterly amazed and did not know what to make of it. Indeed they kept saying to each other, "What on earth can this mean?"

Acts II 1-4, 12 (Phillips)

Holy Spirit

The greatest single need today is to discover again the fact and the power of the Holy Spirit. Millions of people are being crushed by the pressures of life because they possess no power of the living God within. The Church is impotent, unable to rise to its role in modern history, because it has little knowledge of, or faith in, the Holy Spirit. The world is restless, tantalised by the vision of what may be, but cannot find the power to turn dreams into reality.

What a price we are paying for the neglect of the doctrine of the Holy Spirit. It is seen in the distortion of the understanding of God. It is appearing in the low morale, the defeatism of the Church. . . .

The New Testament is a story about power. A line runs through its pages. On the one side is confusion, uncertainty about God, personal helplessness in living, doubt about the meaning of life, fear of death. On the other side is an unshakable faith in God, personal sacrifice and courage, a sense of purpose in history, and the conquest of death. That dividing line runs through the Day of Pentecost. That was the great divide of history, that was the day when there was released into human hearts, all the strength that was focused in history through the life, and death, and Resurrection of Jesus. That power is the Spirit of God, which may be defined simply as God in action today. It is this power which we need. It is a power which is available. It is a power we must find, and find urgently.

Alan Walker

As we read the New Testament we may sometimes be conscious of a vast and timeless energy confined within the thought-forms and restricted knowledge of the first century A.D. Today the experience, knowledge and responsibility of every thinking man is very much greater than that of most of the men of New Testament days. But what changed and inspired those men, what gave them daring, hope, patience, and self-giving love is quite timeless. There is no real reason to suppose that we cannot tap the resources of God just as effectively as they did — no real reason except our modern insulations! If we could but see it, God is inevitably contemporary.

J. B. Phillips (1906-1982)

Holy Spirit

Tuesday

Always there are unmistakable signs when the power of the Spirit goes to work. "Thou hearest the sound thereof." When a man once weak and shifty and unreliable becomes strong and clean and victorious; when a church once stagnant and conventional and introverted throws off its dull tedium and catches fire and becomes alert and missionary-minded; when Christians of different denominations begin to realise there is far more in the risen Christ to unite them than there can be anywhere else in the world or in their own traditions to divide them; when religion, too long taboo in polite conversation, becomes a talking-point again; when decisions for Christ are seen worked out in family and business relationships; when mystic vision bears fruit in social passion — then indeed the world is made to know that something is happening. Something vital is going on. And it is not romanticising to say that we can thank God that all around us in these days the evidences are so indisputably clear. "The wind bloweth where it listeth, and thou hearest the sound thereof." If you have heard that sound, as I hope you have, you can refute all the minimising and depreciating voices in your own heart and in the world around. It is the unanswerable argument for Christ.

James S. Stewart

When men and women are constrained to give themselves without reserve to the grace and power of the Holy Spirit, when ministers, office-bearers and members alike become 'the community of the redeemed', not just 'nice people' but 'new men', sensitive as never before to every call and movement of the Spirit, the great cause which bears Christ's name will move from its present periphery to the centre of things and become, as it was in the time of the Apostles, a mighty force of revolution for God.

It has been said that what people are waiting for today is an 'inspiration'. This is what they were waiting for when the Church was born. There is no mightier event recorded in the New Testament than the coming of the Spirit to the disciples. According to the Scriptures, the disciples became changed men, and the people round about who witnessed this extraordinary surge of new life in the disciples trembled and wondered. They had known nothing like it before.

William Yule

Holy Spirit

For Christians to write anything about God's people without mentioning the Holy Spirit is like arranging a party without considering the Chief Guest, who will at once be the Reviver and the Entertainer of the whole gathering.

Now: it is fundamental to the New Testament that God does not send the wisdom and the power of his Spirit reluctantly, grudgingly, like a sour schoolmaster allowing ten minutes off for bonfire night. The only thing that stops this power and this wisdom from transforming God's laity is *ourselves,* both individually and in our family and our social groupings. We can cramp his style: we often do. That is why we must often be bitterly ashamed with ourselves for our petty status-seeking and comfort-loving and fairly blameless and largely useless private lives. That is why we must not only laugh at but also systematically wrestle with the dead weight of American religiosity and British slovenliness. There is much that we can do.

'But what's the use?' you mutter. 'What can *I* do? I don't have the main stream of the lay revival past my door; and the church at the corner has broken better Christians than me.'

You are quite right, and you are quite wrong. In the first place, even one or two spiritually strong individuals (who may by no means be 'leader types' psychologically) can have a quite fantastic effect if they really put themselves at the disposal of God. In the second place, you should not be, and you will not be, alone for long. Nothing is more certain than that God intends his people to work in groups, in fellowships, together. All over the place, cutting across the whole messy entanglements of denominational barriers, there are springing up informal groups of Christians, clerical and lay together, who really care about God's world. You will find one, if you look hard. And these groups are genuine manifestations of God's Church: they are indeed in some ways 'House Churches' together, and you can find fun and strength and wisdom in them.

Mark Gibbs and T. Ralph Morton

Holy Spirit

Thursday

When we pray, 'Come, Holy Ghost, our souls inspire', we had better know what we are about. He will not carry us to easy triumphs and gratifying successes; more probably He will set us some task for God in the full intention that we shall fail, so that others, learning wisdom by our failure, may carry the good cause forward. He may take us through loneliness, desertion by friends, apparent desertion even by God; that was the way Christ went to the Father. He may drive us into the wilderness to be tempted of the devil. He may lead us from the Mount of Transfiguration (if He ever lets us climb it) to the hill that is called the Place of a Skull. For if we invoke Him, it must be to help us in doing God's will, not ours. We cannot call upon the

Creator Spirit, by whose aid
The world's foundations first were laid

in order to use omnipotence for the supply of our futile pleasures or the success of our futile plans. If we invoke Him, we must be ready for the glorious pain of being caught by His power out of our petty orbit into the eternal purposes of the Almighty, in whose onward sweep our lives are as a speck of dust. The soul that is filled with the Spirit must have become purged of all pride or love of ease, all self-complacence and self-reliance; but that soul has found the only real dignity, the only lasting joy. Come then, Great Spirit, come. Convict the world; and convict my timid soul.

William Temple (1881-1944)

I feel the winds of God today;
Today my sail I lift,
Though heavy oft with drenching spray,
And torn with many a rift;
If hope but light the water's crest,
And Christ my bark will use,
I'll seek the seas at His behest,
And brave another cruise.

Jessie Adams (1863-1954)

Holy Spirit

The Spirit repeatedly brings us back to Jesus' emphasis — that real faith is no other-worldly affair. I know that again and again in recent years He has plucked me out of the clouds of theoretical Christianity back to earth where I belonged.

For when we allow the Spirit to guide us He will concern Himself with how we use our time and spend our money; with honesty and moral integrity and Christlike quality of character; with what is happening to our children; with the health of our relationship with other people and with our God. And, if our need is severe enough, the Holy Spirit will turn our lives upside down. . . .

Do without Him? How could any of us who have embarked on the pilgrimage that is Christianity do without Him? For we who long for something more, for strength and hope and wisdom beyond our selves, discover to our joy that as the Comforter reveals Christ to us, in Him we have our heart's desire.

Catherine Marshall (1914-1983)

O live in us this day,
O clothe thyself, thy purpose yet again
In human clay:
Work through our feebleness thy strength,
Work through our meanness thy nobility,
Work through our helpless poverty of soul
Thy grace, thy glory and thy love.

J. S. Hoyland (1887-1957)

Holy Spirit

Saturday

But the fruit of the Spirit is love, joy, peace, longsuffering, gentleness, goodness, faith, meekness, temperance: against such there is no law.

Galatians V 22-23

Lord, I have accepted the challenge of Your great promise. I have asked for the gift of the Helper. I have bidden Him welcome as he enters my heart to take possession. So now, by faith, I accept Your sure promise that this is done, that I *have* received the Spirit.

I wait patiently now for these tokens of the Helper's presence that shall reveal that He is not only with me but in me.

Help me too never to fall into the trap of thinking of the Helper as a servant to do my bidding; rather create in me the willingness to be Your servant, Lord, for Your work to be done through me. Then only will I know the fullness of the Helper's presence. In Your strong name, I pray. Amen.

Catherine Marshall (1914-1983)

Love

Amor vincit omnia

God is love; and he that dwelleth in love dwelleth in God, and God in him.

1 John IV 16

This love of God, of which we have been thinking and of which so much can be expected, is not so different in quality that we cannot recognise it as love when we meet it. It is love, our old familiar friend, higher and better, more splendid and more generous, but still love, the most precious thing that we know, the quality which even in our duller moments we know can outlast anything. It is not so much that we do not understand what love is, but that we are slow to grasp love's methods of working. We are tempted by love of power, by the show of results, by the short cut, by the pleasing exterior; but love is deceived by none of these things and takes awful patient ways, of which we know very little. Yet, though we are blind and ignorant and stupid, it is of unutterable comfort and gives rise to unspeakable hopes in our hearts to know, not only that God is wonderful and beautiful and good, but that He actually is that strange quality which lives in our inmost heart — love itself.

J. B. Phillips (1906-1982)

Love

Monday

Where Joy and Sorrow meet, there is Love.
And where the deepest joy and the deepest sorrow
meet, there is the most perfect love.

Edward Wilson (1872-1912)

My song is love unknown,
My Saviour's love to me,
Love to the loveless shown, that they might lovely be.
O who am I, that for my sake
My Lord should take frail flesh and die?

He came from his blest throne,
Salvation to bestow:
But men made strange and none the longed-for Christ would know.
But O, my Friend, my Friend indeed;
Who at my need his life did spend!

Sometimes they strew his way,
And his sweet praises sing:
Resounding all the day hosannas to their King.
Then 'Crucify!' is all their breath,
And for his death they thirst and cry.

In life, no house, no home
My Lord on earth might have;
In death, no friendly tomb but what a stranger gave.
What may I say? heav'n was his home:
But mine the tomb wherein he lay.

Here might I stay and sing,
No story so divine;
Never was love, dear King, never was grief like thine!
This is my Friend, in whose sweet praise
I all my days could gladly spend.

Samuel Crossman (c.1624-83)

Love

The Penalty of Love

If love should count *you* worthy, and should deign
One day to seek your door and be your guest,
Pause! ere you draw the bolt and bid him rest,
If in your old content you would remain.
For not alone he enters; in his train
Are angels of the mist; the lonely guest
Dreams of the unfulfilled and unpossessed
And sorrow, and life's immemorial pain.
He wakes desires you never may forget,
He shows you stars you never saw before,
He makes you share with him, for evermore,
The burden of the world's divine regret.
How wise you were to open not! and yet,
How poor if you should turn him from the door!

Sidney Royse Lysaght (1858-1941)

Love

Love bade me welcome; yet my soul drew back,
Guilty of dust and sin.
But quick-eyed Love, observing me grow slack
From my first entrance in,
Drew nearer to me, sweetly questioning
If I lack'd anything.

'A guest,' I answered, 'worthy to be here.'
Love said, 'You shall be he.'
'I, the unkind, ungrateful? Ah, my dear,
I cannot look on Thee.'
Love took my hand and smiling did reply,
'Who made the eyes but I?'

'Truth, Lord; but I have marr'd them: let my shame
Go where it doth deserve.'
'And know you not,' says Love, 'Who bore the blame?'
'My dear, then I will serve.'
'You must sit down,' says Love, 'and taste my meat.'
So I did sit and eat.

George Herbert (1593-1632)

171

Love

Wednesday

That violence wherewith sometimes a man doteth upon one creature is but a little spark of that love, even towards all, which lurketh in his nature. We are made to love, both to satisfy the necessity of our active nature, and to answer the beauties in every creature. By Love our Souls are married and solder'd to the creatures: and it is our duty like God to be united to them all. We must love them infinitely, but in God, and for God: and God in them: namely all His excellencies manifested in them. When we dote upon the perfections and beauties of some one creature, we do not love that too much, but other things too little. Never was anything in this world loved too much, but many things have been loved in a false way: and all in too short a measure.

Thomas Traherne (1637-1674)

O ye who taste that love is sweet,
Set waymarks for all doubtful feet
That stumble on in search of it.

Sing notes of love: that some who hear
Far off, inert, may lend an ear,
Rise up and wonder and draw near.

Lead lives of love; that others who
Behold your life may kindle too
With love, and cast their lot with you.

Christina Georgina Rossetti (1830-1894)

Love

The dying Bishop Lamberton speaks to Robert the Bruce, King of Scots:

"What has God been doing with us this while, Robert, think you? In all our joys and sorrows, our achievements and defeats? What, but building — making *us* build. As I built that cathedral. Stone by stone, building our character. Heart, mind, will, understanding — aye, and compassion, above all. These things we have been attaining unto. Their fullest flowering in us. The body is as nothing, compared with these. All our years, these have been building up, for better or for worse. Now, they are at their height. Think you the All Highest ordained it thus for nothing? The patient moulding, ours and His, the secret strivings of the heart, this edifice that is our life's essence. Just to cast it away, discarded, unused, spurned, like a child's bauble? In all His creation, this is the height of His achievement — not the tides of the oceans, the lands, the sun, moon and stars. Man, at the summit of his earthly character — which is when he dies. Here is God's achievement — and man's, in His image. Purpose and order are in all His works — that is plain to all. Should, then, the greatest work of all be purposeless? . . .

"God is purpose, order, power. But, forget it not — love, also. Else where comes love? Love, the force which drives all else. Love is compassion, understanding. . . .

"If life has taught me anything, Robert, it is that love is of all things great, powerful, eternal, the very sword of God. Not weak, soft, pap — as some would have it! Love is God, therefore it is eternal. Cannot die — God's, or yours, or mine. Here is the greatest comfort in all creation. Love cannot die with the body. It must go on, since it is eternal. See you what this means, my friend?"

Nigel Tranter

173

Love

Friday

Love is a great thing, a great and thorough good; by itself it makes everything that is heavy light, and it bears evenly all that is uneven. For it carries a burden which is no burden and makes everything that is bitter, sweet and savoury. . . . Nothing is sweeter than love, nothing more courageous, nothing higher, nothing wider, nothing more pleasant, nothing fuller nor better in heaven and earth; because love is born of God, and cannot rest but in God, above all created things. He that loveth flies with wings, runneth and rejoiceth because he is free and not bound.

Love feels no burdens, thinks nothing of trouble, attempts what is above all strength, pleads no excuse of impossibility; for it thinks all things lawful for itself and all things possible. It is therefore able to undertake all things, and it completes many things and brings them to a conclusion, where he who does not love faints and lies down. Love watcheth ever and slumbereth not. Though weary, love is never tired; when pressed, it is not straitened; though alarmed, it is not confounded; but as a lively flame and burning torch, it forces its way onwards and upwards, securely passing through all.

Thomas à Kempis (1379-1471)

Love in the New Testament is stern and strong and severe and virile. It is not sloppy and sentimental and weak. . . . Love is all the things St Paul described in I Corinthians 13, but it has steel in it as well as tears and a smashing power greater far than dynamite. Love suffers, entreats and endures, and fools think this is weakness. But those who oppose love take up arms against the whole universe. *They* will be broken, not love. For love is invincible. Love is the only power in the world that can change men's motives as they have got to be changed if our dreams are to come true.

Leslie D. Weatherhead (1893-1976)

Love

Lord, why did you tell me to love all men, my brothers?
I have tried, but I come back to you, frightened. . . .
Lord, I was so peaceful at home, I was so comfortably settled.
It was well furnished, and I felt cosy.
I was alone, I was at peace,
Sheltered from the wind, the rain, the mud.
I would have stayed unsullied in my ivory tower.
But, Lord, you have discovered a breach in my defences,
You have forced me to open my door;
Like a squall of rain in the face, the cry of men has awakened me;
Like a gale of wind a friendship has shaken me,
As a ray of light slips in unnoticed, your grace has stirred me . . .
*   and, rashly enough, I left my door ajar. Now, Lord, I am lost!*
Outside men were lying in wait for me.
I did not know they were so near; in this house, in this street, in
*   this office; my neighbour, my colleague, my friend.*
As soon as I started to open the door I saw them, with outstretched
*   hands, burning eyes, longing hearts, like beggars on church*
*   steps.*

Michel Quoist

Measure thy life by loss instead of gain,
Not by the wine drunk, but by the wine poured forth;
For love's strength standeth in love's sacrifice;
And he who suffers most has most to give.

Source unknown

Joy

Sunday

When the morning stars sang together, and all the sons of God shouted for joy.

Job XXXVIII 7

You never enjoy the world aright, till the sea itself floweth in your veins, till you are clothed with the heavens, and crowned with the stars: and perceive yourself to be the sole heir of the whole world, and more so, because men are in it who are every one sole heirs with you. Till you can sing and rejoice and delight in God, as misers do in gold, and kings in sceptres, you never enjoy the world. . . .

All things were made to be yours, and you were made to prize them according to their value: which is your office and duty, the end for which you were created, and the means whereby you enjoy. The end for which you were created is that by prizing all that God hath done you may enjoy yourself and Him in Blessedness.

Thomas Traherne (1637-1674)

Joy

And joy is everywhere; it is in the earth's green covering of grass; in the blue serenity of the sky; in the reckless exuberance of spring; in the severe abstinence of grey winter; in the living flesh that animates our bodily frame; in the perfect poise of the human figure, noble and upright; in living; in the exercise of all our powers; in the acquisition of knowledge; in fighting evils; in dying for gains we never can share.

Rabindranath Tagore (1861-1941)

Help me, Lord,
to put one step in front of the other
as I follow your lead.
I know you can.
Because wherever I go, you've already been.
Wherever I go, you are already there.
And with me on the journey.
It's good to know that, to experience it.

And Lord, help me to find the joy
that comes with answering your demands.
Help me to live the freedom
that comes from walking in your love.

Eddie Askew

Joy

Tuesday

These things have I spoken unto you, that my joy might remain in you, and that your joy might be full.

John XV 11

It is the great mystery of human life that old grief passes gradually into quiet, tender joy. The mild serenity of age takes the place of the riotous blood of youth. I bless the rising sun each day, and, as before, my heart sings to meet it, but now I love even more its setting, its long slanting rays and the soft, tender, gentle memories that come with them, the dear images from the whole of my long, happy life — and over all the Divine Truth, softening, reconciling, forgiving! My life is ending, I know that well, but every day that is left me I feel how my earthly life is in touch with a new infinite, unknown, but approaching life, the nearness of which sets my soul quivering with rapture, my mind glowing and my heart weeping with joy.

Dostoevsky (1821-1881)

Joy

Where, then, does happiness lie? In forgetfulness, not indulgence, of the self. In escape from sensual appetites, not in their satisfaction. We live in a dark, self-enclosed prison which is all we see or know if our glance is fixed ever downwards. To lift it upwards, becoming aware of the wide, luminous universe outside — this alone is happiness. At its highest level such happiness is the ecstasy which mystics have inadequately described. At more humdrum levels it is human love; the delights and beauties of our dear earth, its colours and shapes and sounds; the enchantment of understanding and laughing, and all other exercise of such faculties as we possess; the marvel of the meaning of everything, fitfully glimpsed, inadequately expounded, but ever-present.

Such is happiness — not compressible into a pill; not translatable into a sensation; lost to whoever would grasp it to himself alone, not to be gorged out of a trough, or torn out of another's body, or paid into a bank, or driven along a motorway, or fired in gun-salutes, or discovered in the stratosphere. Existing, intangible, in every true response to life, and absent in every false one. Propounded through the centuries in every noteworthy word and thought and deed. Expressed in art and literature and music; in vast cathedrals and tiny melodies; in everything that is harmonious, and in the unending heroism of imperfect men reaching after perfection.

When Pastor Bonhoeffer was taken off by his Nazi guards to be executed, as I have read, his face was shining with happiness, to the point that even those poor clowns noted it. In that place of darkest evil, he was the happiest man — he, the executed. I find this an image of supreme happiness.

Malcolm Muggeridge

Joy

Thursday

Strong emotions surge through the gospels. Virile men did not leave their businesses and their homes to follow Christ without intense convictions. Men did not risk persecution and death out of lukewarmness. Those who were healed, who had sight restored, their children given back to them, could not be phlegmatic about it. The exuberance of the men who experienced the Spirit at Pentecost was such that they were accused of being drunk with new wine. Emotion beyond embarrassment, beyond caring what other people thought, all this is there for anyone to read.

I have watched the same process today in those whom the Holy Spirit touches. Feelings are sensitised. Life takes on relish. Joys are heightened. Here is the way one woman described her encounter with the Spirit:

> I saw no new thing, but I saw all the usual things in a miraculous new light. I saw for the first time how wildly beautiful and joyous, beyond any words of mine to describe, is the whole of life. Every human being, every sparrow that flew, every branch tossing in the wind, was caught up in and was a part of the whole mad ecstasy of loveliness, of joy, of importance, of intoxication of life.

In the experience of everyone to whom I have talked about the Spirit, the word *joy* stands out. In the rebirth of our emotional selves this seems to be the essential missing ingredient which the Holy Spirit supplies.

I have written earlier of the joy of childhood. For me it was in the fragrance of mint and honeysuckle, the feel of bare feet on moss, ice-cold apples, the magnificent fury of a thunderstorm, the far horizons of blue Appalachians. And all my life I have felt that this early joy was trying to teach me something, that it was not just a sentiment restricted to childhood. It seemed to reveal something fundamental and basic about the nature of the universe itself. Surely I was right; surely this is the way things are in God's world! But only now do I see how God intends for us to know this. It is the Holy Spirit who is to open our eyes to the joy which undergirds the universe.

Catherine Marshall (1914-1983)

Glen Lyon Hills, Perthshire.
REMEMBERING — *"If only their far snows might claim the yearning, Claim wearied thought."*

Children's Food Queue, Ethiopia.

INDIFFERENCE — "'I was hungry and you said, 'The poor are always with us' ."

CAMPBELL R. STEVEN

In Strathconon, Ross-shire.
I BELIEVE — *"In joy He has been the light of the morning, in trouble the clear shining after rain."*

Devotion.
LOVE — *"O ye who taste that love is sweet."*

Loch Mallachie, Speyside.
QUIET TIME — *"Teach us how to be more still."*

Benmore Avenue, Cowal.

TRUST — *"In all thy ways acknowledge him and he shall direct thy paths."*

Homeless.

WHO IS MY NEIGHBOUR? — "And who is my neighbour?"

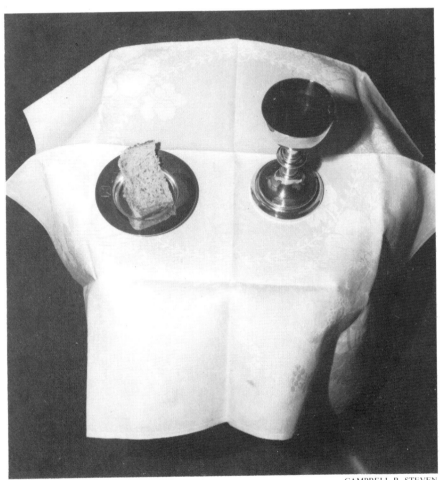

Invitation.

COMMUNION — *"O taste and see that the Lord is good."*

Joy

And he arose, and came to his father. But when he was yet a great way off, his father saw him, and had compassion, and ran, and fell on his neck, and kissed him.

And the son said unto him, Father, I have sinned against heaven, and in thy sight, and am no more worthy to be called thy son.

But the father said to his servants, Bring forth the best robe, and put it on him; and put a ring on his hand, and shoes on his feet:

And bring hither the fatted calf, and kill it; and let us eat, and be merry: for this my son was dead, and is alive again; he was lost and is found.

Luke XV 20-24

O good God, what is that which is wrought in man, that more joy is found in the delivery out of great danger of a soul which had almost been despaired of, than if there had always been good hope thereof, or the danger had been less? . . . And the joy of the solemnity of thy house doth bring the tears from our eyes, when, in thy house, there is read how that younger son was dead, yet is alive again, was lost, but is found.

St Augustine (354-430)

Thou wilt shew me the path of life: in thy presence is fulness of joy; at thy right hand there are pleasures for evermore.

Psalm XVI 11

Joy

Saturday

Rejoice in the Lord alway: and again I say, Rejoice.

Philippians IV 4

O God, give me in my life the fruit of joy. Help me always to be happy and cheerful. Help me still to smile even when things go wrong. Help me always to look on the bright side of things, and always to remember that, even when things are at their worst, there is still something to be thankful for. Don't let me grumble and complain; don't let me be a pessimist and a wet blanket.

And help me to find my happiness, not in doing what I want, but in doing what you want, and not in thinking of myself, but in thinking of others, through Jesus Christ my Lord. Amen.

William Barclay (1907-1978)

Peace and Quiet

Lord, I have time.
I went out, Lord.
Men were coming out.
They were coming and going, walking and running.
Everything was rushing, cars, lorries, the street, the whole town.
Men were rushing not to waste time.
They were rushing after time,
To catch up with time,
To gain time.

Goodbye, sir, excuse me, I haven't time.
I'll come back, I can't wait, I haven't time.
I must end this letter — I haven't time.
I'd love to help you, but I haven't time.
I can't accept, having no time.
I can't think, I can't read, I'm swamped, I haven't time.
I'd like to pray, but I haven't time.

You understand, Lord, they simply haven't the time.

But we must not lose time, waste time, kill time,
For time is a gift that you give us,
But a perishable gift,
A gift that does not keep.

Lord, I have time,
I have plenty of time,
All the time that you give me,
The years of my life,
The days of my years,
The hours of my days,
They are all mine.
Mine to fill, quietly, calmly,
But to fill completely, up to the brim.
To offer them to you, that of their insipid water
You may make a rich wine such as you made once in Cana of
*   Galilee.*
I am not asking you tonight, Lord,
for time to do this and that,
But your grace to do conscientiously, in the time
that you give me, what you want me to do.

Michel Quoist

183

Peace and Quiet

Monday
The Gift of Peace

People who breezily testify to having not a care in the world may deserve, not our envy, but our pity. There is a peace — if it can be called that — which may be possessed by a man who has never faced a real problem, and who has never seen — or if he has seen, never felt — the agony of a pain-filled bed or the heartbreak of a tender relationship that has turned sour.

There is a kind of peace that may come to the unimaginative and insensitive, who shuts his eyes to human need. But this is not the peace of which the New Testament speaks. This operates in the midst of life's pains and perplexities. It depends on faith, or trustful commitment, which involves, of course, submission to God's will — obedience, as we have already seen. No one can expect to enjoy the peace of God who is unwilling to follow the way of God.

In a little book, *The Verdict of Experience,* Howard Stanley writes on this theme, and quotes the words of a distinguished Quaker which, he says, have helped him. 'If you take a few steps along a road and discover as you go that your mind is uneasy and your heart disturbed, turn back. This is not the way for you. But if, on the other hand, you are travelling along a road which is hard to the feet, which tests your strength and endurance, but you find that you are happy and assured, then continue along that road, for it is the way of God's choosing. The peace of God and the will of God go hand in hand.'

The Soldier's Armoury
14th June, 1973

Quiet minds cannot be perplexed or frightened, but go on in fortune or misfortune at their own private pace, like a clock during a thunderstorm.

Robert Louis Stevenson (1850-1894)

184

Peace and Quiet

To make things with our hands, to watch the green blades growing; to make music with our lips; to keep a jewel or two polished in the mind; these are the acts of living which bring peace to the soul.

Agnes A. MacDiarmid

How still, how happy! Those are words
That once would scarce agree together;
I loved the plashing of the surge,
The changing heaven, the breezy weather,

More than smooth seas and cloudless skies
And solemn, soothing, softened airs
That in the forest woke no sighs
And from the green spray shook no tears.

How still, how happy! Now I feel
Where silence dwells is sweeter far
Than laughing mirth's most joyous swell
However pure its raptures are.

Come, sit down on this sunny stone:
'Tis wintry light o'er flowerless moors —
But sit — for we are all alone
And clear expand heaven's breathless shores.

Emily Brontë (1818-1848)

Peace and Quiet

Wednesday

My cell was deep underground. A light bulb shone from the ceiling on bare walls, an iron bedstead with three planks and a straw pallet. Air entered through a pipe high in the wall. The silence here was practically complete — deliberately so. Our guards wore felt-soled shoes and you could hear their hands on the door before key found lock. Now and again there was the far-off sound of a prisoner hammering steadily on his door or screaming. The cell allowed only three paces in each direction, so I lay down and stared at the bulb. It burned all night. Since I could not sleep, I prayed. The outside world had ceased to exist. All the noises I was used to, the wind and rain in the yard, steel boot studs on stone floors, the buzz of a fly, a human voice, were gone. My heart seemed to shrink, as if it too would stop in this lifeless silence.

I was kept in solitary confinement in this cell for the next two years. I had nothing to read and no writing materials; I had only my thoughts for company, and I was not a meditative man, but a soul that had rarely known quiet. I had God. But had I really lived to serve God — or was it simply my profession? Did I believe in God? Now the test had come. I was alone. There was no salary to earn, no golden opinions to consider. God offered me only suffering — would I continue to love Him? . . .

I wondered how you could praise God by a life of silence. At first I prayed gently to be released. I asked, 'You have said in Scripture that it is not good that a man should be alone; why do You keep me alone?' But as days passed into weeks my only visitor was still the guard, who brought wedges of black bread and watery soup and never spoke a word. . . .

Slowly I learned that on the tree of silence hangs the fruit of peace. I began to realise my real personality, and made sure that it belonged to Christ. I found that even here my thoughts and feelings turned to God and that I could pass night after night in prayer, spiritual exercise and praise. I knew now that I was not play-acting, believing that I believed.

Richard Wurmbrand

Peace and Quiet

Thursday

Silence came before creation, and the heavens were spread without a word. Christ was born at dead of night; and though there has been no power like His, 'He did not strive nor cry, neither was His voice heard in the streets.' Nowhere can you find any beautiful work, any noble design, any durable endeavour, that was not matured in long and patient silence ere it spake out in its accomplishment. *There* it is that we accumulate the inward power which we distribute and spend in action, put the smallest duty before us in dignified and holy aspects, and reduce the severest hardships beneath the foot of our self-denial. There it is that the soul, enlarging all its dimensions at once, acquires a greater and more vigorous being, and gathers up its collective forces to bear down upon the piecemeal difficulties of life and scatter them to dust. There alone can we enter into that spirit of self-abandonment by which we take up the cross of duty, however heavy, with feet however worn and bleeding they may be. And thither shall we return again, only into higher peace and more triumphant power, when the labour is over and the victory won, and we are called by death into God's loftiest watch-tower of contemplation.

James Martineau (1805-1900)

Come to us, O Holy Spirit that was in Christ, bringing the peace that He promised should be ours, a peace that is untouched by the strivings of the world, enabling us to play an active part in ending care and anxiety.

The Soldier's Armoury
27th September, 1970

Peace and Quiet

Friday

Thou wilt keep him in perfect peace, whose mind is stayed on thee.

Cast thy burden upon the Lord, and he shall sustain thee; he shall never suffer the righteous to be moved. — I will trust and not be afraid; for the Lord JEHOVAH is my strength and my song; he also is become my salvation. — Why are ye fearful, O ye of little faith? — Be careful for nothing; but in every thing by prayer and supplication with thanksgiving let your requests be made known unto God. And the peace of God, which passeth all understanding, shall keep your hearts and minds through Christ Jesus. — In quietness and in confidence shall be your strength: and ye would not.

The effect of righteousness shall be quietness and assurance for ever. — Peace I leave with you, my peace I give unto you: not as the world giveth give I unto you. Let not your heart be troubled, neither let it be afraid. — Peace, from him which is, and which was, and which is to come.

From Daily Light (1794). (Jan. 13 Morning)
Isaiah XXVI 3; Psalms LV 22; Isaiah XII 2;
Matthew VIII 26; Philippians IV 6, 7; Isaiah XXX 15;
Isaiah XXXII 17; John XIV 27; Revelation I 4

Peace and Quiet

Drop thy still dews of quietness,
Till all our strivings cease;
Take from our souls the strain and stress,
And let our ordered lives confess
The beauty of thy peace.

Breathe through the heats of our desire
Thy coolness and thy balm;
Let sense be dumb, let flesh retire;
Speak through the earthquake, wind, and fire,
O still small voice of calm!

John Greenleaf Whittier (1807-1892)

Deep peace of the Running Wave to you
Deep peace of the Flowing Air to you
Deep peace of the Quiet Earth to you
Deep peace of the Shining Stars to you
Deep peace of the Son of Peace to you

Fiona Macleod

Goodness

Sunday

These are the words of the Lord: Stop at the crossroads; look for the ancient paths; ask, 'Where is the way that leads to what is good?' Then take that way, and you will find rest for yourselves.

Jeremiah VI 16 (N.E.B.)

Love in all sincerity, loathing evil and clinging to the good. Let love for our brotherhood breed warmth of mutual affection. Give pride of place to one another in esteem.

With unflagging energy, in ardour of spirit, serve the Lord.

Let hope keep you joyful; in trouble stand firm; persist in prayer.

Contribute to the needs of God's people, and practise hospitality.

Call down blessings on your persecutors — blessings, not curses.

With the joyful be joyful, and mourn with the mourners.

Care as much about each other as about yourselves. Do not be haughty, but go about with humble folk. Do not keep thinking how wise you are.

Never pay back evil for evil. Let your aims be such as all men count honourable. If possible, so far as it lies with you, live at peace with all men. My dear friends, do not seek revenge, but leave a place for divine retribution; for there is a text which reads, 'Justice is mine, says the Lord, I will repay.' But there is another text: 'If your enemy is hungry, feed him; if he is thirsty, give him a drink; by doing this you will heap live coals on his head.' Do not let evil conquer you, but use good to defeat evil.

Romans XII 9-21 (N.E.B.)

Goodness

For the word of the Lord is right; and all his works are done in truth.
He loveth righteousness and judgment: the earth is full of the goodness of the Lord.

Psalm XXXIII 4,5

Pray remember what I have recommended to you, which is to think often on God, by day, by night, in your business, and even in your diversions. He is always near you and with you; leave Him not alone. You would think it rude to leave a friend alone who came to visit you: why then must God be neglected? Do not then forget Him, but think on Him often, adore Him continually, live and die with Him; this is the glorious employment of a Christian; in a word, this is our profession; if we do not know it we must learn it.

Brother Lawrence (1610-1691)

Goodness

Tuesday

It doesn't take much of a man to be a Christian, but it takes all there is of him.

D. L. Moody (1837-1899)

This book, *Consistent Christianity,* will be of no avail if we all begin to rush hither and thither seeking to be fruitful in every good work in our own strength. Martha was very busy and active in her way. She wanted to be fruitful in her domestic good work. But her service was defective, because it was not balanced properly with a life of devotion. We need to sit at His feet first, and listen to His word, like Mary, if our works are to be really pleasing to Him. Martha was busy trying to act, before she first paused to discover exactly what it was that He wanted her to be doing. Our lives must consist of these two complementary elements, of devotion to Him on the one hand, and work for Him on the other. Like the two oars with which a boat is rowed, there must be a balance between them. Too much of one and too little of the other will only cause us to move in circles. If all the accent is on devotion, without our love for Him being shown forth in the practical keeping of His commandments, then we shall make no progress. If all the accent is on activity and works, without the time spent in personal devotion to Him, the result will be the same: sterility. Such a distinction between work and devotion is, of course, only one of convenience. They blend into each other. Work is all the sweeter because it is compounded with the fragrance of devotion. It was said of the twelve that they were chosen 'that they should be with him, and that he might send them forth . . .' So it is with ourselves: devotion and service are both part of His plan for us. It is not that we go into the secret place with Him, and then go out from Him into the world. He is with us always. We go out with Him. As His sheep we go in and out and find pasture. The Shepherd, to whom we go in, is also the Shepherd who leads us out.

Michael Griffiths

Goodness

If Christ lives in us, controlling our personalities, we will leave glorious marks on the lives we touch. Not because of our lovely characters, but because of his.

Eugenia Price

A Christian is not one who believes differently from others but who is different. By the work of the Spirit of God deep changes have taken place in the heart, and these are the basis of great changes in the life. God is working in us to will the good and then to do it; first right desires and decisions, then right conduct.

This ultimately means that the Christian must be marked by certain moral qualities which make for beauty of character. There is to be about us an uprightness of conduct and a transparency of motive which make us stand out from others in this evil world. Then there is to be a sympathy and approachableness which are the marks of a follower of the Lord Jesus. All these and other qualities of character combine to give a true Christian testimony which is not in word only, but in disposition and deed and which speaks loudly and unanswerably all the day long. The beauty of the Lord, the marks of His character, are seen in us. It is a real comeliness which is at once an absence of the ugly and a blending of the desirable into a true beauty of character.

Fred Mitchell

Goodness

Thursday

Do all the good you can,
By all the means you can,
In all the ways you can,
In all the places you can,
At all the times you can,
To all the people you can,
As long as ever you can.

John Wesley (1703-1791)

From "God Calling" (A Devotional Diary):

You are to help to save others. Never let one day pass when you have not reached out an arm of Love to someone outside your home — a note, a letter, a visit, help in some way.

Be full of Joy. Joy saves. Joy cures. Joy in Me. In every ray of sunlight, every smile, every act of kindness, or love, every trifling service — joy.

Each day do something to lift another soul out of the sea of sin, or disease, or doubt into which man has fallen. I still walk today by the lakeside and call My disciples to follow Me and to become fishers of men.

The helping hand is needed that raises the helpless to courage, to struggle, to faith, to health. Love and laugh. Love and laughter are the beckoners to faith and courage and success. Trust on, love on, joy on.

Refuse to be downcast. Refuse to be checked in your upward climb. Love and laugh. I am with you. I bear your burdens. Cast thy burden upon Me and I will sustain thee. And then in very lightheartedness you turn and help another with the burden that is pressing too heavily upon him or her.

How many burdens can you lighten this year? How many hearts can you cheer? How many souls can you help?

And in giving you gain: "Good measure, pressed down and running over."

Ed. A. J. Russell

194

Goodness

Friday

How long it takes us to learn that, in the deepest sense, Christian character is God-made and not man-made. If we are anxious to be good men, is God less anxious on the same theme? If He has set His heart on our purification and our sanctification, will He not, in His own time, in His own way, lead us there at last? Does it not look as if there are certain people He means us to meet, certain books He means us to read, certain experiences He means us to go through before we pass "into the city"?

G. Johnstone Jeffrey (1881-1961)

The Easy Way Out

It is easier to abstain from smoking than to love my neighbour.
It is easier to give money to charity than to spend myself helping others.
It is easier to attend church than to worship God.
It is easier to be a member on the roll of a church than to surrender control of my life and become a member of Christ's body.

It is not wrong to be a generous, non-smoking, regularly attending church member, but we could choose to be all these things and still avoid the awkward and uncompromising demands of Jesus Christ.

Jesus was not "respectable". He ate with unwashed hands and sinners. He chose uneducated workers as his cronies and he insulted well-meaning and religious people with intemperate language and extravagant claims.

It is easier to be respectable than Christian.

Glasgow Church Notes. November 1969

Goodness

Saturday

O faithful Lord, grant to us, we pray Thee, faithful hearts devoted to Thee, and to the service of all men for Thy sake. Fill us with pure love of Thee, keep us steadfast in this love, give us faith that worketh by love, and preserve us faithful unto death; through Jesus Christ our Lord. Amen.

Christina Georgina Rossetti (1830-1894)

O Heavenly Father, give me a heart like the heart of Jesus Christ, a heart more ready to minister than to be ministered unto, a heart moved by compassion towards the weak and the oppressed, a heart set upon the coming of Thy kingdom in the world of men.

Grant, O Father, that Thy loving kindness in causing my own lines to fall in pleasant places may not make me less sensitive to the needs of others less privileged, but rather more incline me to lay their burdens upon my own heart. And if any adversity should befall myself, then let me not brood upon my own sorrows, as if I alone in the world were suffering, but rather let me busy myself in the compassionate service of all who need my help. Thus let the power of my Lord Christ be strong within me and His peace invade my spirit. Amen.

John Baillie (1886-1961)

Faith

Now faith means putting our full confidence in the things we hope for, it means being certain of things we cannot see. It was this kind of faith that won their reputation for the saints of old. And it is after all only by faith that our minds accept as fact that the whole scheme of time and space was designed by God — that the world which we can see is operating on principles that are invisible.

Hebrews XI 1-3 (Phillips)

To Jesus the Unseen Dimension and Order were continuously real. The love, the generosity, and the power of the Father were constant realities, and it must not only have amazed but grieved Him more than we can guess to find men either unwilling or unable to use the power of faith.

Again and again He urges men to "have faith in God;" and both by His own teaching and His own example it is plain that He is continually urging men to put the weight of their confidence, not in earthly schemes and values, but in the unseen Heavenly Order, of which the supreme Head is the Father. To live like this, to live as though the spiritual realities were infinitely more important than the appearance of things, might fairly be said to be a basic teaching of Jesus. To live "by faith" is to Him the truly natural way of living, and although it may demand effort and persistence, He does not hold it out as a way of living merely for the spiritual elite. . . . Throughout the Gospels Jesus seems to be urging men to dare to use their faith-faculty — to knock, to seek, to ask. His general implication is that there are boundless resources in the Unseen World available for men of faith.

J. B. Phillips (1906-1982)

Faith

Monday

I do beg of you to recognise, then, the extreme simplicity of faith; namely, that it is nothing more nor less than just believing God when He says He either has done something for us, or will do it; and then trusting Him to keep His word. It is so simple that it is hard to explain. If any one asks me what it means to trust another to do a piece of work for me, I can only answer that it means committing the work to that other, and leaving it without anxiety in his hands. All of us have many times trusted very important affairs to others in this way, and have felt perfect rest in thus trusting, because of the confidence we have had in those who have undertaken them. . . . You could not live among your fellow-men and go through the customary routine of life a single day, if you were unable to trust your fellow-men, and it never enters into your head to say you cannot. But yet you do not hesitate to say, continually, that you cannot trust your God! And you excuse yourself by the plea that you are "a poor weak creature" and "have no faith." . . .

Away with such unworthy doubtings! Take your stand on the power and trustworthiness of your God, and see how quickly all difficulties will vanish before a steadfast determination to believe. Trust in the dark, trust in the light, trust at night and trust in the morning, and you will find that the faith that may begin perhaps by a mighty effort, will end, sooner or later, by becoming the easy and natural habit of the soul. It is a law of the spiritual life that every act of trust makes the next act less difficult, until at length, if these acts are persisted in, trusting becomes, like breathing, the natural unconscious action of the redeemed soul.

Hannah Pearsall Smith (1832-1911)

Faith

Christ called for faith in Himself. He never called for intellectual comprehension. He sent out to preach His gospel men who had not any creed or any intellectual faith, only a dumb sort of faith that Christ was more than man. I believe that He sends me out also to help make a better world. Surely that is not an irrational conceit or sentimental twaddle. Christ says that we must begin with faith, but that we can prove the truth of that faith ourselves.

It is not extraordinary that we must begin with faith. It is natural because we have to begin everything else with faith. Faith is an inherent quality of finiteness. It cannot be foregone. We cannot live without it. We cannot make any progress without it. No faith, no business; no faith, no fun; no faith, no victory. . . .

The faith in Christ upon which I have based my life has given me a light on life's meaning which has satisfied my mind, body, and soul. The hope that through that faith He would reveal a way of life here which justifies it, has been more than answered; and it seems to me ever more reasonable to hold that it will 'carry on' just as gloriously when we have passed beyond the limits of what material machines can reveal to us.

Wilfred Grenfell (1865-1940)

It isn't proved, you fool, it can't be proved.
How can you prove a victory before
It's won? How can you prove a man who leads
To be a leader worth the following,
Unless you follow to the death?

G. A. Studdert Kennedy (1883-1929)

Faith

Wednesday

There are two kinds of believing: first a believing about God which means that I believe that what is said of God is true. This faith is rather a form of knowledge than a faith. . . . Men possessing it can say, repeating what others have said: I believe that there is a God. I believe that Christ was born, died, rose again for me. But what the real faith is, and how powerful a thing it is, of this they know nothing. . . . They think that faith is a thing which they may have or not have at will, like any other natural human thing; so when they arrive at a conclusion and say "Truly the doctrine is correct,and therefore, I believe it," then they think that this is faith.

When faith is of the kind that *God* awakens and creates in the heart, then a man trusts in Christ. He is then so securely founded on Christ that he can hurl defiance at sin, death, hell, the devil and all God's enemies. He fears no ill, however hard and cruel it may prove to be. Such faith which throws itself upon God, whether in life or in death, alone makes a Christian man. It kills the past and reconstitutes us utterly different men in heart, disposition, spirit and in all the faculties. . . . Oh! there is something vital, busy, active, powerful about this faith that simply makes it impossible ever to let up in doing good works. The believer does not stop to ask whether good works are to be done, but is up and at it before the question is put. Faith is a lively, reckless confidence in the grace of God. So it is that a man unforced acquires the will and feels the impulse to do good to everybody, serve everybody and suffer everything for the love and praise of God who has bestowed such grace upon him. . . . Pray to God that He work this faith in you: otherwise you will never, never come by it, feign all that you will, or work all you can.

Martin Luther (1483-1546)

Faith

"Nothing, I suppose, in the long story of human cruelty has exceeded the Nazi concentration camps and the vile philosophy of life which produced them."

So wrote Father Trevor Huddleston in his Foreword to that terrible, deeply moving book, 'Dying We Live', the collection of farewell letters written by men and women living in the shadow of death before their execution because they could not acquiesce in the Hitler way of life, because they could not renounce their faith.

"It is," he continues, "natural for us today to wish to close the door for ever upon those dark and terrible days, when the full horror of Belsen and Buchenwald and Dachau was revealed. . . .

"To adopt such an attitude is, I believe, a kind of treason to those who died. But it is also to miss a glorious opportunity of learning what Faith can do, and this book states again and again, not in abstract theory but in living, human affirmation the meaning of Faith.

"To a generation such as ours, and especially to the young whose eyes are turned to the future, nothing is more absolutely essential than to grasp this meaning. It is so easy, and so deadly, to write and talk as if Faith were a soft option: to be enjoyed, if you have it; to be regretted if you have not. Whereas, in fact, Faith demands what Love demands: an act of the will; a hold, firm and forceful, upon reality. It is a positive and glorious and flaming thing, which only glows more splendid in the darkness.

"It is this Faith that you will find here. Do not turn aside from it, I beg you: for you need it as much as those who suffered so greatly in the winning of it."

Trevor Huddleston

Friday

Finding Faith

Faith is not learned from books, but, like Peter,
by following Jesus into "impossible" situations,
launching out into the deeps at His command,
walking out into the stormy waters of life,
and finding that somehow, "it works".

Faith is not learned sitting in the arm-chair,
but on the knife-edge between faith and folly,
when life and death are at stake,
when only faith in God
remains between you and disaster.

Faith is not learned while we go on our way,
buttressed up with worldly securities,
but when we throw everything we have
into the battle for His Kingdom.

I cannot learn faith,
and at the same time surround myself with "security".
I cannot discover God's power,
and at the same time live for my own comfort.
I cannot know the strength of His Spirit,
and at the same time attempt only those things within my power.

O Christ,
If you ever call on me to leave everything
and to follow you in some great venture,
give me grace not to miss my chance.
If you ever need to strip me of all I have,
so that I am alone in life, with nothing but you,
give me grace to welcome the experience.
If I rely more than I realise upon earthly securities,
then show me where I have gone wrong,
and deepen my faith, at whatever the cost.

Anon. "Life and Work"

Faith

Dear Daughter —

You say I'm clinging to an outworn creed;
That Jesus Christ is out of date — passé;
That I must put another in His place,
A new messiah for this present day!

And when I cannot, you're surprised and hurt,
Annoyed — impatient and provoked with me
Because I fail to see in him the "truth",
The answer to the world's perplexity.

You smile and say, "It is not given to all
To grasp, at once, its vast complexity,"
That "when the time is ripe" I'll know the "truth"
And wonder at my blind stupidity.

How can I answer best this avalanche,
Impassioned with the certainty of youth?
What was the evil quirk of circumstance
That caught you off guard in your search for truth?

How can I give you back your childhood faith,
Restored in all its sweet simplicity?
How can I show you Christ, the Perfect One,
Who was and is, and evermore shall be?

He is the Truth, the Life, the Light, the Way!
All I could need or want, I find in Him;
Friend of the friendless; Courage for the day;
Constant Companion when the path is dim.

How could I put another in His place,
Who has been more than friend or life to me?
How meet the coming years without His face,
Waiting at journey's end to welcome me?

Call me old-fashioned — stubborn — what you will,
Steadfast, unmovable, I shall remain,
Rooted and grounded in the Word, until
He shall appear, who maketh all things plain!

Katherine Melville

Humility

Sunday

Immense as our admiration must be for all who can talk to magnificent purpose about their own uncommon selves, one may admire, too, the magnificence of the unbroken silence of others.

C. E. Montague (1867-1928)

Pride goeth before destruction, and an haughty spirit before a fall. Better it is to be of an humble spirit with the lowly, than to divide the spoil with the proud.

Proverbs XVI 18-19

He that ruleth over men must be just, ruling in the fear of God. And he shall be as the light of the morning, when the sun riseth, even a morning without clouds; as the tender grass springing out of the earth by clear shining after rain.

II Samuel XXIII 3-4

Blessed are the meek, for they shall inherit the earth. . . . Whosoever will be great among you, let him be your minister; and whosoever will be chief among you, let him be your servant: even as the Son of man came not to be ministered unto, but to minister, and to give his life a ransom for many.

Matthew V 5 and XX 26-28

Humility

'The harvest which the Spirit produces is . . . strength of gentleness' (Galatians V 22, 23. Barclay).

Unconcern with self. If there is one Christian grace that is misunderstood more than any other it is meekness, or humility. There is, of course, a humility which is sheer humbug. Charles Dickens's Uriah Heep ('I am so very 'umble, Master Copperfield, so very 'umble') is the classic illustration from fiction, but it is observable in real life also. Christian meekness is far different from the kind advertised by the Uriah Heeps. The Christian is never conscious of humility; it is not a pose: how indeed can one pose this quality? Christian meekness arises from unconcern with self. We may feel that few Christians rise to this high standard; that it is 'quite out of this world'. And of course it is. None of Paul's nine Christian graces is natural to man. They are possible of realisation only as men are indwelt by God's Spirit.

Something must be said here by way of warning. Christian meekness is not an inferiority complex. Though the Christian is never self-assertive and for Christ's sake defers to others, he does not feel inferior. He recognises sensibly and with gratitude and wonder his own place in God's Kingdom. The difference between meekness and a sense of inferiority is recognised by the discerning.

Further, meekness is not weakness. William Barclay's translation is helpful here. And Jesus, who said, 'the meek shall inherit the earth' is the great illustration of the truth that 'gentleness (humility) is strength'.

But note, our prayer must not be, 'Lord, make me lowly', but 'Lord, possess me fully'. That is the secret of all the Christian virtues.

The Soldier's Armoury
Sunday, June 20th, 1971

Humility

Tuesday

As Jesus Christ does not only teach humility, but also bestows it, let us begin by asking Him to give us a love for that virtue. . . . No prayer could be more pleasing to Jesus Christ; we can feel sure of that; He will infallibly grant our request if we sincerely wish it to be granted. But many who pray for humility would be extremely sorry if God were to grant it to them. This is one of the points on which people are most easily deluded. Some book, or meditation, or Communion touches their heart; they feel the attraction of this virtue, and ask God to give it to them; but they forget that to love, desire, and ask for humility is loving, desiring and asking for humiliations, for these are the companions, or rather the food of humility, and without them it is no more than a beautiful but meaningless idea. Now, if the bare thought of humiliation fills us with horror; if we repel it with our whole strength; if pride and self-love get the better of us on every occasion; and if, instead of stiffening ourselves against them, we yield to them and cannot for a moment endure anything that wounds them, we are flattering ourselves if we think we love humility. The fact is that we dislike it, and our prayer is a delusion. We shall do well, then, to examine ourselves a little on this point before offering our petition to God; and instead of giving rein to our imagination, and making proposals that we are too weak to carry out, see whether we be resolved and prepared to bear the lightest and most ordinary humiliations. Otherwise such a prayer can have no result except self-deception; for our inmost feelings would nullify it if we were really abhorring what we seemed to be asking for.

But there are truly those, though not very many, who ask God in all sincerity to grant them humility and offer themselves to carry all the humiliating crosses that He is pleased to send them. This offer on their part is a real consecration. From that moment they should feel that they are not their own, but belong to Jesus Christ and are fighting under His standard.

Jean Nicolas Grou (1731-1803)

Humility

They came to the upper room on that evening with their feet hot and sweaty, with the dust of the roads coating feet and sandals. But there was nobody present to do the slave's work of washing their feet. It must have been obvious to all that feet were unwashed, for, reclining at the table in the manner of that time, with your head and your hands by the table, supporting yourself on one elbow, the feet of the others at the table were only just over your shoulder. Anyone who has lived in hot climates knows the smell of unwashed feet! But if you had just been competing to see who was the most important, you were not going to step down and admit you were the junior present. There was a long, painful, smelly silence. . . . It is Jesus who gets up, stripping off His outer clothes, girding Himself with a towel to perform the menial task of washing the feet of His own disciples. There must have been an embarrassing silence as the water splashed in the basin and the Master knelt and washed dirty feet. That this One who is so pure and clean should humble Himself to wash off *my* dirt, to defile Himself with *my* uncleanness. His words to gruffly protesting Peter make it clear that this must be submitted to, for it prefigured the cross, when He was to take the sin and filthiness of all mankind upon His pure and holy heart. That He who is so great, so gloriously holy, should take this on Himself — this is humility. If we have been shrinking from being slaves, too proud to be slaves, we are utterly shamed to see what He did. 'If I then, your Lord and Teacher, have washed your feet, you also ought to wash one another's feet. For I have given you an example, that you also should do as I have done to you. Truly, truly, I say to you, a slave is not greater than his master. . .' In other words, I have become your slave — now you become slaves to others as well.

Michael Griffiths

Humility

God dwells among the lowliest of men. He sits on the dust heap among the prison convicts. He is with the juvenile delinquents. He stands at the door begging bread. He throngs with the beggars at the place of alms. He is among the sick, and with the unemployed in front of the free employment bureau.

Toyohiko Kagawa (1888-1960)

Here is thy footstool and there rest thy feet where live the poorest, and lowliest, and lost.

When I try to bow to thee, my obeisance cannot reach down to the depth where thy feet rest among the poorest, and lowliest, and lost.

Pride can never approach to where thou walkest in the clothes of the humble among the poorest, and lowliest, and lost.

My heart can never find its way to where thou keepest company with the companionless among the poorest, the lowliest, and the lost.

Rabindranath Tagore (1861-1941)

Christ's humility was simply the surrender of Himself to God, to allow God to do in Him what He pleased, whatever men around might say of Him, or do to Him.

Andrew Murray (1828-1917)

Humility

Saturday

The Lowly Way
I strove for Power, I sought for Fame,
To keep the Crown of the Causeway my aim,
In the Temple of Honour to carve my name;
But I found no rest for my soul.

Then I met with a Man, and heard Him say:
"Come, walk with Me the Lowly Way:
The humble in heart, at the end of the day,
Alone finds rest for his soul."

I went with the Man, and looked in His face,
And the lust for Power and the Pride of Place
Were slain in my heart by His gentle grace;
And so I found rest for my soul.

Herbert Reid

And Jesus said to them all, If any man
will come after me, let him deny himself,
and take up his cross daily, and follow me.

For whosoever will save his life shall
lose it: but whosoever will lose his life
for my sake, the same shall save it.

Luke IX 23, 24

Holy Week

On the next day much people that were come to the feast, when they heard that Jesus was coming to Jerusalem, took branches of palm trees, and went forth to meet him, and cried, Hosanna: Blessed is the King of Israel that cometh in the name of the Lord.

And Jesus, when he had found a young ass, sat thereon; as it is written, Fear not, daughter of Sion: behold, thy King cometh, sitting on an ass's colt.

John XII 12-15

In the East in the time of Jesus the ass was a noble beast. . . . The ass was the beast on which kings rode when they came in peace; only in war did they ride upon horses. The entry of Jesus was the claim to be King.

But at the same time it was the claim to be the King of peace. It was upon the ass of peace and not upon the horse of war that Jesus came. He came deliberately refusing the role of the warrior Messiah and claiming to be the Prince of peace. He was appealing for a throne, but the throne was in the hearts of men. In that entry into Jerusalem Jesus, in a dramatic symbolic action which spoke more loudly than any words, was making one last appeal to men, and saying to them: 'Will you not, even now, even yet, accept me as your Lord and King, and enthrone me within your hearts?'

Jesus' entry into Jerusalem was an action of supreme courage; it was an assertion of royalty and an offer of love; it was at one and the same time royalty's claim and love's appeal.

William Barclay (1907-1978)

Holy Week

Monday

As the cheering of the crowds echoed in his ears that morning he knew already that the die was cast. With tragic irony the orchestra of hell was playing a royal overture for the Son of man, who was delivered to the evil one. The trial of Jesus before Pilate was as nothing to the trial that was on between light and darkness, love and hate, hope and despair. Even the fearful torments that were to be inflicted on his body were as nothing to the agony of his descent to hell, the moment of utter darkness when meaning was drained out of life, when the evil one was triumphant, and he cried: "My God, my God, why hast thou forsaken me?" All that happened during Holy Week was the living out by Jesus of his own prayer. This was the final test when the skies of evil opened and the cosmic storm broke upon him with final fury. "Lead me not into temptation," "Do not bring me to the test" — was not that even his last prayer in the Garden of Gethsemane, a prayer that ended with the confident "nevertheless" — "nevertheless not as I will, but as thou wilt." For, even as this last test had to come, he knew that the Father was there to deliver him from evil.

Do you see now why he said to the disciples in the garden, "Watch and pray, that ye enter not into temptation"? It was this temptation he had in mind, the ultimate assault of the devil on the soul of man. And he knew that neither these disciples, nor you and I, are capable of withstanding such a storm. But — and this is the inner meaning of Holy Week — we need never pass in our mortal weakness into this place where God seems absent and the evil one is rampant. Our Lord has been there for us. He rode into the valley of death and desolation, not as a knight in shining armour, but as the lowly, the innocent one, borne by a donkey to an ignominious death. He was in solemn truth led into temptation, brought to the final test. And when the deed was done, and the skies had cleared, he emerged the victor. He was delivered from evil. His disciples then knew, and have known ever since, that the awful test is over, that no one any more need descend into hell. Thus we look back to the lonely figure who rode into Jerusalem and we know that indeed this is the King of kings, the Lord of lords, for he is the Deliverer from evil.

David H. C. Read

Holy Week

What, then, was Jesus doing in his life and in his death? The answer must be that in his life and in his death Jesus was demonstrating to men the eternal, unchangeable, unconquerable love of God. He was demonstrating to men that God is the Father who loves undefeatably and whose one desire is that the lost son should come home. When Jesus entered the world, when he healed the sick, comforted the sad, fed the hungry, forgave his enemies, he was saying to men: 'God loves you like that.' When he died upon the Cross, he was saying: 'Nothing that men can ever do to God will stop God loving them. There is no limit to the love of God. There is no end beyond which that love will not go. God loves you like that.' That is why nothing less than death on the Cross would do. If Jesus had refused or escaped the Cross, if he had not died, it would have meant that there was some point in suffering and sorrow at which the love of God stopped, that there was some point beyond which forgiveness was impossible. But the Cross is God saying in Jesus: 'There is no limit to which my love will not go and no sin which my love cannot forgive.'

William Barclay (1907-1978)

It is infinitely easier to suffer in obedience to a human command than to accept suffering as free, responsible men.

It is infinitely easier to suffer with others than to suffer alone.

It is infinitely easier to suffer as public heroes than to suffer apart and in ignominy.

It is infinitely easier to suffer physical death than to endure spiritual suffering.

Christ suffered as a free man, alone, apart and in ignominy, in body and in spirit.

Dietrich Bonhoeffer (1906-45)

Holy Week

Wednesday

And Pilate answered and said again unto the people, What will ye then that I shall do unto him whom ye call the King of the Jews?

And they cried out again, Crucify him.

Then Pilate said unto them, Why, what evil hath he done? And they cried out the more exceedingly, Crucify him.

Mark XV 12-14

So they came to a place called Golgotha (which means 'Place of a skull') and there they offered him a draught of wine mixed with gall; but when he had tasted it he would not drink.

After fastening him to the cross they divided his clothes among them by casting lots, and then sat down there to keep watch.

Matthew XXVII 33-36 (N.E.B.)

And sitting down they watched Him there,
The soldiers did.
There, while they played with dice,
He made His sacrifice,
And died upon the Cross to rid
God's world of sin.

He was a gambler too,
My Christ,
He took His life and threw
It for a world redeemed.
And e'er His agony was done
Before the westering sun went down,
Crowning that day with crimson crown,
He knew
That He had won.

G. A. Studdert Kennedy (1883-1929)

Holy Week

Longinus

We nailed him there
Aloft between the thieves, in the bright air.
The rabble and the readers mocked with oaths,
The hangman's squad were dicing for his clothes.
The two thieves jeered at him. Then it grew dark,
Till the noon sun was dwindled to a spark,
And one by one the mocking mouths fell still.
We were alone on the accursed hill
And we were still, not even the dice clicked,
Only the heavy blood-gouts dropped and ticked
On to the stone; the hill is all bald stone.
And now and then the hangers gave a groan.
Up in the dark, three shapes with arms outspread.
The blood-drops spat to show how slow they bled.
They rose up black against the ghastly sky.
God, lord, it is a slow way to make die
A man, a strong man, who can beget men.
Then there would come another groan, and then
One of those thieves (tough cameleers those two)
Would curse the teacher from lips bitten through,
And the other bid him let the teacher be.
I have stood much, but this thing daunted me:
The dark, the livid light, and long, long groans
One on another, coming from their bones.
And it got darker and a glare began
Like the sky burning up above the man.
The hangman's squad stood easy on their spears
And the air moaned, and women were in tears,
While still between his groans the robber cursed.
The sky was grim: it seemed about to burst.
Hours had passed: they seemed like awful days.
. . . Jesus cried
Once more and drooped, I saw that he had died.
Lord, in the earthquake God had come for him.

John Masefield (1878-1967)

Holy Week

Friday

The Sentry

Yes, I was bored with the event;
The same pattern as before,
Murderers and thieves caught in the act;
Condemned to die at last, the robbers
Death by crucifixion.
But then by some strange chance
My Captain of the Guard fell sick
And languished, whilst I remained
On watch until the third hour.
   Ah then, such strange events befell,
   For He whom they named Jesus,
   Nailed fast upon his cross
   Called unto the night hour,
   "Father forgive them . . ."
And behold, the hill was bathed in light;
Whilst on the wind winged forms
Appeared, and lifted Him away!
Appalled, with burning heart,
My spear-hand gripped the shaft,
Then as He rose
Plunged the point deep
Into His side, to keep my charge.
   Then, blinded, my senses left me
   And to this hour I know not the outcome
   Of that day, save what they tell me;
   And that this arm bears witness
   To the deed; for here imprinted
   In the flesh, a cross has burned itself
And now all Romans know
That Paulus was the man
Who wounded Him.

Frank Jenkins

Holy Week

Good Friday?

Of course it was a common way to kill.
Two thieves died with Him on the selfsame day,
And hundreds, later, living torches, hung
And burned on crosses by the Appian Way.
This Jesus, He was luckier than most —
It often took two days before they died;
His suffering was mercifully brief
Compared with others whom they crucified.
The Cross, indeed, was far too commonplace
To win, just by itself, His case for God.
They looked for signs and wonders, not mere death —
Some demonstration that was really odd.

How can that ancient wrong put right for us
All in mankind that's sinful and obscene?
Can horror shake us into faith, today?
It entertains us on our TV screen!
Torture is carnal; pain is of the flesh;
Can spirit be redeemed by agony?

What counts is surely the huge confidence
That God would somehow, surely, justify.
You can't do more to show your trust in Him
Than leave it all to Him to see you through;
You can't surrender more than life itself
To show you're sure He won't abandon you.

They took the body down and buried it.
It could itself do nothing; it was dead.
Dead things can't rise; they utterly depend
On someone else. All independence fled
They need another Power than their own —
As we do, bound in bondage to our sin,
Although we seem to think we need no help —
Have "come of age" — need only will, to win.
Delusion! We are dead: dead as the Christ
When taken from the Cross. And only if
We wholly trust and are at one with Him
Can we, like Him, be raised by God to life.

Norman M. Bowman.

Lord Christ, Thou gavest Thyself for me;
behold here I am, and here I give myself to Thee.

Jeremiah Dyke (? -1620)

Easter

Sunday

And when the sabbath was past, Mary Magdalene, and Mary the mother of James, and Salome, had bought sweet spices, that they might come and anoint him.

And very early in the morning the first day of the week, they came unto the sepulchre at the rising of the sun.

And they said among themselves, Who shall roll us away the stone from the door of the sepulchre?

And when they looked, they saw that the stone was rolled away: for it was very great.

And entering into the sepulchre, they saw a young man sitting on the right side, clothed in a long white garment; and they were affrighted.

And he saith unto them, Be not affrighted: Ye seek Jesus of Nazareth, which was crucified: he is risen; he is not here: behold the place where they laid him.

But go your way, tell his disciples and Peter that he goeth before you into Galilee: there shall ye see him, as he said unto you.

And they went out quickly, and fled from the sepulchre; for they trembled and were amazed.

And they told all these things unto the eleven, and to all the rest. . . .

And their words seemed to them as idle tales, and they believed them not.

Then arose Peter, and ran unto the sepulchre; and stooping down, he beheld the linen clothes laid by themselves, and departed, wondering in himself at that which was come to pass.

Mark XVI 1-8
Luke XXIV 9, 11, 12

Easter

Christ is Risen!

It is recorded that in the early 1920's a Russian politician was sent to address a great anti-God rally in Kiev. In a fervent speech he attacked the Christian faith with all the power at his command, and afterwards questions were invited. There was a short silence, and then a priest of the Orthodox Church gave the crowd the simple and ancient Easter greeting: "Christ is risen!" Instantly the crowd rose and made a thunderous reply: "He is risen indeed!"

Against such a conviction no argument can prevail.

Kenneth Budd

He lives! He lives! Christ Jesus lives today;
He walks with me and talks with me
Along life's narrow way.
He lives! He lives! Salvation to impart.
You ask me how I know He lives?
He lives within my heart.

Alfred H. Ackley

Thine be the glory, risen, conquering Son,
Endless is the victory thou o'er death hast won.

Edmond Budry (1854-1932)

219

Easter

Tuesday

It is a familiar sound: the wisdom of this world jeering at the wisdom of God, the pride of reason denouncing the credibility of the faith as the credulity of the faithful. Preach an abstract pantheism, and no one will disturb you. Preach an impersonal God — the sum-total of the ethical and religious values — and you will be left in peace. But Resurrection — this is another matter. This is the scandal. This is the palpable absurdity. These Christians — how credulous they are! Twenty centuries have echoed the laughter of the Areopagus. Here in the Resurrection of Jesus is the fact which at the first launched Christianity upon the world and conquered the throne of the Caesars; here is the rock on which the Church was built and has stood for two thousand years; here is the good news which, a million times, has dried the tears of the desolate and solaced the bruised heart's dumb agony.

James S. Stewart

Most glorious Lord of Lyfe! that, on this day,
Didst make Thy triumph over death and sin;
And having harrow'd hell, didst bring away
Captivity thence captive, us to win:
This joyous day, deare Lord, with joy begin;
And grant that we, for whom Thou didest dye,
Being with Thy deare blood clene washt from sin,
May live for ever in felicity!

Edmund Spenser (1552-1599)

Easter

Something happened between the Friday night and the evening of Easter Sunday to change the disciples from a terrified group of deserters, leaderless, starting at every sound, to men of such courage, determination and unquenchable faith that they withstood everything the Jewish leaders could do to silence them. On the Friday night they were shocked into helplessness by the death of Jesus; Peter, who might have rallied them, was off somewhere in the bottomless abyss of his shame.

Something happened in what has been called "thirty-six hours that changed the world." For within days these same disciples were out in the streets of Jerusalem, with Caiaphas and Annas and all the rest still in power, declaring that Jesus had arisen from the dead, and getting people to believe them. No one has ever yet explained away this change, quite out of character, and for me it is basic. From it much follows. The New Testament itself is witness to the Resurrection: the joy and triumph of the Resurrection ring through it from first to last; it thrills and vibrates with the presence and power of the living Christ. If Christ had died and stayed dead the story of this brief and tragic life would never have been written and I doubt if we would ever even have heard his name. The Church is witness to the Resurrection, for it was founded in its tiny, unlikely beginnings on belief in the risen Christ, and withstood persecution in the early days in the power of that belief. It has gone on growing and spreading in spite of cruel pressure from without and debilitating corruption from within. If Christ is not risen then Christianity is the biggest confidence trick in all history. . . . Experience witnesses to the Resurrection. In forty years I have seen hundreds of people, of all sorts, face life with a radiance of joy, a tireless compassion for others and an unconquerable courage and faith which I can only explain by saying that Christ is alive for them, in them and through them. My own personal experience bears the same witness, for things have happened to me of such a nature that they left me with no option but to say: "Christ was there." Not to believe this would be to me like looking in the mirror and not seeing my own face.

R. Leonard Small

Easter

Thursday

Now we're ready for the Easter text: "For thine is the kingdom, and the power, and the glory, for ever. Amen." That's the doxology, the hymn of praise, the roll of drums and the clash of cymbals with which the Church closes the Prayer of prayers. And what else is being said or sung in a thousand languages wherever Christians meet on Easter morning? I call it the defiant doxology because it rises out of the Resurrection faith of the Church in defiance of the world, the flesh, and the devil. In spite of the immense authority and terrible responsibility of the rulers of this world we still declare: "*Thine* is the kingdom"; in spite of the stupendous new powers that have been given to modern man, the man of flesh, secular man, we still confess: "*Thine* is the power"; in spite of the resplendent antics of demonic forces, the seductions of the current cults of magnificent despair, and the hypnotic fascination of the absurd and the abyss, we still raise the shout of adoration: "*Thine* is the glory." Easter means that in a world of jet diplomacy, intercontinental missiles, cybernetics, extrasensory perception, LSD, space probes, far-out cults, and everything-a-go-go, there are still men and women who can get up in the morning and say: "Glory be to the Father, and to the Son, and to the Holy Ghost; as it was in the beginning, *is now,* and ever shall be: world without end." . . .

The man or woman who underscores each prayer with the Resurrection doxology, who knows in each moment of triumph the humility, and in each moment of disaster the ultimate confidence that says: "Thine is the kingdom, and the power, and the glory", has known the presence of the risen Christ. . . . God knows how desperate are the problems that confront us at this time, and how serious the decisions that weigh upon us all. But the missing note in so much Christian argument and activity around us today is surely the ultimate gaiety of spirit that can throw open a window, like Pope John in the Vatican not long ago, and beam upon a snarling world the radiant belief that Christ is alive, that God's in his heaven, and that his Spirit is at work in every corner of his creation. Argue, if you like, about the need for a doctrine of the Trinity. I only know that there are times when I can do nothing else than cry out: "Glory be to the Father, and to the Son, and to the Holy Ghost."

David H. C. Read

Easter

Friday

I am not talking about a spirit of optimism, or about a God who shines forever out there in space like the sun beyond these threatening clouds. I am talking about a God who came here, about Jesus Christ, who lived like us through storm and sunshine, who was hurt by what hurts us, who was crushed by the kingdom of evil, delivered to the powers of this world, and overwhelmed by the demonic fury of hell unleashed. He died. That was the moment when all prayers could cease, when the world was darkness and all life absurd. And on the third day God brought him back to life, and life has never been the same.

It was not a myth. It was Jesus. It was not a beautiful idea. It was Jesus, standing by an empty tomb and saying: Mary. It was Mary saying: *Master*. It was Mary telling the others, and the others telling their friends, and their friends telling the world. The Resurrection doxology is born into the hearts of people like you and me by the infection of a faith that is unbroken across two thousand years.It is not shaken by any change in our ways of thought, or deflected by any invention of men. Surrounded by the threatening forces of the modern world, and taunted by the philosophies of despair and the cult of the absurd, we join the chorus of the Church in heaven and on earth: "Thine is the kingdom, and the power, and the glory." For the living Christ is with us now, and his word is the same: "Peace I leave with you, my peace I give unto you: not as the world giveth, give I unto you. Let not your heart be troubled, neither let it be afraid."

David H. C. Read

Easter

Saturday

But Thomas, one of the twelve, was not with them when Jesus came. The other disciples therefore said unto him, We have seen the Lord. But he said unto them, Except I shall see in his hands the print of the nails, and put my finger into the print of the nails, and thrust my hand into his side, I will not believe.

And after eight days again his disciples were within, and Thomas with them: then came Jesus, the doors being shut, and stood in the midst, and said, Peace be unto you.

Then saith he to Thomas, Reach hither thy finger, and behold my hands; and reach hither thy hand, and thrust it into my side: and be not faithless, but believing. And Thomas answered and said unto him, My Lord and my God.

John XX 24-28

Thomas had been shattered by the sight of Jesus on the cross. His sufferings were so real to him that anything that forgot them would be meaningless. Talk about seeing Jesus still was a mockery unless it was the same Jesus, with his wounds. Only Thomas was allowed to touch Jesus, and then only his wounds.

Pascal wrote: It seems to me that Jesus Christ after His resurrection allowed only His wounds to be touched: noli me tangere. We must unite ourselves to His sufferings alone.

Part of our experience of the resurrection is the recognition of suffering in the purpose of life. The resurrection is not the denial of the death of Jesus but the victory of his death. And we see the power of the resurrection in the suffering of other men — not in our compassion for their suffering but in their ability to suffer and to overcome. Our difficulty to believe in the resurrection lies in our unwillingness to believe this. We do not want to touch his wounds.

"When pain ends, gain ends too.
To me that story — ay, that Life and Death
Of which I wrote 'it was' — to me it is;
Is not God now in the world His power first made?
Is not His love at issue still with sin,
Closed with and cast and conquered, crucified
Visibly when a wrong is done on earth?
Love, wrong, and pain, what see I else around?
Yea, and the Resurrection . . ."

Robert Browning

From 'Towards Easter and Beyond',
with notes by Rev. T. Ralph Morton

224

Presence of Christ

Where is the Lord Jesus most surely to be found today? Where is what a sacramental theology would call "the real presence of Christ?" No doubt in Word and Sacrament and worship, in all the ordinances of the faith, here in this church, yonder in your own room when you kneel to pray. Yes, but also and most certainly in the flesh and blood of every needy soul throughout God's earth today. This, if only we had eyes to see and a heart to understand, is where Christ the King comes forth to meet us. Did He not tell us this Himself? "I was hungry, and you gave Me no meat; sick and in prison, and you visited Me not. Then shall they answer Him, Lord, when saw we Thee hungry or sick or in prison, and did not minister to Thee? Then shall He answer them, Inasmuch as you did it not to one of the least of these, you did it not to Me."

Here is the real presence: every homeless refugee, every hungry child, every racially segregated soul from whom a Western culture stands traditionally and patronisingly aloof; and to come nearer home — that troublesome neighbour, that handicapped sufferer, that poor bungler who has made a wretched mess of his life, that woman who carries a hidden tragedy in her heart, that paganised youth who will tell you he has no use for your religion or your God. This is the real presence; and if we are not prepared to see and serve Him there, in His needy brethren, all our expressions of love to God are worthless and our religious professions frivolous.

Can we face the challenge? The burden of this world's need could break us, the yoke of its callousness crush us — if it were not for one thing: that this is precisely the yoke, the burden, that Christ carried triumphantly through the cross to the resurrection, and is still carrying for ever. So that, in the deepest sense, it is not we who have to be strengtheners and reinforcers of others. It is Christ in us — the living contemporaneous Christ moving out into these other lives. This is the incredible glory of our calling as Christians. And it is along this road that we make the great discovery, that His yoke is easy, and His burden light.

James S. Stewart

Presence of Christ

Monday

I think that we ought to make it quite clear that we are not talking about a third party who is somewhere else when we're talking about this Jesus — He is here — this is the whole point of it. It seems to me that if the Church really got hold of this, how vitalised the worship of the Church would be, how energised its mission, if it saw Christ in the very midst — "Where two or three are gathered together there am I in the midst of them." This is the real thrill. I can understand a man not believing it — I can almost understand a man refusing to have anything to do with it; but what I cannot understand is a man believing it and not being thrilled by it. . . . I start every day by saying to myself His words, "Lo, I am with you always, even unto the end of the world." And I know that whatever happens in the future, He is quite certain to be there.

James S. Stewart

The claim that Jesus is not findable is a denial of history, and it is a denial of the experience of some of the finest men and women the world has ever seen, who, for the sake of the truth of that experience, have sallied forth on the most desperate exploits in the spiritual history of the world. Many of them have never seen visions or heard voices, but through questing faith and adventurous prayer there has come to them such an inward reinforcement of personality which no adverse circumstance can undermine, such a serenity of heart which nothing can invade, such an infectious gaiety which no grief or depression can quell, such an outgoing love to others, including even critics and enemies — their lives have been so changed, changed as none other has ever changed lives save Jesus of Nazareth, that the most reasonable way of explaining their experience is to assert that they have found Him for themselves.

Leslie D. Weatherhead (1893-1976)

Presence of Christ

Christ in Flanders

We had forgotten You, or very nearly —
You did not seem to touch us very nearly —
Of course we thought about You now and then;
Especially in any time of trouble —
We knew that You were good in time of trouble —
But we are very ordinary men.

And there were always other things to think of —
There's lots of things a man has got to think of —
His work, his home, his pleasure, and his wife;
And so we only thought of You on Sunday —
Sometimes, perhaps, not even on a Sunday —
Because there's always lots to fill one's life.

And, all the while, in street or lane or byway —
In country lane, in city street, or byway —
You walked among us, and we did not see.
Your Feet were bleeding as You walked our pavements —
How did we miss Your Footprints on our pavements?
Can there be other folk as blind as we?

Now we remember; over here in Flanders —
(It isn't strange to think of You in Flanders) —
This hideous warfare seems to make things clear.
We never thought about You much in England —
But now that we are far away from England —
We have no doubts, we know that You are here.

You helped us pass the jest along the trenches —
Where, in cold blood, we waited in the trenches —
You touched its ribaldry and made it fine.
You stood beside us in our pain and weakness —
We're glad to think You understand our weakness —
Somehow it seems to help us not to whine.

We think about You kneeling in the Garden —
Ah! God! the agony of that dread Garden —
We know You prayed for us upon the Cross.
If anything could make us glad to bear it —
'Twould be the knowledge that You willed to bear it —
Pain — death — the uttermost of human loss.

Though we forgot You — You will not forget us —
We feel so sure that You will not forget us —
But stay with us until this dream is past.
And so we ask for courage, strength, and pardon —
Especially, I think, we ask for pardon —
And that You'll stand beside us to the last.

L.W.
(Reprinted from 'The Spectator' of September 11th, 1915.)

227

Presence of Christ

Wednesday

[In hiding from the Germans in Holland during the war, sanctuary was found temporarily in the low-beamed attic of a friendly house.] There I spent most of my time in true solitary confinement, more mental than physical. My thoughts had always been my own, but here, here it was different; one could not utter these thoughts, mould them, discuss them and get fresh ideas.

Never before did I have such close fellowship with Him, the invisible Christ, whose existence people deny. Our acquaintance became strong, our friendship secure, my dependability in Him absolutely unshakeable, a certainty which I have proved in every smallest detail till this very day.

Some of His attitudes have puzzled me. I still don't understand the depth of all His suffering for those who care to associate with Him. The free entry into a living union with Him, if an individual trusts in that divine blood, shed for him or her. I have proved this union with Christ and have also experienced that His promises are dependable and pregnant with fulfilment. With Him one can live through the toughest problems, the most dangerous situation, the loneliest experience. He promised to be with us always, and He is with us in every difficulty. One just cannot doubt Him, when He has proved Himself dependable in every aspect of life.

With warm love He surrounded me in that bare attic. He gave me courage when the air raid sirens sounded their fearful piercing tone. When others ran to the shelters, He stayed with me. His Holy Spirit, able to be everywhere at the same time, covered me with security. I knew myself loved, even when no human being considered my need. His cross became my symbol of ultimate victory. It was the cross which pointed at all times to the Victory after suffering and death.

From 'Selected to Live',
Memories by Johanna-Ruth Dobschiner

Presence of Christ

I will fear no evil — for Thou art with me.

Is not this the great lesson about calamity that Jesus taught? He did not tell His men that they would escape trouble because they were His. He rather told them the opposite. Jesus doesn't say, 'I will deliver you from the waters.' He says something which one day we shall perceive to be much more wonderful. He says, 'When you pass through the waters, I shall be there, too.' And what does that presence do? Is it merely comfort? Is it merely sharing our sad experiences with us? Is it merely companionship? It is all this and more. That presence enables us so to make an adjustment to the shadowed experiences of life that they produce a completely different result in personality. The normal result of a gloomy experience is gloom; of pain, resentment; of calamity, despair; of bereavement, rebellion. But those who have walked through shadowed valleys *with Him,* emerge with an experience that makes us catch our breath in awe and wonder and admiration. There is nothing in a shadowed experience which automatically makes men noble. Rather the reverse. But the alchemy of His perceived presence turns the dull lead to shining gold and even pain into a sacrament. 'I used to wonder why God did not save His loved ones from sorrow,' said a great saint to me, 'but it was in the valley of tears I found how near He was and how gentle His hand. It is not an evil thing that we should have to cry if it is He who wipes our tears away. It gives us an experience of Him we otherwise might not have had. And all experiences of Him are blessed.' 'I will fear no evil for Thou art with me.'

Leslie D. Weatherhead (1893-1976)

Why not make a rendezvous with Christ at a certain point of your daily journey? Some corner of a familiar street? Some stretch of the road we travel each day to work? Or some portion of the road home that you can keep sacred for Him? Soon you will come to expect Him in that place. Even in 100 yards you can say much to each other. Such a place will become a shrine to you. A Royal Mile. And every day He will be there and waiting.

John H. Sammon (1890-1962)

Friday

The Second Crucifixion

Loud mockers in the roaring street
Say Christ is crucified again:
Twice pierced His gospel-bearing feet,
Twice broken His great heart in vain.

I hear, and to myself I smile,
For Christ talks with me all the while.

No angel now to roll the stone
From off His unawaking sleep,
In vain shall Mary watch alone,
In vain the soldiers vigil keep.

Yet while they deem my Lord is dead
My eyes are on His shining head.

Ah! never more shall Mary hear
That voice exceeding sweet and low
Within the garden calling clear:
Her Lord is gone, and she must go.

Yet all the while my Lord I meet
In every London lane and street.

Poor Lazarus shall wait in vain,
And Bartimaeus still go blind;
The healing hem shall ne'er again
Be touch'd by suffering humankind.

Yet all the while I see them rest,
The poor and outcast, on His breast.

No more unto the stubborn heart
With gentle knocking shall He plead,
No more the mystic pity start,
For Christ twice dead is dead indeed.

So in the street I hear men say,
Yet Christ is with me all the day.

Richard Le Gallienne (1866-1947)

Presence of Christ

Footprints

The following poem was written by the Bishop of Iran whose son had been murdered. The poem was written in Persian and translated into English by his wife.

One night I dreamed I was walking along a beach with my LORD.
Many scenes from my life flashed across my mind.
In each scene I noticed footprints. Sometimes there were two sets of footprints;
At other times there was only one.
This bothered me, because I noticed that during the low periods of my life,
When I was suffering from anguish, sorrow or defeat,
I could see only one set of footprints.
So I said "my LORD, you promised me that if I followed you,
You would be with me always.
But I have noticed that during the most trying periods of my life,
There has been only one set of footprints.
Why when I needed you most were you not there?"
The LORD replied "The times when you saw only one set of footprints,
my   child, was when I carried you."

Christ be with me, Christ within me,
Christ behind me, Christ before me,
Christ beside me, Christ to win me,
Christ to comfort and restore me,
Christ beneath me, Christ above me,
Christ in quiet, Christ in danger,
Christ in hearts of all that love me,
Christ in mouth of friend and stranger.

St. Patrick (372-466);
version by Cecil Frances Alexander (1818-1895)

And, lo, I am with you alway, even unto the end of the world.

Matthew XXVIII 20

Quiet Time

Sunday

I will hear what God the Lord will speak: for he will speak peace unto his people.

Psalms 85 8

Father, Who hast told us to listen to Thy voice, give us ears to hear Thy lightest whisper. The daily work and the rush of life around us, and the clamour of our own fears and self concern, make such a noise that it is difficult to be quiet before Thee, and so we lose the sound of Thy voice. Teach us how to be more still. Teach us how to shut our doors around us to all other thoughts, and to make a deep silence in our hearts. Then speak to us, and we shall be strong to hear, strong to do, strong to follow Thee utterly. Through Jesus Christ our Lord. Amen.

Prayers of Health and Healing
(altered)

There is a viewless, cloistered room,
As high as heaven, as fair as day,
Where, though my feet may join the throng,
My soul can enter in, and pray.

One hearkening, even, cannot know
When I have crossed the threshold o'er;
For He alone, who hears my prayer,
Has heard the shutting of the door.

Quiet Time

How can you expect to keep your powers of hearing when you never want to listen? That God should have time for you, you seem to take as much for granted as that you cannot have time for Him.

Dag Hammarskjöld (1905-1961)

The Archbishop. How do you know you are right?
Joan.   I always know. My voices —
Charles.   Oh, your voices, your voices. Why don't the voices come to me? I am king, not you.
Joan.   They do come to you; but you do not hear them. You have not sat in the field in the evening listening for them. When the angelus rings you cross yourself and have done with it; but if you prayed from your heart, and listened to the thrilling of the bells in the air after they stop ringing, you would hear the voices as I do.

From Saint Joan, Scene V.
George Bernard Shaw (1856-1950)

Quiet Time

Tuesday

Come ye yourselves apart and rest awhile,
Weary, I know it, of the press and throng;
Wipe from your brow the sweat and dust of toil,
And in My quiet strength again be strong.

Edward H. Bickersteth

On one never-to-be-forgotten Sunday morning (in 1872), I found myself one of a small company of silent worshippers, who were content to sit down together without words, that each one might feel after and draw near to the Divine Presence, unhindered at least, if not helped, by any human utterance. Utterance I knew was free, should the words be given; and, before the meeting was over, a sentence or two were uttered in great simplicity by an old and apparently untaught man, rising in his place amongst the rest of us. I did not pay much attention to the words he spoke, and I have no recollection of their purport. My whole soul was filled with the unutterable peace of the undisturbed opportunity for communion with God, with the sense that at last I had found a place where I might, without the faintest suspicion of insincerity, join with others in simply seeking his presence. To sit down in silence could at least pledge me to nothing; it might open to me (as it did that morning) the very gate of heaven. And, since that day, now more than seventeen years ago, Friends' meetings have indeed been to me the greatest of outward helps to a fuller and fuller entrance into the spirit from which they have sprung; the place of the most soul-subduing, faith-restoring, strengthening and peaceful communion, in feeding upon the bread of life, that I have ever known.

Caroline Stephen (1835-1909)

Quiet Time

That God speaks directly to man, and often in an extremely concrete manner, is affirmed unequivocally by the Bible and confirmed by the experience of countless believers in every age. . . . Abraham, Moses, and Peter were committed to adventures they would never have imagined. It can happen to us all, at any time — whenever it pleases God — to hear the "small voice", of which Gandhi also spoke.

Yes, it can happen. I have even known people who have told me they would at once recognise that voice if it were to speak again, they would be able to distinguish it from any other voice. . . . Personally, I have never heard a voice. This is what I have to reply to those who say to me, "I tried to meditate, to have a quiet time, as you recommend, but I heard nothing." If people are prompted to say this by a superiority complex, they conclude triumphantly that it is impossible to hear the voice of God; but if they suffer from an inferiority complex they think they have been rejected by God, since he speaks to other people but not to them! . . .

We always walk, therefore, on a knife-edge between scepticism and illuminism, between a systematic doubt about God's guidance and the presumptuous claim to know what his will is. . . . My own frequent experience is that God may repeat his commands with importunate insistence when we are in doubt as to whether they come from him. I have sometimes written an order down twenty or thirty times in my notebook during my "quiet times" before recognising its authenticity and making up my mind to obey it. Despite all the risk of making a mistake, sincerely to seek God's guidance remains the surest method of living the adventure of our lives in accordance with his purpose for us. . . .

What, then, is the answer? Well, I think that it is only when we give up the idea that we *must* be clear, and let ourselves be led by God blindly, if I may put it so, rather than demanding that he show us clearly at each step what our road is, that we shall get out of the difficulty. . . . Religion means binding ourselves to God, abandoning ourselves to him, asking him to guide us, even if we do not understand his guidance.

Paul Tournier

Quiet Time

Thursday

We highly prize silent waiting upon the Lord in humble dependence upon him. We esteem it to be a precious part of spiritual worship, and trust that no vocal offering will ever exclude it from its true place in our religious meetings. Let not the silence be spent in indolent or vacant musing but in patient waiting in humble prayerful expectancy before the Lord.

Yearly Meeting of Friends, 1884, 1886

In silence, without rite or symbol, we have known the Spirit of Christ so convincingly present in our quiet meetings that his grace dispels our faithlessness, our unwillingness, our fears, and sets our hearts aflame with the joy of adoration. We have thus felt the power of the Spirit renewing and recreating our love and friendship for all our fellows. This is our Eucharist and our Communion.

Yearly Meeting of Friends, 1928

Give unto us, O Lord, that quietness of mind in which we can hear Thee speaking to us, for Thine own Name's sake.

Anon.

Quiet Time

I believe my early morning readings are the secret of my own happiness in life. Read chiefly the New Testament, and in it chiefly the Gospels, and of them chiefly St.John's, and write out what you think each verse means in your own words as you read it, and in between each morning's reading put down shortly what has happened to you — I mean a sort of diary, only make it a mixture of self-examination and your prayers. Write out a short prayer or a short thanksgiving for anything that happens out of the way, no matter whether it has pleased you or not; for having once given your life and your will to God as a reasonable offering, *everything* that happens to you is sanctioned by Him because He allows only such things to happen to you, when once you have put your life in His hands, as can do you some good. Nine times out of ten you will be able to see. The tenth perhaps you won't — just make a note of it and ask God to show you. Only be quite sure that you have not given up your will to Him merely in so many words, but in reality, and then you will have every reason to take things exactly as they happen to come and find a blessing in the worst of them. God lives in and with those who get into this habit of thought, only it takes some perseverance to get out of the way of grumbling and impatience. I have been at it for some eight years now and I haven't succeeded yet, but it's worth sticking to.

Edward Wilson (1872-1912)

Quiet Time

Saturday

I have no wish to judge others, but my own experience is that, unless I can start the day with God in an adequate and unhurried "morning watch", my spiritual life all too easily declines and sinks to a second best. I fear that this is the trouble with far too many of us Christians. We live perfectly good and respectable lives, but there is nothing shining or infectious about them. They have lost the radiance they should possess because we have spent so little time in the presence of Christ.

It is costly to make time for prayer and to persevere faithfully in it. It is costly to deny ourselves those extra minutes in bed that we may have adequate time for quiet converse with God before the rush of the day's work and the noise of worldly traffic come crowding in. But this is a cost which I am sure we must be prepared to pay, if our faith in God is to remain so strong and sure that it can quicken a like faith in our friends and acquaintances who are looking for some light by which to see their way through life, some compass by which to steer their course.

Jack Winslow

Let us then labour for an inward stillness —
An inward stillness and an inward healing;
That perfect silence, where the lips and heart
Are still, and we no longer entertain
Our own imperfect thoughts and vain opinions,
But God alone speaks in us, and we wait
In singleness of heart, that we may know
His will, and in the silence of our spirits
That we may do His will, and do that only.

Henry Wadsworth Longfellow (1807-1882)

The Bible

Monday

It is one of the curious phenomena of modern times that it is considered perfectly respectable to be abysmally ignorant of the Christian Faith. Men and women who would be deeply ashamed of having their ignorance exposed in matters of poetry, music, ballet or painting, for example, are not in the least perturbed to be found ignorant of the New Testament. Indeed it is perfectly obvious from the remarks let slip on the radio by intellectuals, and from their own writings, that apart from half-remembered scraps left over from childhood's memory they have no knowledge of the New Testament at all. Very, very rarely does a man or woman give honest intelligent adult attention to the writings of the New Testament and then decide that Jesus was merely a misguided man. Even less frequently will he conclude that the whole Christian religion is founded upon a myth. The plain fact is not that men have given the New Testament their serious attention and found it spurious, but that they have never given it their serious attention at all. Let our intelligent men and women be urged, goaded, even shamed into reading this remarkable collection of early Christian literature for themselves. Let this ignorance of what Christianity teaches and practises be shown up for the intellectual affectation that it really is. Let the ill-informed critic of the Christian religion read particularly the Acts of the Apostles. Here is a simple, unvarnished, conscientious account of the behaviour and actions of quite a small group of people who honestly believed that Jesus was right in His claims. Let the critics put aside for a moment their contempt for (and ignorance of) the Church as it is today, and let them feel afresh the astonishing impact of this tiny group of devoted men and women.

J. B. Phillips (1906-1982)

The Bible

Do you really want to enter into the spirit of the gospel message? Then you must approach in a spirit of reverence and generosity in order to hear and to see (that is, to contemplate) Jesus Christ who reveals himself here and now through the events of his life and the words he spoke.

Whether you realise it or not, you are hungry for the bread of the gospels. . . . You crave words of life, of eternal life. Respect this inner hunger you experience, this call of love asking to be loved by the God who is love. You are experiencing a hunger for the living Word, for the living Word who came down from heaven and is communicated by the gospels.

Perhaps you will object: I speak to God but he never answers. You are mistaken. From all eternity you have been called to dialogue with God. At every stage of human history God has sought to enter into dialogue with man: 'God, who at sundry times and in diverse manners spoke in times past to the fathers by the prophets, last of all in these days has spoken to us by his Son.' If you find yourself complaining of the silence of God, it's because you don't open your ears and your heart to the words of the gospels. It is in the gospels that God wishes to enter into conversation with you. Answer his call. It is in this way that you will be able to enter into conversation with Jesus Christ. The lover finds his joy in revealing himself more and more fully to his beloved. God, who so loved the world that he gave his only-begotten Son, delights in revealing himself to man through the medium of Sacred Scripture. Are you attentive to this revelation God makes of himself in Jesus Christ? Would you let your fiancee's letter lie unopened on your desk? Why then do you let the gospels stand unopened on your bookshelves? Today a letter has arrived for you from the Son of God. What is Jesus Christ saying to you for today? . . .

You can receive these words of life over and over again; their depths are unfathomable, for 'the word of God is living and efficient and keener than any two-edged sword.'

Michel Quoist

Wednesday

In the beginning was the Word, and the Word was with God, and the Word was God. The same was in the beginning with God. All things were made by him; and without him was not any thing made that was made. In him was life; and the life was the light of men. The light shines on in the dark, and the darkness has never quenched it.

John I 1-4 (K.G.V.); 5 (N.E.B.)

Anthony Bloom, Archbishop of the Russian Orthodox Church in Great Britain and Ireland, hated Christianity in his youth. In order to check upon a certain lecturer's arguments he asked his mother for a New Testament, counting the chapters in each Gospel so as to read the shortest. Describing his experience he says, 'While I was reading the beginning of Mark's Gospel, before I reached the third chapter, I became aware of a presence. I saw nothing. I heard nothing. It was no hallucination. It was a simple certainty that the Lord was standing there and that I was in the presence of Him whose life I had begun to read with such revulsion and such ill will. This was my basic and essential meeting with the Lord. From then on I knew that Christ did exist.'

The primary purpose of the Bible, as in Anthony Bloom's experience, is to create a living relationship with Christ. This is what saves a man from sin and from himself. It is not faith *in* the Bible, much less knowledge *of* the Bible, which saves; only that trustful relationship with God through Christ which the Bible so often, and so astonishingly, creates.

Yet how can reading of past events make possible a relationship with the living Christ? The answer is found in the work of the Holy Spirit. He makes Jesus our contemporary. Without Him Bible reading may make us students: it could never make us saints.

The Soldier's Armoury
Wednesday, September 10th, 1969

The Bible

The translator is bound to feel the enormous spiritual energy, indeed, in its truest sense, the inspiration of the Gospels, the Acts, and the Epistles. It is not, to speak personally, that particular doctrines, or the seeds of particular dogmas, strike the mind afresh. On the contrary, it is the sheer spiritual zest and drive of the New Testament which fill one with both wonder and wistfulness. It is as though in these pages there lies the secret of human life. The secret is not a mere theory or ideal, but a fresh quality of living worked out in terms of ordinary human life and circumstance. Above all, the general impression is of something supernatural, of supra-human truth and a supra-human way of living. The wistfulness arises, of course, from the comparison between the shining, blazing certainty of the New Testament writers and the comparatively tentative and uncertain faith and hope we meet so often in present-day Christianity. . . .

As the work went on, steadily and inexorably there stood up from these pages a Figure of far more than human stature and quality. One tried to sense, and indeed to transmit, something of the difference in the style of the four evangelists. . . . Very naturally, a composite portrait forms in the mind after many months of study of these four remarkable compositions. But to the present translator it is by no means only the Figure that they succeed in creating between them that is so impressive. The feeling grows that behind these early attempts to set down what was reliably remembered about this Man, there stands the Man Himself! It is His Presence, His Character, which springs to life at the stimulation of these artless pages. . . . Here, through the incomplete and sometimes almost naive records, one is in contact with something so tremendous in its significance that at first the mind cannot grasp it, but only as it were gasps incredulously.

J. B. Phillips (1906-1982)

The Bible

Friday

There is one Book that speaks to me of God;
it struck within
a sacred flame that did not die.
This Bible tells of other men who felt as lost as I
who came with childlike trust
and found he did not lie.
Is it so hard to believe
when we record the day he came
to cut our time in two?
Who else but Jesus showed us God made flesh,
the perfect Man who cannot be denied?
What other launched a life like his
to lift this world in love,
then cheated death to send us power from on high?
And now
when earth-men walk among the stars
I know that the Creator walked my world.

William Alfred Pratney

No one can read this book without being convinced that there is Someone here at work besides mere human beings. Perhaps because of their very simplicity, perhaps because of their readiness to believe, to obey, to give, to suffer, and if need be to die, the Spirit of God found what surely He must always be seeking — a fellowship of men and women so united in love and faith that He can work in them and through them with the minimum of let or hindrance. Consequently it is a matter of sober historical fact that never before has any small body of ordinary people so moved the world that their enemies could say, with tears of rage in their eyes, that these men "have turned the world upside down!"

J. B. Phillips (1906-1982)

The Bible

The Bible is a very rare book in Roumania. The old people who bought their Bibles when they were young are holding on to them. The young people are searching to find Bibles.

Every time that a Christian from another country visits Roumania he asks them how he can help them. He always receives the same answer, every time, time and time again. "Give us more and more Bibles!"

I have had the occasion to see old people receiving Bibles who were shaking, weeping with joy, and who fell on their knees to thank God. I saw people kissing Bibles just like people kissing a child that had been away from home for a long time. I saw Believers who had prayed for five, six and even ten years for God to send them a Bible. I heard the young and old, men and women who thanked God with tears for His mercy and love and who prayed for you who are far away — whom they do not know, but who helped them to receive a Bible.

> A Christian leader in the underground
> Church in Communist Roumania.

A Prayer of Thanks for the Bible

O God, we thank Thee on this day for the sacred Scriptures; for the comfort the Bible has brought to the sorrowful, for guidance offered to the bewildered, for its gracious promises to the uncertain, for its strength given to the weak, and for its progressive revelation of Thyself.

We thank Thee for the men of God who speak to us still from its pages and for the men of God whose learning has made those pages live.

We thank Thee most of all that it reveals to us Thy Son, the Word made flesh. Help us so to ponder this record of Thy ways with men that Thy word may be indeed a lamp unto our feet and a light unto our path. Through Jesus Christ our Lord. Amen.

> Leslie D. Weatherhead (1893-1976)

Prayer

Sunday

*Moreover the word of the Lord came
unto Jeremiah the second time, while
he was yet shut up in the court of
the prison, saying, Thus saith the Lord . . .*

*Call unto me, and I will answer thee,
and shew thee great and mighty things,
which thou knowest not.*

*Ask, and it shall be given you; seek,
and ye shall find; knock, and it shall
be opened unto you:
For every one that asketh receiveth;
and he that seeketh findeth; and to
him that knocketh it shall be opened.*

*. . . and dost promise, that when two
or three are gathered together in thy
Name thou wilt grant their requests.*

Jeremiah XXXIII 1-3
Matthew VII 7-8
A Prayer of St. Chrysostom

246

Prayer

To deny the possibility of prayer is to deny the teaching of Jesus. To deny that teaching is to destroy Him.

Yet once again, we base our belief in the possibility of prayer upon the history and experience of men. When science makes experience the universal test of reality, how can men rationally exclude the experience of the saints of all ages in this matter? They tell us they have asked and had; sought and found; knocked and the door has been opened. In answer to this it is affirmed that they were all perfectly sincere in believing so, but they were mistaken. Such a statement is a test of patience to which I am not equal. To be told that not one or two, but hundreds, thousands, tens of thousands of human beings, not of one age or temperament or geographical position, but in every age, of all temperaments and from every clime, through weeks and months and years and decades and centuries and milleniums, have all been deceived, is to be asked to believe something far more incredible than anything which Christianity affirms as true. If the testimony of seers, prophets, psalmists, saints, confessors and martyrs is all to go for nothing, yet may God help me to share their delusion, for it has been a glorious delusion, and the dynamic by which all the best work of the centuries has been done.

G. Campbell Morgan (1863-1945)

More things are wrought by prayer
Than this world dreams of. Wherefore, let thy voice
Rise like a fountain for me night and day.
For what are men better than sheep or goats
That nourish a blind life within the brain
If, knowing God, they lift not hands of prayer
Both for themselves and those who call them friend?
For so the whole round earth is every way
Bound by gold chains about the feet of God.

Alfred, Lord Tennyson (1809-1892)

Prayer

Tuesday

Tell God all that is in your heart, as one unloads one's heart to a dear friend. People who have no secrets from each other never want subjects of conversation; they do not weigh their words, because there is nothing to be kept back. Neither do they seek for something to say; they talk out of the abundance of their hearts, just what they think. Blessed are they who attain to such familiar, unreserved intercourse with God.

François de Fénelon (1651-1715)

Be not afraid to pray — to pray is right.
Pray, if thou canst, with hope; but ever pray,
Though hope be weak, or sick with long delay;
Pray in the darkness, if there be no light.
Far is the time, remote from human sight,
When war and discord on the earth shall cease:
Yet every prayer for universal peace
Avails the blessed time to expedite.
Whate'er is good to wish, that ask of Heaven,
Though it be that thou canst not hope to see:
Pray to be perfect, though material leaven
Forbid the spirit so on earth to be:
But if for any wish thou darest not pray,
Then pray to God to cast that wish away.

Hartley Coleridge (1796-1849)

Prayer

Instead of calling prayers unanswered, it is far truer to recognize that "No" is as real an answer as "Yes", and often far more kind. . . .

In one of the most impressive passages in his "Confessions", St. Augustine pictures his mother, Monica, praying all one night, in a sea-side chapel on the North African coast, that God would not let her son sail for Italy. She wanted Augustine to be a Christian. She could not endure losing him from her influence. If under her care, he still was far from being Christ's what would he be in Italy, home of licentiousness and splendour, of manifold and alluring temptations? And even while she prayed there passionately for her son's retention at home, he sailed, by the grace of God, for Italy, where, persuaded by Ambrose, he became a Christian in the very place from which his mother's prayers would have kept him. The form of her petition was denied; the substance of her desire was granted. As St. Augustine himself puts it: "Thou, in the depth of Thy counsels, hearing the main point of her desire, regardedst not what she then asked, that Thou mightest make me what she ever desired." It would be a sorry world for all of us if our unwise petitions did not often have "No" for their answer.

Harry Emerson Fosdick (1878-1969)

Prayer

Thursday

"My life," wrote Mary Slessor, "is one long daily, hourly, record of answered prayer. For physical health, for mental overstrain, for guidance given marvellously, for errors and dangers averted, for enmity to the Gospel subdued, for food provided at the exact hour needed, for everything that goes to make up life and my poor service, I can testify with a full and often wonder-stricken awe that I believe God answers prayer. I know God answers prayer. I have proved during long decades while alone, as far as man's help and presence are concerned, that God answers prayer. Cavillings, logical or physical, are of no avail to me. It is the very atmosphere in which I live and breathe and have my being, and it makes life glad and free and a million times worth living. I can give no other testimony. I am sitting alone here on a log among a company of natives. My children, whose very lives are a testimony that God answers prayer, are working round me. Natives are crowding past on the bush road to attend palavers, and I am at perfect peace, far from my own countrymen and conditions, because I know God answers prayer. Food is scarce just now. We live from hand to mouth. We have not more than will be our breakfast today, but I know we shall be fed, for God answers prayer."

W. P. Livingstone

Prayer

The power to see our duty through, that is the answer we get to prayer, to see it through unbeaten and unbroken to the end. That is the answer we get, and it is the only answer that Christ ever promised. He was quite honest about it. He did not say, "If any man will be My disciple, I will give him cushions to sit on, and a nice soft job to play with." He said, "If any man will be My disciple, let him take up his cross and follow after Me." In plain words, He said, "Follow Me and you'll get hell." But His promise was this, "If any man follows Me honest and true and really tries, the world may do its damnedest, but that man will find his manhood, and enjoy the peace of God inside." That was Christ's promise, and that promise He has kept all down the history of the years.

No man ever followed Christ with all his heart who did not find the secret of fine manhood and the peace of God. His first followers were men of prayer and they were burned at the stake, tortured and flung to lions for a feast, and butchered to make a Roman holiday. Prayer did not quench the flames that burned them or shut the lions' mouths, but it won them strength to see it through and die like gods with songs upon their lips and gladness in their souls.

So it has been always. Prayer does not make millionaires, but it does make men. If you are out in life for a soft job and a good time, don't be a Christian; if you are out for manhood, and the real happiness that true manhood brings, then follow Christ.

The spirit of Christ is the answer to prayer and it can come not only to the man who prays, but through him it can be poured out upon his pals for whom he prays. It can run like fire through a battalion, a division, an army or a world, if there are enough fine men who seek it by prayer.

G. A. Studdert Kennedy (1883-1929)

Prayer is the power of God needed to fight
the battles of life and of faith.

Paul Schneider (1897-1939)

Prayer

Saturday

I asked for strength that I might achieve;
He made me weak that I might obey.
I asked for health that I might do greater things;
I was given grace that I might do better things.
I asked for riches that I might be happy;
I was given poverty that I might be wise.
I asked for power that I might have the praise of men;
I was given weakness that I might feel the need of God.
I asked for all things that I might enjoy life;
I was given life that I might enjoy all things.
I received nothing that I asked for, all that I hoped for.
My prayer was answered.

Nurses' Christian Fellowship of Scotland
News Letter. October-December, 1966

When we depend upon man, we get what man can do.
When we depend upon prayer, we get what God can do.

Shop window sign in Selma, California

252

Prayers

Mother Teresa's Way of Love

Love to pray — feel often during the day the need for prayer, and take trouble to pray. Prayer enlarges the heart until it is capable of containing God's gift of himself. Ask and seek, and your heart will grow big enough to receive him and keep him as your own.

Days

Let me not see each day,
As one in a succession
Of all the days behind, ahead,
A dull procession,
But as a day apart, unlike the rest,
God's hand has given,
To take from Him and see it as the best
Of all the days long past, or still to come,
He gives it me
To use in ways unknown just yet.
It may hold joy beyond all earthly thought,
Or in its sorrow
I may find the Presence that I sought.

Let me not see each day
As one in a succession
Of all the days behind, ahead,
But a possession,
A gift from God's own hand,
With Him to fashion
Some rare and golden hours, eternal, fair,
Here on its threshold stand,
And know this day He comes with me to share
These moments, which in perfect love His will and purpose
*   planned.*

Doris G. Cox

253

Prayers

Monday

Prayer of General Lord Astley (1579-1652) before the Battle of Edgehill, A.D. 1642.

O Lord, Thou knowest how busy we must be this day;
if we forget Thee, do not Thou forget us;
for Christ's sake. Amen.

May the mind of Christ my Saviour
Live in me from day to day,
By His love and power controlling
All I do and say.

May the Word of God dwell richly
In my heart from hour to hour,
So that all may see I triumph
Only through his power.

May the peace of God my Father
Rule my life in everything,
That I may be calm to comfort
Sick and sorrowing.

May the love of Jesus fill me,
As the waters fill the sea;
Him exalting, self abasing,
This is victory.

May I run the race before me,
Strong and brave to face the foe,
Looking only unto Jesus,
As I onward go.

Kate B. Wilkinson (1859-1928)

Prayers

Prayer of Lady Jane Grey, born 1537, executed with her husband 1554.

O merciful God, be Thou unto me a strong tower of defence, I humbly entreat Thee. Give me grace to await Thy leisure, and patiently to bear what Thou doest unto me; nothing doubting or mistrusting Thy goodness towards me; for Thou knowest what is good for me better than I do. Therefore do with me in all things what Thou wilt; only arm me, I beseech Thee, with Thine armour, that I may stand fast; above all things, taking to me the shield of faith; praying always that I may refer myself wholly to Thy will, abiding Thy pleasure, and comforting myself in those troubles which it shall please Thee to send me, seeing such troubles are profitable for me; and I am assuredly persuaded that all Thou doest cannot but be well; and unto Thee be all honour and glory. Amen.

Prayer of Dag Hammarskjöld, former Secretary-General of the United Nations.

Give us
A pure heart
That we may see Thee,
A humble heart
That we may hear Thee,
A heart of love
That we may serve Thee,
A heart of faith
That we may live Thee.

Prayers

Wednesday

Prayer of Dietrich Bonhoeffer, written at Christmas, 1943, while he was awaiting execution in a Nazi concentration camp because of his opposition to Hitler.

O God, early in the morning do I cry unto Thee.
Help me to pray, and to think only of Thee.
I cannot pray alone.
In me there is darkness,
But with Thee there is light.

I am lonely, but Thou leavest me not.
I am feeble in heart, but Thou leavest me not.
I am restless, but with Thee there is peace.
In me there is bitterness, but with Thee there is patience.

Thy ways are past understanding, but Thou knowest the way for me.

Lord, whatsoever this day may bring, Thy name be praised.
Be gracious unto me and help me.
Grant me strength to bear whatsoever Thou dost send,
And let not fear overrule me.
I trust Thy grace, and commit my life wholly into Thy hands.
Whether I live or whether I die, I am with Thee,
And Thou art with me, O my Lord and my God.
Lord, I wait for Thy salvation, and for the coming of Thy
*   Kingdom.*

O God, who hast been the Refuge of my fathers through many generations, be my Refuge today in every time and circumstance of need. Be my Guide through all that is dark and doubtful. Be my Guard against all that threatens my spirit's welfare. Be my Strength in time of testing. Gladden my heart with Thy peace; through Jesus Christ my Lord. Amen.

John Baillie (1886-1961)

Prayers

From the last prayer of Robert Louis Stevenson:

Be with our friends, be with ourselves. Go with each of us to rest; if any awake, temper to them the dark hours of watching; and when the day returns, return to us, our sun and comforter, and call us up with morning faces and with morning hearts — eager to labour — eager to be happy, if happiness shall be our portion — and if the day be marked for sorrow, strong to endure it.

O God, take control of me all through today.
Control my tongue,
so that I may speak
no angry word;
no cruel word;
no untrue word;
no ugly word.
Control my thoughts,
so that I may think
no impure thoughts;
no bitter, envious, or jealous thoughts;
no selfish thoughts.
Control my actions,
so that all through today
my work may be my best;
I may never be too busy to lend a hand to those who need it;
I may do nothing of which afterwards I would be ashamed.
All this I ask for Jesus' sake. Amen.

William Barclay (1907-1978)

Prayers

Friday

Prayer of astronaut Frank Borman, Apollo 8 commander, broadcast as his spacecraft orbited the moon on Christmas Eve, 1968.

Give us, O God, the vision which can see Thy love in the world in spite of human failure.

Give us the faith to trust Thy goodness in spite of our ignorance and weakness.

Give us the knowledge that we may continue to pray with understanding hearts, and show us what each one of us can do to set forward the coming of the day of universal peace.

If we with earnest effort could succeed
To make our life one long connected prayer,
As lives of some perhaps have been and are;
If, never leaving Thee, we had no need
Our wandering spirits back again to lead
Into Thy presence, but continue there,
Like angels standing on the highest stair
Of the sapphire throne — this were to pray indeed.
But if distractions manifold prevail,
And if in this we must confess we fail,
Grant us to keep at least a prompt desire,
Continual readiness for prayer and praise,
An altar heaped and waiting to take fire
With the least spark, and leap into a blaze.

Richard Trench (1807-1886)

Prayers

Saturday

Lord, we believe that in knowing and serving you all men can rise to the full height of their humanity.

But we do not see it happening. What we see is a world divided between the overfed and the hungry, between the comfortable and the homeless, between some entrenched in privilege and others clamorous for their rights. We see goodwill made ineffective by stupidity, and honest men failing to measure up to the demands of a crisis. We see the peacemakers and bridgebuilders pushed aside because progress towards justice seems too slow.

Yet also in this world, and identified with it, we see Jesus. We see his life of love; we see his Cross. Not only as they were long ago, but as they are now, wherever his Spirit is allowed by men and women to govern human actions and purify human motives.

And so we recover faith about the world, and through faith we find hope. You, Father, are the source of this faith and hope: and you are the source of the love which alone can make the hope come true. May those who believe this learn how to avoid obstructing your love. May all who revere you make haste to promote justice and to practise compassion and to overcome the terrible strength of evil with the power of good.

More Contemporary Prayers (ed. Caryl Micklem)

Almighty and eternal God, so draw our hearts to Thee, so guide our minds, so fill our imaginations, so control our wills, that we may be wholly Thine, utterly dedicated unto Thee; and then use us, we pray Thee, as Thou wilt, but always to Thy glory and the welfare of Thy people, through our Lord and Saviour, Jesus Christ.

William Temple (1881-1944)

Healing

Sunday

Prove me now herewith, saith the Lord of hosts, if I will not open you the windows of heaven, and pour you out a blessing, that there shall not be room enough to receive it.

Malachi III 10

In the past eight years it has been a joy to me to see many people freed, healed, or strengthened by the power of Jesus Christ released through prayer. Many of the things I have seen are so wonderful as to sound incredible to those who have not themselves experienced them. These saving actions of God include spiritual healings (such as being freed instantly from long-standing alcoholism), emotional healings (such as from schizophrenia and deep mental depression), and physical healings (such as growths disappearing in a matter of minutes). For some these healings are immediate; for some they are gradual and take months, and for still others nothing at all seems to happen. But I would estimate that about 75 per cent of the people we pray for, for physical or emotional ailments, are either healed completely or experience a noticeable improvement. Almost everyone regards the prayer as a real blessing and experiences the presence of Christ in a very direct way.

I would encourage any of you who question all this — and we usually do question the authenticity of healing through prayer when we first hear about it — to check it out for yourself. Healing is caused by far more than the power of suggestion or even what can be achieved through the love of a compassionate person.

Francis MacNutt

Healing

Then he called his twelve disciples together, and gave them power and authority over all devils, and to cure diseases. And he sent them to preach the kingdom of God, and to heal the sick.

Luke IX 1-2

The American doctor Rebecca Beard has told how she herself became convinced of the reality of spiritual healing and came to give it a primary place in her own practice. Though as a Christian she wished to believe in the power of prayer, she had the scientist's desire for clear demonstration before committing herself. She asked God for proof in the form of some illness that is called incurable being instantaneously and completely healed without any agency but prayer. The answer came through a friend of hers, suffering from cancer and the dreaded cachexia. Her emaciated body could hardly carry the hugely enlarged abdomen. But she possessed unshakeable faith that God would heal her. Cancelling all social obligations she did simple domestic work, rested, walked in the open air, read her Bible, sang hymns and prayed. Finally one night the miracle happened. She had a vision of Jesus nailed to the cross which was being lowered into the hole dug for it. She cried out "Oh, my Jesus" and put out her hand to steady His body and ease the suffering. Her hand dropped to her abdomen and she woke. Suddenly she realised that the huge accumulation was gone. In the morning her doctor came and for a moment was speechless with astonishment. Then the questions came short and fast in his excitement. "What passed? What came away? Water? Blood? What was it?" To all she answered truthfully, "Nothing". At last he said quietly, "No one but God could perform a miracle like that." When she was weighed she was found to have lost thirty-eight and a half pounds in three hours. Every organ was "fresh and virginal as though she had never been ill." This was the miracle Rebecca Beard had asked for. Her doctoring took on a new power from that day.

Jack Winslow

Healing

Tuesday

And when Jesus was entered into Capernaum, there came unto him a centurion, beseeching him, and saying, Lord, my servant lieth at home sick of the palsy, grievously tormented. And Jesus saith unto him, I will come and heal him.

The centurion answered and said, Lord, I am not worthy that thou shouldest come under my roof: but speak the word only, and my servant shall be healed. . . .

When Jesus heard it, he marvelled, and said to them that followed, Verily I say unto you, I have not found so great faith, no, not in Israel. . . .

And Jesus said unto the centurion, Go thy way; and as thou hast believed, so be it done unto thee. And his servant was healed in the selfsame hour.

Matthew VIII 5-8, 10, 13

During the following days [at the conference] the lives of many were transformed as they were baptised in the Holy Spirit, and faith was encouraged by the further healings that took place. One man had been assigned to a wheelchair for the rest of his life, following an accident in which his spine was fractured. It was a common sight to see people lovingly carry him up the numerous steps of the University in his chair. By the middle of the conference, he was walking up them carrying his two young children in either arm. The healing had occurred during a time of prayer, when he was very aware of God's presence. The Lord told him to get out of his chair. It was impossible for him to stand because of his physical condition, but he obeyed and was immediately healed. No human ministry had taken place or was needed. Praise our wonderful God!

Colin Urquhart

Healing

Is any sick among you? Let him call for the elders of the church; and let them pray over him, anointing him with oil in the name of the Lord: and the prayer of faith shall save the sick, and the Lord shall raise him up; and if he have committed sins, they shall be forgiven him.

James V 14-15

I have often told how, a few weeks later, after my own Pentecost, I called on an elderly woman in the church who had suffered for many years with angina pectoris and arthritis of the spine. She was in bed much of the time. Said she:

'I've heard what's happening to some of you people at the church, and I believe it. If you lay your hands on me I'm going to be healed!'

I did lay hands on her, not feeling any great faith, but she had enough for both of us! I left the room right away without waiting to see what happened, but the next week she came to visit me at *my* house. 'See what I can do!' she said, and literally skipped round the front room! A year later she wrote to me in Seattle, 'I'm 84 now, and I get a bit tired sometimes; but last night when my neighbour, who is 72, locked herself out of her house, I climbed in the window and let her in!'

It wasn't just me. People were praying for one another and they were being healed. Why not? After all Jesus had said, 'These signs shall follow them that believe. . . . They shall lay hands on the sick, and they shall recover.'

Dennis Bennett

Healing

Thursday

When Peter saw this, he said to the people, "Men of Israel, why are you surprised at this? Why do you stare at us, as if we had made him walk by any power or piety of ours? . . . Jesus it is who has given strength to this man whom you see and know, by faith in His name; it is the faith He inspires which has made the man thus hale and whole before you all."

Acts III 12, 16 (Moffatt)

When our son Steve was eight years old he fell from the upper bunk of his bed and lay on the floor screaming with pain in his right arm. X rays showed a pathological fracture of his arm which was not caused by the accident but due to an unusually large bone cyst which had been developing for some time. The cyst, growing inside the bone of his upper arm, had reduced it to the fragility of an eggshell.

The two orthopaedic specialists who examined Steve impressed us with the seriousness of his condition. He would be in a cast from his neck to his waist for at least six months, then in a sling for another extended period. We were advised to "teach him how to play chess" because physical activity would aggravate his condition.

Our prayer group prayed over Steve, asking Jesus to accelerate this healing process. We encouraged him to speak to the cells in his arm, asking them to fill in all the empty places with strong, bony tissue. After six weeks the cast was removed and X rays were taken to determine proper alignment.

The physician seemed somewhat incredulous as he compared the latest X rays to the originals and could find no evidence of a fracture or a bone cyst. No further treatment was necessary and when I asked about limiting Steve's activity, he replied, "A kid who heals that fast can do anything he pleases."

Perhaps talking to a mountain and expecting it to move isn't so far fetched after all.

Barbara Leahy Shlemon

Healing

And Jesus stood still, and called the two blind men, and said, What will ye that I shall do unto you?
They say unto him, Lord, that our eyes may be opened.

Matthew XX 32-33

From Cape Town to Port Elizabeth and another crowded church for a powerful meeting. At the end of the meeting I received one of the most moving testimonies I have heard. It was very brief and to the point. Before me stood a young woman in her early twenties. Tears were streaming down her face. "What has the Lord done for you tonight?" I asked her gently.

Through the tears she replied: "When I came to the meeting I was blind; and now I can see. God has healed me. I can see clearly, I can see you."

The healing was confirmed by the friends who had brought her to the meetings and who stood beside her radiant with joy. My only regret was that there was no time to obtain more details of the healing; there were so many others queueing to give their testimonies. Perhaps others were not as dramatic but every healing is important. If God touches your life to heal even a minor ailment it is a great privilege and honour.

Whenever I hear people question whether God heals today (incredibly some still doubt this), I often think back to the simple testimony of that girl. "When I came to the meeting I was blind; and now I can see."

On one occasion I was listening to a minister give me all his reasons why God doesn't heal today, substantiating h s arguments from Scripture, of course. There is usually little point in arguing; I simply asked him this question. "Do you expect me to say to a young woman who has just told me that when she came to the meeting she was blind and now she can see, that she must be mistaken because God doesn't heal today?" He gave me no answer.

Colin Urquhart

265

Healing

Saturday

The peace of God, which passeth all understanding.

Philippians IV 7

The criticism is sometimes made that those who are not healed when they seek the Church's help lose their faith in God, but I have never found this to be so. On the contrary, I have many times seen prayers answered in very helpful ways, even when healing does not come. The gospel has the last word and it is full of encouragement.

Even in terminal illness there is a gracious ministry to offer which goes beyond mere comfort, though that is valuable enough. The prayerful approach often eases pain and lifts deep fears. It is healing in a very real sense when the sick man is freed from pain-racked hours and days, and, no longer needing sedation, is able to share his last hours with his loved ones with a clearer mind. Not the least important part of the healing work that is our heritage is found here. We surround our loved ones with prayer and see those prayers answered as they slip quietly away — without pain and without fear — to the adventures that await them in a new world. Thanks be to God!

Bert Jordan

So I believe in healing because God has made it abundantly plain to me that this is not the fad of a few cranks, but that he, himself, is active as he has always been, in caring for those he has made. One joy is that he is strongly active 'at such a time as this', when the need is so great, for church after church is awakening to this realisation and one sees the ministry of healing becoming an integral part of their life.

Reginald East

Thanks

One of the saddest things about the atheist is that he has no one to thank.

Hugh Silvester

I waited patiently for the Lord; and he inclined unto me, and heard my cry.
He brought me up also out of an horrible pit, out of the miry clay, and set my feet upon a rock, and established my goings.
And he hath put a new song in my mouth, even praise unto our God: many shall see it, and fear, and shall trust in the Lord.
Blessed is the man that maketh the Lord his trust, and respecteth not the proud, nor such as turn aside to lies.
Many, O Lord my God, are thy wonderful works which thou hast done, and thy thoughts which are to us-ward: they cannot be reckoned up in order unto thee: if I would declare and speak of them, they are more than can be numbered.

Psalm XL 1-5

And it came to pass, as he went to Jerusalem, that he passed through the midst of Samaria and Galilee.
And as he entered into a certain village, there met him ten men that were lepers, which stood afar off: and they lifted up their voices, and said, Jesus, Master, have mercy on us.
And when he saw them, he said unto them, Go shew yourselves unto the priests. And it came to pass, that, as they went, they were cleansed.
And one of them, when he saw that he was healed, turned back, and with a loud voice glorified God, and fell down on his face at his feet, giving him thanks: and he was a Samaritan.
And Jesus answering said, Were there not ten cleansed? But where are the nine? There are not found that returned to give glory to God, save this stranger. And he said unto him, Arise, go thy way: thy faith hath made thee whole.

Luke XVII 11-19

267

Thanks

Monday

It is more important to thank God for blessings received than to pray for them beforehand. For that forward-looking prayer, though right as an expression of dependence upon God, is still self-centred in part, at least, of its interest; there is something which we hope to gain by our prayer. But the backward-looking act of thanksgiving is quite free from this. In itself it is quite selfless. Thus it is akin to love.

William Temple (1881-1944)

O Lord, I thank Thee in deepest sincerity for hearing my prayer. In my trouble, in my bitter anxiety, I had no one to turn to but Thee. Now, in gratitude for what Thou hast done, my heart is full, full to overflowing. Grant, O Lord, that I many not forget. Grant rather that I may be quick to remember how royally I have been answered, so that my trust may be deepened, my dependence on Thee made more complete. Amen.

Anon.

Thanks

Thankfulness is a way of looking at life, and it brings its blessing even though it may be difficult. If Jesus could practise thanksgiving in spite of all the difficulties of his day, you and I will find reason for thankfulness in the commonplace routine of our private lives. Thus we shall find ourselves strengthened in spirit to meet the pressing problems that are everywhere. Today my step will be a little lighter because I have said in my heart, 'Father, I thank Thee.'

Hugh Ivan Evans

O God, we thank Thee for this universe, our great home; for its vastness and its riches, and for the manifoldness of the life which teems upon it and of which we are part. We praise Thee for the arching sky and the blessed winds, for the driving clouds and the constellations on high. We praise Thee for the salt sea and the running water, for the everlasting hills, for the trees, and for the grass under our feet. We thank Thee for our senses by which we can see the splendour of the morning, and hear the jubilant songs of love, and smell the breath of the springtime. Grant us, we pray Thee, a heart wide open to all this joy and beauty, and save our souls from being so steeped in care or so darkened by passion that we pass heedless and unseeing when even the thornbush by the wayside is aflame with the glory of God.

Walter Rauschenbusch (1861-1918)

Thanks

Wednesday

I thank Thee, God, that I have lived
In this great world and known its many joys;
The song of birds, the strong, sweet scent of hay
And cooling breezes in the secret dusk,
The flaming sunsets at the close of day,
Hills, and the lonely, heather-covered moors,
Music at night, and moonlight on the sea,
The beat of waves upon the rocky shore
And wild, white spray, flung high in ecstasy:
The faithful eyes of dogs, and treasured books.
The love of kin and fellowship of friends,
And all that makes life dear and beautiful.
I thank Thee, too, that there has come to me
A little sorrow and, sometimes, defeat,
A little heartache and the loneliness
That comes with parting, and the word, "Goodbye,"
Dawn breaking after dreary hours of pain,
When I discovered that night's gloom must yield
And morning light break through to me again.
Because of these and other blessings poured
Unasked upon my wondering head,
Because I know that there is yet to come
An even richer and more glorious life,
And most of all, because Thine only Son
Once sacrificed life's loveliness for me —
I thank Thee, God, that I have lived.

Elizabeth Craven

Thanks

O God, we give thanks to Thee for all the happiness we have known in the years that have gone; for every moment of loveliness and joy and beauty; for every experience of Thyself when we have been sure of Thee and known that only in Thy will could our souls ever find rest. We thank Thee for tasks we have been allowed to do, friendships that have made us glad, and service in which we have forgotten ourselves.

Grant that no present depression, or grief, or weakness, may allow us to forget the gladness we have known. Though the mists come down upon the soul, mists of failure and doubt and even despair, may we remember the mountains are still there, majestic, strong and sure. The sun will shine again upon their snow-clad summits. May we, even in the darkness, keep on, climbing upward toward them. Keep at least our memories bright with praise and love, and may the memory of those moments of insight and certainty and dedication send us forth now with newborn purpose and rekindled desire to know and do Thy blessed will. Through Jesus Christ our Lord. Amen.

Leslie D. Weatherhead (1893-1976)

Thanks

Friday
Thankfulness from the Heart

It pleases God that by the help of his grace we should work away at our praying and our living, directing all our powers to him until in the fullness of joy we have him whom we seek — Jesus.

Thankfulness and prayer belong together. Thanksgiving is the deep inward certainty which moves us with reverent and loving fear to turn with all our strength to the work to which God stirs us, giving thanks and praise from the depths of our hearts.

Sometimes thanksgiving overflows into words and says, 'Good Lord, I thank you. Blessed be your name.' And sometimes when our hearts are dry and without feeling, or when we are assaulted by temptation, then we are driven by reason and grace to call upon our Lord with our voice, rehearsing his blessed Passion and great goodness.

The simple enjoyment of our Lord is in itself a most blessed form of thanksgiving. This is so in his sight.

Lady Julian of Norwich (1342-1443)

Thanks

Christ turns all our sunsets into dawns.

Clement of Alexandria (?150-?216)

For the strength of His body and the firmness of His tread,
For the beauty of His spirit and the laughter in His eyes,
For the courage of His heart and the greatness of His deeds,
For the depth of His love and the men it makes anew,
For the strength of His friendship when we dare to trust His love,
For the knowledge of His presence at each turn of the road,
We thank Thee, Lord.

Godfrey S. Pain

Trust

Sunday

Trust in the Lord with all thine heart and lean not unto thine own understanding. In all thy ways acknowledge him, and he shall direct thy paths.

When I sit in darkness, the Lord shall be a light unto me. — When thou passest through the waters, I will be with thee; and through the rivers, they shall not overflow thee: when thou walkest through the fire, thou shalt not be burned; neither shall the flame kindle upon thee. For I am the Lord thy God, the Holy One of Israel, thy Saviour. — I will bring the blind by a way that they knew not; I will lead them in paths that they have not known: I will make darkness light before them, and crooked things straight. These things will I do unto them, and not forsake them.

Yea, though I walk through the valley of the shadow of death, I will fear no evil: for thou art with me; thy rod and thy staff they comfort me. — What time I am afraid, I will trust in thee. In God I will praise his word, in God I have put my trust; I will not fear what flesh can do unto me. — The Lord is my light and my salvation; whom shall I fear? The Lord is the strength of my life; of whom shall I be afraid?

Proverbs III 5-6
From Daily Light (Nov. 20 Morning)
Micah VII 8; Isaiah XLIII 2, 3;
Isaiah XLII 16; Psalms XXIII 4;
Psalms LVI 3, 4; Psalms XXVII 1

Trust

Remember always that there are two things which are more utterly incompatible even than oil and water, and these two are trust and worry. Would you call it trust, if you should give something into the hands of a friend to attend to for you, and then should spend your nights and days in anxious thought and worry as to whether it would be rightly and successfully done? And can you call it trust, when you have given the saving and keeping of your soul into the hands of the Lord, if day after day, and night after night, you are spending hours of anxious thought and questionings about the matter? When a believer really trusts anything, he ceases to worry about the thing he has trusted. And when he worries, it is a plain proof that he does not trust. Tested by this rule, how little real trust there is in the Church of Christ! No wonder our Lord asked the pathetic question, "When the Son of Man cometh, shall He find faith on the earth?" He will find plenty of work, a great deal of earnestness, and doubtless many consecrated hearts; but shall He find faith, the one thing He values more than all the rest? Every child of God, in his own case, will know how to answer this question. Should the answer, for any of you, be a sorrowful No, let me entreat you to let this be the last time for such an answer; and if you have ever known anything of the trustworthiness of our Lord, may you henceforth set to your seal that He is true, by the generous recklessness of your trust in Him! . . . You have trusted Him in a few things, and He has not failed you. Trust Him now for everything, and see if He does not do for you exceeding abundantly, above all that you could ever have asked or even thought, not according to your power or capacity, but according to His own mighty power, working in you all the good pleasure of His most blessed will.

Hannah Pearsall Smith (1832-1911)

Trust

Tuesday

It is quite clear that the whole teaching of Jesus Christ about God, expressed alike in His words and in the whole fashion and mould of His character, implies that God is always nearer, mightier, more loving, and more free to help every one of us than any one of us ever realizes. This alone is what makes His incessant summons to faith, and to more faith, coherent and reasonable. This again seems to me to imply that mankind generally is under a kind of hypnotic spell about God, which is always contracting and chilling their thoughts of Him, and leading to all kinds of depressing and terrifying illusions about Him. The story of the growth of the disciples' faith is the story of the breaking of that evil spell. If we transport ourselves in imagination into the little company of His disciples, it is not difficult to imagine what the effect upon them of His continual demand for faith in God must have been. Taken along with His own unbroken confidence of God's presence, power, and love, He must have seemed like one holding a continued dialogue with the Unseen One. Yet a doubt must have sometimes crept in. Was it not rather a monologue? No man but He heard the other Voice . . . Was He mad? . . . The issue, as He meant that it should, gradually became inevitable. Either He was a dreamer, or they and all other men were dreamers, walking in the darkness and deeming it to be light.

Such, I doubt not, was the early struggle of faith. The issue does not seem to me vitally different today. We are all alike wrapped up in the great earth-dream, and He alone was fully awake of all the sons of men; or we men and women of the twentieth century are broad awake to the reality, and He was dreaming His solitary dream.

David S. Cairns (1862-1946)

Trust

And I said to the man who stood at the gate of the year: 'Give me a Light
that I may tread safely into the unknown.'
And he replied: 'Go out into the darkness and put your hand into the hand
of God; that shall be to you better than a light, and safer than a known way.'

Minnie Louise Haskins (1875-1957)

God is my strong salvation;
What foe have I to fear?
In darkness and temptation
My light, my help is near.

Though hosts encamp around me,
Firm to the fight I stand;
What terror can confound me,
With God at my right hand?

Place on the Lord reliance;
My soul, with courage wait;
His truth be thine affiance,
When faint and desolate.

His might thine heart shall strengthen,
His love thy joy increase;
Mercy thy days shall lengthen;
The Lord will give thee peace.

James Montgomery (1771-1854)

Thursday

Petition

Teach us, O Father, to trust Thee with life and with death,
And (though this is harder by far)
With the life and the death of those that are dearer to us than our
life.

Teach us stillness and confident peace
In Thy perfect will,
Deep calm of soul, and content
In what Thou wilt do with these lives Thou hast given.

Teach us to wait and be still,
To rest in Thyself,
To hush this clamorous anxiety,
To lay in Thine arms all this wealth Thou hast given.

Thou lovest these souls that we love
With a love as far surpassing our own
As the glory of noon surpasses the gleam of a candle.

Therefore will we be still,
And trust in Thee.

J. S. Hoyland (1887-1957)

Above all, do not spend the whole time of prayer talking yourself. Bring the needs of the world, and the problems of your life, before God; then leave them with Him and wait for a while in silence not only from speech, but as far as possible from thought, just desiring with all your force that in these things God's will may be done, and resting in the quiet assurance of His love and power. There is no limit to what God will do by means of us if we train ourselves to trust Him enough.

William Temple (1881-1944)

Trust

What is before us, we know not, whether we shall live or die; but this we know, that all things are ordered and sure. Everything is ordered, with unerring wisdom and unbounded love, by Thee, our God, Who art love. Grant us in all things to see Thy hand; through Jesus Christ our Lord. Amen.

Charles Simeon (1759-1836)

Child of my love, fear not the unknown morrow,
Dread not the new demand life makes of thee;
Thy ignorance does hold no cause for sorrow
Since what thou knowest not is known to Me.

Thou canst not see today the hidden meaning
Of my command, but thou the light shall gain;
Walk on in faith, upon my promise leaning,
And as thou goest, all shall be made plain.

One step thou seest — then go forward boldly,
One step is far enough for faith to see;
Take that, and thy next duty shall be told thee,
For step by step thy Lord is leading thee.

Stand not in fear, thine adversaries counting;
Dare every peril, save to disobey;
Thou shalt march on, all obstacles surmounting,
For I, the Strong, will open up the way.

Wherefore, go gladly to the task assigned thee,
Having my promise, needing nothing more
Than just to know, where'er the future find thee,
In all thy journeying I go before.

Frank J. Exeley

Trust

Saturday

Cause me to hear thy lovingkindness in the morning; for in thee do I trust:
cause me to know the way wherein I should walk; for I lift up my soul unto
thee.

Psalm CXLIII 8

I am trusting Thee, Lord Jesus,
Trusting only Thee,
Trusting Thee for full salvation,
Great and free.

I am trusting Thee for pardon:
At Thy feet I bow,
For Thy grace and tender mercy
Trusting now.

I am trusting Thee to guide me:
Thou alone shalt lead,
Every day and hour supplying
All my need.

I am trusting Thee for power:
Thine can never fail;
Words which Thou Thyself shalt give me
Must prevail.

I am trusting Thee, Lord Jesus;
Never let me fall;
I am trusting Thee for ever,
And for all.

Frances Ridley Havergal (1836-79)

Strength for the Task

And Moses said unto the Lord, O my Lord, I am not eloquent, neither heretofore, nor since thou hast spoken unto thy servant: but I am slow of speech, and of a slow tongue.

And the Lord said unto him, Who hath made man's mouth? or who maketh the dumb, or deaf, or the seeing, or the blind? have not I the Lord?

Now therefore go, and I will be with thy mouth, and teach thee what thou shalt say.

Exodus IV 10-12

Then said I [Jeremiah], Ah, Lord God! behold, I cannot speak: for I am a child.

But the Lord said unto me, Say not, I am a child: for thou shalt go to all that I shall send thee, and whatsoever I command thee thou shalt speak.

Be not afraid of their faces: for I am with thee to deliver thee, saith the Lord.

Then the Lord put forth his hand, and touched my mouth. And the Lord said unto me, Behold, I have put my words in thy mouth.

Jeremiah I 6-9

And ye shall be brought before governors and kings for my sake, for a testimony against them and the Gentiles.

But when they deliver you up, take no thought how or what ye shall speak: for it shall be given you in that same hour what ye shall speak.

For it is not ye that speak, but the Spirit of your Father which speaketh in you.

Matthew X 18-20

281

Strength for the Task

Monday

Without me ye can do nothing.

John XV 5

If I stoop
Into a dark, tremendous sea of cloud,
It is but for a time; I press God's lamp
Close to my breast; its splendour, soon or late,
Will pierce the gloom: I shall emerge one day.

Robert Browning (1812-1889)

I believe that God both can and will bring good out of evil. For that purpose he needs men who make the best use of everything. I believe God will give us all the power we need to resist in all times of distress. But he never gives it in advance, lest we should rely upon ourselves and not on him alone. A faith as strong as this should allay all our fears for the future. I believe that even our errors and mistakes are turned to good account. It is no harder for God to cope with them than with what we imagine to be our good deeds. I believe God is not just timeless fate, but that he waits upon and answers sincere prayer and responsible action.

Dietrich Bonhoeffer (1906-1945)

Strength for the Task

With God all things are possible.

Mark X 27

And Hezekiah spake comfortably to them, saying,
Be strong and courageous, be not afraid or dismayed for the king of Assyria, nor for all the multitude that is with him; for there be more with us than with him:
With him is an arm of flesh; but with us is the Lord our God to help us, and to fight our battles. And the people rested themselves upon the words of Hezekiah king of Judah.

II Chronicles XXXII 6-8

One of the greatest discoveries a man can make is to awake to the fact that the power with which he has to do his work is not his power at all, and that consequently his own sufficiency, his past experience and his present feelings may be disregarded and his whole reliance placed on the unchanging forces of truth, goodness and love which he may allow to work in and through him. The scale by which the possibilities of his achievement are measured is thus entirely changed.

Anon.

If I am really on the business of the Divine King . . . then all the resources of our Father's empire of reality must needs be at my call for the legitimate requirements of my errand. That he who is on the King's business should have the right to work miracles at need is no subject for surprise or incredulity. The real marvel is elsewhere; it lies in the fact that we mortals should be actually entrusted with the King's business.

A. G. Hogg (1875-1954)

Strength for the Task

Wednesday

Who are we to set a limit on God's ability to use even our meagre gifts and talents in His cause?

It was a young insignificant woman, a London housemaid, who felt the urge to become a missionary in China and who led a hundred Chinese children to safety through Japanese occupied territory. God was able to use Gladys Aylward's talent for overcoming obstacles to save a hundred lives.

It was a shy retiring housewife, who, having suffered the loss of her little daughter, opened her home to homeless prostitutes. God was able to use the sorrow of a bereaved mother to save countless homeless girls. At the end of her life, and despite the often sordid nature of her work, Josephine Butler was able to say, "There is nothing in this world so ugly that God cannot raise up to meet it a corresponding beauty that can blaze it out of existence."

A hospital chaplain's assistant in writing of her experiences amongst the sick says this, "God works in a mysterious way, for in those who suffer most are found the gifts of contentment and peace and an amazing courage. To us who visit, they give an enrichment of spirit."

There is nothing in the world so ugly that God cannot raise up enough beauty to meet it. There is no pain so great that God cannot transform it. There is no talent so small that God cannot increase it. There is no one so unimportant that God cannot use him or her to bring in His Kingdom.

It's only if we believe this that we can dare to offer to God our hands and feet and our lips in His service. And it's only when through our prayers we are in touch with the very source of love and power that we can discover how our tiny talent, whatever it may be, can be used by God so that we may indeed be "His Witnesses."

Excerpt from "Late Call" on the
theme "Ye are my witnesses"

Strength for the Task

I remember passing through the "pain barrier" which athletes sometimes describe when I trained in a commando course in the Royal Navy. Faced with tough physical demands in the rope crossing of small rivers, climbing walls in full kit, crawling through mud and barbed wire, utter exhaustion brought you near to tears of frustration. A few dropped out, but if you crawled on, even cursing the whole idea as you went, you eventually got through. And it felt great!

We all meet pain barriers of one sort or another, and we don't need to be athletes to understand them. There are times when a relationship goes wrong or a serious obstacle gets in our way, and all we feel is pain. Being Christian doesn't necessarily ease the pain, and certainly doesn't make the problem disappear. (However much the athlete trains he always has to cope with the pain barrier.) We can pray for a miracle, Christians often do. Sometimes miracles happen, but my Christian experience shows that more often we just have to face the moment as it comes. We have to find that extra bit of strength from our prayer, scrape that extra bit of courage from the faith that God knows and cares, and hang on to the encouragement of friends around. Yes, I know we have to put it into the Lord's hands, but even then we have to take some responsibility ourselves. That's the hard part.

Yet, however hard the road, however long it takes, there comes a point where we break through our personal pain barrier onto the smoother road ahead. The pain recedes, the rhythm returns, and we're running again. And the real miracle is not that something spectacular happened, but that we found the courage and strength to keep going, to hang on. Then we can look back and find that the Lord was with us, even when we felt most lonely and vulnerable. Especially then. The important thing is to keep moving ahead.

"No one who sets his hand to the plough," said Jesus, "and then keeps looking back is fit for the kingdom of God" (Luke IX: 62).

Eddie Askew

Strength for the Task

Friday

The story of the writing of *God Calling*, a little pocket-sized book with world sales of over one million copies, is altogether amazing. "Two poor, brave women were courageously fighting against sickness and penury. They were facing a hopeless future and one of them even longed to be quit of this hard world for good. And then He spoke. And spoke again! Day after day He came and cheered them. And though they still had their sorrows they had joy and a new courage. For He inspired them with His promises for their future when His loving purpose should be revealed; and He gently rallied them on their unbelief."

By way of introduction one of the "Two Listeners" wrote:

The tender understanding of some of Our Lord's messages was at times almost heart-breaking: but His loving reproofs would leave no hurt. Always, and this daily, He insisted that we should be channels of Love, Joy and Laughter in His broken world. This was the Man of Sorrows in a new aspect.

We, or rather I, found this command very difficult to obey, although to others it might have been simple. To laugh, to cheer others, to be always joyful when days were pain-racked, nights tortured by chronic insomnia, when poverty and almost insupportable worry were our daily portion, when prayer went unanswered and God's face was veiled and fresh calamities came upon us?

Still came this insistent command to love and laugh and be joy-bringers to the lives we contacted. Disheartened, one of us would gladly have ceased the struggle and passed on to another and happier life.

But He encouraged us daily, saying that He would not break the instruments that He intended to use, that He would not leave the metal in the crucible longer than was necessary for the burning away of the dross. Continually He exhorted us not to lose heart, and spoke of the joy that the future held for us.

Ed. A. J. Russell

Strength for the Task

From "God Calling":

Never feel inadequate. Obey my commands. They are steps in the ladder that leads to success. Above all, keep calm, unmoved.

Go back into the silence to recover this calm when it is lost even for one moment. You accomplish more by this than by all the activities of a long day. At all costs keep calm, you can help nobody when you are agitated. I, your Lord, see not as man sees.

Never feel inadequate for any task. All work here is accomplished by My Spirit, and that can flow through the most humble and lowly. It simply needs an unblocked channel. Rid yourself of self and all is well.

Pray about all, but concentrate on a few things until those are accomplished. I am watching over you. Strength for your daily, hourly task is provided. Yours is the fault, the sin, if it is unclaimed, and you fail for lack of it.

Ed. A. J. Russell

A doctor, cured of acute rheumatoid arthritis, writes: "In this Year of the Disabled I write to encourage stricken people to seek their own slow miracles.

"Twenty-two years ago a fearsome future confronted a close family friend who was a musician. The imminent terror of blindness and the need for operations on the eyes, followed by weeks of eye occlusion, confronted her. I wrote the following which, with her permission, I reproduce. I offer it with humbleness and thanks for my own slow miracle:

"And He smiled at me and said 'Grasp hold of this hand for it is here beside you and will lead you through the darkness of the time ahead. Its warmth will warm you, and from its strength will flow your strength, and from its gentle power will come your courage, for this is the hand of love; though wounded it is unharmed and strong and waits your touch to guide you to the sunlight of the morning'."

Philip Kent, M.R.C.S., L.R.C.P.,
general practitioner

Witnessing

Sunday

There was another most interesting character at that cross. We do not know his name, but he made his own impression on the Christian community, for the story is told in no less than three of the Gospels. He was the centurion in charge of the execution squad. He had the closest view of anyone on that grim occasion. He watched Jesus suffer with dignity. He noticed that Jesus was concerned entirely for others, the soldiers who had nailed him there, the mother who had borne him, and the criminals executed with him. He had heard the priests mocking Jesus; he had seen the crowd jeering. He had felt the uncanny darkness; he had heard the great cry as Jesus died. And he burst out with a confession of faith in this man he had just executed. 'Truly this man was the Son of God,' is the bit Matthew and Mark record. Luke's account is more politically slanted: 'Certainly this man was innocent.' Maybe he said both, convinced not only of the innocence of Jesus but of his superhuman quality. Quite what a Roman centurion would have meant by 'Son of God' we cannot be sure. It was one of the titles by which the Emperor liked to be known: so on any showing it was a fantastic confession of loyalty to a crucified member of a subject race. But we can hardly doubt that the evangelists meant us to see far more in that cry. It was the primitive Christian credal confession: Jesus Christ is Son of God and Saviour. Here was the man who killed Jesus recognising in him the way back to God!

Michael Green

Witnessing

Monday

The simple truth, whether we like it or not, is that religion can be a substitute for Christianity. Will you ask yourself this: is your experience one of a vague religious sense, say that there is a God, a purpose behind all things, an inspired Bible, a historic person called Christ whose teaching you admire and whose personality you love, or is it Christianity? Is it, in other words, that you are committed to a way of life, that you are entering more and more fully into a living and definite experience with Christ which is changing your life? If it is the first you have nothing to pass on. If it is the second you cannot, however reticent, but long to find some way or another in which others can be brought into that experience which is changing you. . . .

Do let us take this matter of our relation to others seriously. No man is fully won to Christ unless his personlity is reaching out to bring others into the experience. It is incredible that we can possess the real thing and keep it as dark as some of us keep our religion. After all, a chill falls upon the spirit if one contemplates what would have happened if the earliest Christians of all had done no more to spread their experience than we have done. Supposing they had settled down in Jurusalem, a little body of men and women meeting together every week in the Upper Room, exchanging experiences, worshipping together, singing hymns, listening to sermons from one another. The Christian Church would have been extinct within half a century of Christ's death.

But what did happen at once? They went throughout the known world preaching this glorious good news, that there was a transforming communicable experience of salvation for every man and woman. Nor did they say to themselves what I have heard people say: "Very well then, I suppose I had better begin to tell others." The thing simply burst from them. They could not keep it in.

Leslie D. Weatherhead (1893-1976)

Witnessing

Tuesday

A year ago I was ill in a New Jersey hospital and my doctor (who had been a missionary) was talking with me about the difference, as he saw it, between the all-out keenness with which medical resources were mobilized for the very humblest and the apathy of Christians in the Christian cause. He said that a few nights before a negro had come into the hospital, dangerously wounded after a drunken fracas. He was a known bully, and dying of a knife-wound in his belly. But the hospital, though it had no hope of saving him, and though he was a drunken ne'er-do-well of whom society might deem itself well rid, used its most expensive methods for him and did for him all that it could have done for anyone — and this out of professional loyalty and keenness. My doctor wished that Christians and Churches were as unlimited in their sacrifice and their commitment.

Of course, the reason is that we do not really believe. We assent, but we do not *believe*. When men really believe that the Son of God died for the sins of men and that through Him we are brought into that kind of family relation to the Creator of all the worlds which is typified in Christ's use of the word 'Abba', they do not keep the news to themselves.

William Paton

Witnessing

Thursday

'He went about doing good.' So we might say in our own age of two or three who have been personally known to us, 'He or she went about doing good.' They are the living witnesses to us of His work. If we observe them we shall see that they did good because they were good — because they lived for others and not for themselves, because they had a higher standard of truth and therefore men could trust them, because their love was deeper and therefore they drew others after them. These are they of whom we read in Scripture that they bear the image of Christ until His coming again, and of a few of them that they have borne the image of His sufferings, and to us they are the best interpreters of His life. They too have a hidden strength which is derived from communion with the Unseen; they pass their lives in the service of God, and yet only desire to be thought unprofitable servants. The honours or praises which men sometimes shower upon them are not much to their taste. Their only joy is to do the will of God and to relieve the wants of their brethren. Their only or greatest sorrow is to think of the things which, from inadvertence or necessity, they have been compelled to leave undone. Their way of life has been simple; they have not had much to do with the world; they have not had time to accumulate stores of learning. Sometimes they have seen with superhuman clearness one or two truths of which the world was especially in need. They may have had their trials too — failing health, declining years, the ingratitude of men — but they have endured as seeing Him who is invisible.

Benjamin Jowett (1817-1893)

Witnessing

Nothing promotes atheism and impiety more than the great disagreement between the faith and practice of men professing to be Christians. . . . You call yourself a Christian. Pray how are you distinguished from an heathen?

Thomas Wilson (1663-1755)

The Gospel according to You

If none but you in the world today
Had tried to live in the Christ-like way,
Could the rest of the world look close at you
And find the path that is straight and true?

If none but you in the world so wide
Had found the Christ for your daily guide,
Would the things you do and the things you say
Lead others to live in His holy way?

Ah! friend of Christ, in the world today
Are many who watch you upon your way;
Who look to the things you say and do
To measure the Christian standard true.

Men read and admire the Gospel of Christ,
With its love unfailing and true;
But what do they say and what do they think
Of the Gospel according to you?

You are writing each day a letter to men —
Take care that the writing is true:
For the only Gospel that some men will read
Is the Gospel according to YOU.

Witnessing

Saturday

Make me a witness, Lord,
so faulty I and weak,
My trembling word can scarce he heard,
so loud my failings speak.
Make me a witness, Lord,
that all at home may see
A constant daily growth in grace
and glory give to Thee.
Make me a witness, Lord,
to those I daily meet,
That I may be Thy messenger
in neighbourhood and street.
Make me a witness, Lord,
that souls may on Thee call
And glorify Thy name adored,
King Jesus, Lord of all.

Lord, speak to me, that I may speak
In living echoes of Thy tone;
As Thou hast sought, so let me seek
Thy erring children lost and lone.
O lead me, Lord, that I may lead
The wandering and the wavering feet;
O feed me, Lord, that I may feed
Thy hungering ones with manna sweet.
O strengthen me, that, while I stand
Firm on the rock, and strong in Thee,
I may stretch out a loving hand
To wrestlers with the troubled sea.
O fill me with Thy fulness, Lord,
Until my very heart o'erflow
In kindling thought and glowing word,
Thy love to tell, Thy praise to show.
O use me, Lord, use even me,
Just as Thou wilt, and when, and where,
Until Thy blessed face I see,
Thy rest, Thy joy, Thy glory share.

Frances Ridley Havergal (1836-1879)

These that have turned the world upside down are come hither also.

Acts XVII 6

In His Service

If ye shall ask any thing in my name, I will do it.

John XIV 14

Marianne Adlard

There are saints of God who for long, long years have been shut off from all the activities of the Church, and even from the worship of the sanctuary, but who, nevertheless, have continued to labour together in prayer with the whole fellowship of the saints. There comes to me the thought of one woman, Marianne Adlard by name, who, to my knowledge, since 1872 in this great babel of London, has been in perpetual pain, and yet in constant prayer. She is today a woman twisted and distorted by suffering, and yet exhaling the calm and strength of the secret of the Most High. In 1872 she was a bed-ridden girl in the North of London, praying that God would send revival to the church of which she was a member, and yet into which even then she never came. She had read in the little paper called *Revival,* which subsequently became *The Christian,* the story of the work being done in Chicago among ragged children by a man called Moody. She had never seen Moody, but putting that little paper under her pillow, she began to pray, "O Lord, send this man to our church." She had no means of reaching him or communicating with him. He had already visited the country in 1867, and in 1872 he started again for a short trip with no intention of doing any work. However, the pastor of the church of which this girl was a member, met him and asked him to preach for him. He consented, and after the evening service he asked those who would decide for Christ to rise, and hundreds did so. He was surprised, and imagined that his request had been misunderstood. He repeated it more clearly, and again the response was the same. Meetings were continued throughout the following ten days, and four hundred members were taken into the church. In telling this story Moody said, "I wanted to know what this meant. I began making enquiries and never rested until I found a bed-ridden girl praying that God would bring me to that church. He had heard her, and brought me over four thousand miles of land and sea, in answer to her request."

G. Campbell Morgan (1863-1945)

In His Service

Monday

God may choose people, but he chooses them for special responsibilities, not for special favours.

Mrs Mary Whitehouse

One is almost overwhelmed with the speed and power of the enemy. Am I really the 'little Canute' which the 'Financial Times' calls me? Is there no way at all in which the terrible trends of our time can be reversed and a new spirit arise?

One has, somehow, to get oneself out of the picture. To realise that it is all in the hands of God and trust him. One of the hardest things for me just now is to accept how the strain of the battle is showing in my face and telling on my health. I suppose I've aged ten years in the last three and particularly during the last weeks.

This is the Cross — to realise there is no glamour, no appreciation to be asked or expected, nothing but ridicule, pain and loss. Friendship there is, and love, but even this does not touch the central core of loneliness in a battle of this kind. It is in this loneliness, and in this alone, that one finds Christ. In Him, and in Him alone, not in family or in friends must I seek comfort or sustenance.

Mary Whitehouse, from her Diary

In His Service

Blessed are they which are persecuted for righteousness' sake: for theirs is the kingdom of heaven.

Matthew V 10

Martin Luther King

How do you explain a man as great as Martin Luther King? He lived by the personal power of the Spirit of God. I once heard him tell a small group of people his experience in Montgomery, Alabama. It was at Montgomery that he was thrust into national leadership through the bus boycott which developed in that city. It was there he began his march to becoming a man of destiny.

Soon after the boycott began, white bigotry turned on him. Hour by hour his telephone rang with hateful voices threatening to kill his child, to bomb his home, to destroy his wife, to burn his church.

After three days, in the middle of the night, the telephone rang again. Following his listening to a tirade of hate he went into the kitchen of his home to make a cup of coffee. There his will began to fail and his courage seeped away. He felt that next day he must flee to safety.

Then something happened. These were his words: 'At that moment I experienced the presence of the Divine as I had never experienced Him before. It seemed as though I could hear the quiet reassurance of an inner voice saying: "Stand up for righteousness, stand up for truth, and God will be at your side for ever".' Then he added: 'Almost at once my fears left me and they have never come back.' That he lived in this conquest of fear is shown by his words just before his assassination: 'Maybe I've got the advantage over most people. I have conquered the fear of death.'

Alan Walker

In His Service

Wednesday

These things I have spoken unto you, that in me ye might have peace. In the world ye shall have tribulation: but be of good cheer; I have overcome the world.

John XVI 33

Dietrich Bonhoeffer

Bonhoeffer is then taken to Flossenburg where he is given the death sentence. After it has been delivered, the prison doctor catches a glimpse of him through the half opened door of one of the huts, still in his prison clothes, and kneeling in fervent prayer to the Lord his God. 'The devotion and evident conviction of being heard that I saw in the prayer of this intensely captivating man,' the doctor was subsequently to recall, 'moved me to the depths.' The next morning, naked under the scaffold in the sweet spring woods, Bonhoeffer kneels for the last time to pray. Five minutes later his life is ended.

As this happens, five years of the monstrous buffooneries of war are drawing to a close. Hitler's Reich that was to last for a thousand years will soon reach its ignominious and ruinous end; the liberators are moving in from the east and the west with bombs and tanks and guns and cigarettes and Spam; the air is thick with rhetoric and cant. Looking back now after twenty-four years, I ask myself where in that murky darkness any light shines. Not among the Nazis, certainly, nor among the liberators, who, as we know, were to liberate no one and nothing. The rhetoric and the cant have mercifully been forgotten; what lives on is the memory of a man who died, not on behalf of freedom or democracy or a steadily rising Gross National Product, not for any of the twentieth century's counterfeit hopes and desires, but on behalf of a cross on which another man died two thousand years before. As on that previous occasion, on Golgotha, so amidst the rubble and desolation of 'liberated' Europe, the only victor is the man who died, as the only hope for the future lies in his triumph over death. There never can be any other victory or any other hope.

Malcolm Muggeridge

298

In His Service

Archbishop Janani Luwum

His grave was dug in the sun-baked earth outside the west door of the cathedral in the centre of Kampala just four years ago. Crowds packed the cathedral for the deeply moving funeral service — tears were glistening on brown cheeks. This death shocked a country that was already shattered. Despite President Idi Amin's devastation of Uganda, his murder of Archbishop Janani Luwum numbed the city.

A clumsy lie about a fatal car accident could not conceal the terrible truth. The Archbishop had been brutally shot by Amin only four months before the anticipated celebrations marking 100 years since missionaries had first taken the Gospel to Uganda.

Why was Janani put to death? His crime was that he cared beyond normal caring. He was a man with a great capacity to love, and he cared deeply for his people. His anxiety was for ordinary men and women who were being taken to prison and were never seen again. His courage led him to gather the other bishops together to write a joint letter respectfully and politely 'speaking the truth in love' to the President. Janani knew that he was probably signing his own death warrant.

His funeral service symbolised the suffering and the hope that have marked the Church in Uganda since 1885 when a handful of boys, the first Christian converts, were burned at the stake rather than deny their Lord.

The suffering of mourning was accentuated by the fact that at the service the grave remained empty — President Amin had withheld the Archbishop's body. As the bishops left the cathedral a former archbishop turned to the crowd: 'Brothers and sisters, look at the empty grave!' His voice was steady and confident, 'Isn't that a wonderful sign — this empty grave is not needed because Janani has risen.'

His words released the emotions of the great crowd. One voice, and then thousands picked up the notes of the hymn, resounding over the hill dominating Kampala, 'Up from the grave he arose!' Tears streamed down faces for the beloved Archbishop, and yet there was exultation that God's ultimate victory was sure and certain — even Idi Amin at his worst could not destroy this fact.

Anne Townsend

In His Service

Friday

We express our deep concern for all who have been unjustly imprisoned, and especially for our brethren who are suffering for their testimony to the Lord Jesus. We promise to pray and work for their freedom. At the same time we refuse to be intimidated by their fate. God helping us, we too will seek to stand against injustice and to remain faithful to the Gospel, whatever the cost. We do not forget the warnings of Jesus that persecution is inevitable.

From The Lausanne Covenant, 1974

Rev. Tom Allan

Mr Allan often said, 'We must do something for these people.' This simple sentence is an important clue to the practicality of his ministry in which so many who might have thought no one else cared about them knew that Tom Allan at any rate was deeply concerned about their welfare.

There was Alec, for instance, who came into the church one night after a service, dazed with drink, and found himself telling the minister, who came and sat alongside him in the pew, how his home life was breaking up because of his drinking. Mr Allan found out where he lived and promised to visit him next day. The following day, however, in the cold light of sobriety, Alec ordered the minister out of his home with abusive oaths. Today Alec will tell you that he came to know Christ as his Saviour because Mr Allan came back and back again and showed him the love of Jesus in a practical way.

'He made me feel, in spite of all that I'd done, that I mattered still to God,' said one whose life had reached the depths of degradation. 'He didn't tell me off, nor did he make light of my sin, but showed me how I could seek God's forgiveness.'

Perhaps, too, we should ask the young girl whose way of living has been changed from prostitution to respectable citizenship. It didn't happen overnight and it began when Mr Allan took this girl for a cup of coffee and spent time talking with her in a cafe. Mary was saving hard for a special jacket — the height of fashion at that moment — and some of us will count it a privilege to have seen the expression on Mr Allan's face and the tears in his eyes, as this 17-year-old tearaway presented him, of her own accord, with the money which she had saved with such terrific effort, 'to help somebody that needs it more than me.'

From the memorial tribute to the Rev. Tom Allan
'A Fraction of His Image'

In His Service

Mother Teresa

Our works are only an expression of our love for Christ. Our hearts need to be full of love for him and since we have to express that love in action, naturally then the poorest of the poor are the means of expressing our love for God.

'Mother Teresa Speaks'

Each day Mother Teresa meets Jesus; first at the Mass, whence she derives sustenance and strength; then in each needing, suffering soul she sees and tends. They are one and the same Jesus; at the altar and in the streets. Neither exists without the other. We who are imprisoned in history; castaways on the barren shores of time, past, present and to come — we seek another Jesus. A Jesus of history, which is actually a contradiction in terms; like an eternity clock or an infinity tape-measure. Jesus can only exist now; and, in existing now, makes now always. Thus, for Mother Teresa the two commandments — to love God and to love our neighbour — are jointly fulfilled; indeed, inseparable. In her life and work she exemplifies the relation between the two; how, if we do not love God we cannot love our neighbour, and if we do not love our neighbour we cannot love God.

Malcolm Muggeridge

Courage

Sunday

Have not I commanded thee? Be strong and of a good courage; be not afraid, neither be thou dismayed: for the Lord thy God is with thee whithersoever thou goest . . . only be strong and of a good courage.

Joshua I 9 & 18

Then Nebuchadnezzar in his rage and fury commanded to bring Shadrach, Meshach, and Abed-nego. Then they brought these men before the king.

Nebuchadnezzar spake and said unto them, Is it true, O Shadrach, Meshach, and Abed-nego, do not ye serve my gods, nor worship the golden image which I have set up?

Now if ye be ready that at what time ye hear the sound of the cornet, flute, sackbut, psaltery, and dulcimer, and all kinds of musick, ye fall down and worship the image which I have made; well: but if you worship not, ye shall be cast the same hour into the midst of a burning fiery furnace; and who is that God that shall deliver you out of my hands?

Shadrach, Meshach, and Abed-nego, answered and said to the king, O Nebuchadnezzar, we are not careful to answer thee in this matter.

If it be so, our God whom we serve is able to deliver us from the burning fiery furnace, and he will deliver us out of thine hand, O king.

But if not, be it known unto thee, O king, that we will not serve thy gods, nor worship the golden image which thou hast set up.

Then was Nebuchadnezzar full of fury, and the form of his visage was changed against Shadrach, Meshach, and Abed-nego: therefore he spake, and commanded that they should heat the furnace one seven times more than it was wont to be heated.

And he commanded the most mighty men that were in his army to bind Shadrach, Meshach, and Abed-nego, and to cast them into the burning fiery furnace.

Daniel III 13-20

Courage

And the Lord said unto Moses, Wherefore criest thou unto me? Speak unto the children of Israel, that they go forward.

Exodus XIV 15

So I saw in my dream that Christian made haste and went forward, that if possible he might get lodging there. Now, before he had gone far, he entered into a very narrow passage, which was about a furlong off of the porter's lodge; and looking very narrowly before him as he went, he espied two lions in the way. Now, thought he, I see the dangers that Mistrust and Timorous were driven back by. (The lions were chained, but he saw not the chains). Then he was afraid, and thought also himself to go back after them, for he thought nothing but death was before him. But the porter at the lodge, whose name is Watchful, perceiving that Christian made a halt as if he would go back, cried unto him, saying, Is thy strength so small? Fear not the lions, for they are chained, and are placed there for trial of faith where it is, and for discovery of those that had none. Keep in the midst of the path, and no hurt shall come unto thee.

Then I saw that he went on, trembling for fear of the lions, but taking good heed to the directions of the porter; he heard them roar, but they did him no harm. Then he clapped his hands, and went on till he came and stood before the gate where the porter was.

John Bunyan (1628-1688)

Courage

Tuesday

When thou goest out to battle against thine enemies, and seest horses, and chariots, and a people more than thou, be not afraid of them: for the Lord thy God is with thee, which brought thee up out of the land of Egypt.

And it shall be, when ye are come nigh unto the battle, that the priest shall approach and speak unto the people, and shall say unto them, Hear, O Israel, ye approach this day unto battle against your enemies: let not your hearts faint, fear not, and do not tremble, neither be ye terrified because of them;

For the Lord your God is he that goeth with you, to fight for you against your enemies, to save you.

Deuteronomy XX 1-4

O Thou, my God! Do Thou, my God, stand by me, against all the world's wisdom and reason. Oh, do it! Thou must do it! Yea, Thou alone must do it! Not mine, but Thine, is the cause. For my own self, I have nothing to do with these great and earthly lords. I would prefer to have peaceful days, and to be out of this turmoil. But Thine, O Lord, is this cause; it is righteous and eternal. Stand by me, Thou true eternal God! In no man do I trust. All that is of the flesh and savours of the flesh is here of no account. God, O God! Dost Thou not hear me, O my God? Art Thou dead? No. Thou canst not die; Thou art only hiding Thyself. Hast Thou chosen me for this work? I ask Thee how I may be sure of this, if it be Thy will; for I would never have thought, in all my life, of undertaking aught against such great lords. Stand by me, O God, in the Name of Thy dear Son, Jesus Christ, who shall be my Defence and Shelter, yea, my Mighty Fortress, through the might and strength of Thy Holy Spirit. God help me. Amen.

Martin Luther (1483-1546)

Courage

God and one are always a majority.

Mary Slessor (1848-1915)

Mary Slessor

Among the Okoyong, when she spoke about their bad customs, they would not listen. . . . A slave was blamed for using witchcraft and condemned to die. Ma knew he was innocent, and went and stood beside him in front of the armed warriors of the chief, and said:

"This man has done no wrong. You must not put him to death."

"Ho, ho," they cried, "that is not good speaking. We have said he shall die, and he must die."

"No, no; listen," and she tried to reason with them, but they came round her waving their swords and guns, and shouting at the pitch of their voices. She stood in the midst of them as she had stood in the midst of the Dundee roughs, pale, but calm and unafraid. Perhaps it was her wonderful courage which did not fail her even when the swords were flashing about her head, perhaps it was the strange light that shone in her face that awed and quietened them, but the confusion died down and ceased. Then the chiefs agreed for her sake not to kill the man, but they put heavy chains upon his arms and legs, and starved and flogged him until he was a mass of bleeding flesh. Ma felt she had not done much, but it was a beginning.

W. P. Livingstone

305

Courage

Thursday

And I said, Should such a man as I flee?

Kagawa of Japan

Toyohiko looked at the hut and felt sick. It was six feet by nine, like every other one in the lane. Its walls were made of bamboo, but there was no paper in the windows or in the flimsy entrance door. The floors were fouled by dogs, and vermin crawled everywhere. Toyohiko held his heaving stomach, prayed for courage and went inside, where a thin partition divided the hut into two tiny rooms. Borrowing a broom, he began to clean up. Darkness, falling quickly, had almost come before he had finished. The ex-convict went away, and Toyohiko, because he had had no money to buy oil for his lamp, sat cross-legged on the floor, listening, thinking and praying.

Outside the unceasing noise of the slums went on — a shrill clatter of sound, broken by children's cries, the sharp outbreaks of quarrels and slurred voices of drunken men and women. The smell of the slums had already begun to cling to his clothes and his body. Alone except for a diseased dog which had slunk inside the hut, he wondered if he was mad to have done this thing which no one could understand. On the other side of the bridge it had seemed the only step to take. If these people were to be won for Christ, he must come and live amongst them. Now he wondered if he could even spend a whole night there. His mind ranged backwards to the quiet beauty of Awa, to the ceremonious tea-drinking of his uncle's house and the peace of the college library. His breath dragged up from his weak lungs, painfully and slowly. Still praying, he fell asleep.

Cyril J. Davey

306

Courage

I can do all things through Christ which strengtheneth me.

Philippians IV 13

Gladys Aylward — China Missionary

The Governor of the Yangcheng prison, small, pale-faced, his mouth set into a worried line, met her at the entrance. Behind were grouped half a dozen of his staff.

"We are glad you have come," he said quickly. "There is a riot in the prison; the convicts are killing each other."

"So I can hear," she said. "But what am I here for? I'm only the missionary woman. Why don't you send the soldiers in to stop it?"

"The convicts are murderers, bandits, thieves," said the Governor, his voice trembling. "The soldiers are frightened. There are not enough of them."

"I'm sorry to hear that," said Gladys. "But what do you expect me to do about it? I don't even know why you asked me to come."

The Governor took a step forward. "You must go in and stop the fighting."

"I must go in . . . !" Gladys's mouth dropped open; her eyes rounded in utter amazement. "Me! Me go in there! Are you mad? If I went in they'd kill me!"

The Governor's eyes were fixed on her with hypnotic intensity. "But how can they kill you? You tell everybody that you have come here because you have the living God inside you."

The words bubbled out of the Governor's mouth, his lips twisted in the acuteness of distress. Gladys felt a small, cold shiver down her back. When she swallowed, her throat seemed to have a gritty texture.

"The — living God?" she stammered.

"You preach it everywhere — in the streets and villages. If you preach the truth, if your God protects you from harm, then you can stop this riot."

Gladys stared at him. Those men — murderers, thieves, bandits, rioting and killing each other inside those walls! How could she . . .? "I must try," she said to herself. "I must try. O God, give me strength. All right," she said. "Open the door. I'll go in to them." She did not trust her voice to say any more.

Alan Burgess

Courage

Saturday

I cannot provide you with that staff for your journey; but perhaps I can tell you a little about it, how to use it and lose it and find it again, and cling to it more than ever. You shall cut it — so it is ordained — every one of you for himself, and its name is Courage. You must excuse me if I talk a good deal about courage today. There is nothing else much worth speaking about to undergraduates or graduates or white-haired men and women. It is the lovely virtue — the rib of Himself that God sent down to His children. Courage is the thing. All goes if courage goes.

From the Rectorial Address given by Sir J. M. Barrie at St Andrews University on 3rd May, 1922

But the big courage is the cold-blooded kind, the kind that never lets go even when you're feeling empty inside, and your blood's thin, and there's no kind of fun or profit to be had, and the trouble's not over in an hour or two but lasts for months and years. One of the men here was speaking about that kind, and he called it 'Fortitude.' I reckon fortitude's the biggest thing a man can have — just to go on enduring when there's no guts or heart left in you.

Peter Pienaar in John Buchan's 'Mr Standfast'

The Bishop of Birmingham, speaking about his imprisonment by the Japanese while Bishop of Singapore, during the last war, said: 'Without God's help I doubt whether I should have come through. Long hours of ignoble pain were a severe test. In the middle of the torture they asked me if I still believed in God. When by God's help I said, "I do," they asked why God did not save me, and by the help of His Holy Spirit I said: "God does save me. He does not save me by freeing me from pain or punishment, but He saves me by giving me the spirit to bear it;" and when they asked me why I did not curse them, I told them it was because I was a follower of Jesus Christ, who taught us that we were all brethren.'

Facing Facts!

Who Is My Neighbour?

And behold, a certain lawyer stood up, and tempted him, saying, Master, what shall I do to inherit eternal life?

He said unto him, What is written in the law? how readest thou?

And he answering said, Thou shalt love the Lord thy God with all thy heart, and with all thy soul, and with all thy strength, and with all thy mind; and thy neighbour as thyself.

And he said unto him, Thou hast answered right: this do, and thou shalt live.

But he, willing to justify himself, said unto Jesus, And who is my neighbour?

And Jesus answering said, A certain man went down from Jerusalem to Jericho, and fell among thieves, which stripped him of his raiment, and wounded him, and departed, leaving him half dead.

And by chance there came down a certain priest that way: and when he saw him, he passed by on the other side.

And likewise a Levite, when he was at the place, came and looked on him, and passed by on the other side.

But a certain Samaritan, as he journeyed, came where he was: and when he saw him, he had compassion on him.

And went to him, and bound up his wounds, pouring in oil and wine, and set him on his own beast, and brought him to an inn, and took care of him.

And on the morrow when he departed, he took out two pence, and gave them to the host, and said unto him, Take care of him; and whatsoever thou spendest more, when I come again, I will repay thee.

Which now of these three, thinkest thou, was neighbour unto him that fell among the thieves?

And he said, He that shewed mercy on him. Then said Jesus unto him, Go, and do thou likewise.

Luke X 25-37

Who Is My Neighbour?

Monday

In another walk to Salisbury, Mr George Herbert saw a poor man with a poorer horse, that was fallen under his load: they were both in distress, and needed present help; which Mr Herbert perceiving, put off his canonical coat, and helped the poor man to unload, and after to load, his horse. The poor man blessed him for it, and he blessed the poor man; and was so like the Good Samaritan, that he gave him money to refresh both himself and his horse; and told him, 'That if he loved himself he should be merciful to his beast.' Thus he left the poor man: and at his coming to his musical friends at Salisbury, they began to wonder that Mr George Herbert, which used to be so trim and clean, came into that company so soiled and discomposed: but he told them the occasion. And when one of the company told him 'He had disparaged himself by so dirty an employment,' his answer was, 'That the thought of what he had done would prove music to him at midnight; and that the omission of it would have upbraided and made discord in his conscience, whensoever he should pass by that place: for if I be bound to pray for all that be in distress, I am sure that I am bound, so far as it is in my power, to practice what I pray for. And though I do not wish for the like occasion every day, yet let me tell you, I would not willingly pass one day of my life without comforting a sad soul, or shewing mercy; and I praise God for this occasion. And now let's tune our instruments.'

Izaak Walton (1593-1683)

310

Who Is My Neighbour?

Tuesday

There are only two duties which our Lord requires of us, namely, the love of God and the love of our neighbour. . . . In my opinion, the surest sign for discovery whether we observe these two duties is the love of our neighbour; since we cannot know whether we love God, though we may have strong proof of it; but this can be more easily discovered respecting the love of our neighbour. And be assured that the further you advance in that love the more you will advance in the love of God likewise.

St. Teresa (1515-1582)

On a visit to Newcastle a year or two ago I was told of a man, a keen church member, who had died with tragic suddenness. Men were still, in their own way, "writing his obituary," in other words, remarking upon what they remembered of him with affection and esteem. They remembered that for fifty years he had been a business man of utter integrity, exercising an ever-increasing influence in his chosen profession. They remembered that for forty of these years he had been an Elder and for most of them Session Clerk in the church that he loved. But what they remembered most was that for the last year of his life he had got up half an hour earlier than he needed to do and gone round by the home of an old couple with no help, cleaned out the fireplace, lit the fire, and made their breakfast ready, before he went to his office. No one will question that it will be important when the books of his life are made up that he exercised that influence in the community and served thus lovingly and faithfully in the Church of his Lord. But, if Jesus' teaching is to be taken seriously, the most important part of his record will be: "Inasmuch as ye have done it unto these two of the least of my brethren, ye have done it unto me."

R. Leonard Small

Who Is My Neighbour?

Wednesday

The love of our neighbour is the only door out of the dungeon of self, where we mope and mow, striking sparks, and rubbing phosphorescence out of the walls, and blowing our own breath in our own nostrils, instead of issuing to the fair sunlight of God, the sweet winds of the universe. The man thinks his consciousness is himself; whereas his life consisteth in the inbreathing of God, and the consciousness of the universe of truth. To have himself, to know himself, to enjoy himself, he calls life; whereas, if he would forget himself, tenfold would be his life in God and his neighbours. The region of man's life is a spiritual region. God, his friends, his neighbours, his brothers all, is the wide world in which alone his spirit can find room. Himself is his dungeon. If he feels it not now, he will yet feel it one day — feel it as a living soul would feel being prisoned in a dead body, wrapped in sevenfold cerements, and buried in a stone-ribbed vault within the last ripple of the sound of chanting people in the church above. His life is not in knowing that he lives, but in loving all forms of life. He is made for the All; for God, who is the All, is his life. And the essential joy of his life lies abroad in the liberty of the All. His delights, like those of the Ideal Wisdom, are with the sons of men. His health is in the body of which the Son of Man is the head. The whole region is open to him — nay, he must live in it or perish.

George MacDonald (1824-1905)

Who Is My Neighbour?

If you feel that because you are a Church member, the ex-mental patient, the alcoholic and all the rest, are not your neighbour, remember that it is because you are a Church member that they *are* your neighbour, and this is where friendship begins.

Geoffrey Shaw (1927-1978)

If ever I am jaded and depressed there is one certain cure. It is to get out among other people, visit them in their homes, share their interests and their happiness, try to stand beside them in their trouble and their sorrow. So often one finds that others have so much more to endure, and yet contrive to keep cheerful. Depression feeds itself all the more when it remains alone. It is when we forget ourselves that we begin to find gladness again.

Hugh O. Douglas (1911-1986)

Too many of our people, decent and agreeable folk as they are, are singularly content to be comforted themselves, instead of being comforters of others. . . .

Happiness may be defined as 'A great love and much serving.'

Ernest D. Jarvis (1888-1964)

Who Is My Neighbour?

Friday

The spectre of famine now stretches across the length and breadth of Africa. And in its wake death and destruction on an unprecedented scale.

This has been a tragic year for the continent of Africa. A year in which it has regularly appeared and re-appeared in the news headlines.

. . . Starvation in Ethiopia came to the world's attention in March — three million people still face immediate famine and will need very generous food aid to survive the next six months.

. . . Few will forget the vivid T.V. pictures of the plight of Ghanaian refugees heading home from Nigeria.

. . . The long-standing war in Chad escalated dramatically.

. . . Tensions and conflicts continue to disrupt life in Uganda and Southern Africa.

. . . So the story goes on.

And above it all — accentuating the difficulties — hangs the dark cloud of drought and famine bringing its cruel and tragic legacy. The drought is creeping across the continent from North to South and from West to East — stretching across nearly the whole of the Sub-Saharan middle of Africa and reaching right down the eastern side.

Even if some areas get rain this year the legacy of the drought will reverberate for years to come. And drought in its turn brings ruined harvests. Consequently in Africa this Christmas millions face the imminent prospect of starvation. . . .

'Love came down at Christmas'. The very birth of Jesus shows his identification with the poor and needy. It tells us something about the great love of God for each and every one. Our response in the face of such love should also be love — to love God with all our heart, soul and mind, and to love our neighbour as ourself.

Tear Fund leaflet, Christmas 1983

I sought my soul, my soul I could not see;
I sought my God, but God eluded me;
I sought my brother — and I found all three.

Who Is My Neighbour?

Saturday

The Calcutta house of the Missionaries of Charity is bursting at the seams, and as each new house is opened there are volunteers clamouring to go there. As the whole story of Christendom shows, if everything is asked for, everything — and more — will be accorded; if little, then nothing. It is curious, when this is so obvious, that nowadays the contrary proposition should seem the more acceptable, and endeavour be directed towards softening the austerities of the service of Christ and reducing its hazards with a view to attracting people into it. After all, it was in kissing a leper's hideous sores that St Francis found the gaiety to captivate the world and gather round him some of the most audacious spirits of the age, to whom he offered only the glory of being naked on the naked earth for Christ's sake. If the demands had been less, so would the response have been. I should never have believed it possible, knowing India as I do over a number of years, to induce Indian girls of good family to tend outcasts and untouchables brought in from Calcutta streets, yet this, precisely, is the very first task that Mother Teresa gives them to do when they come to her as postulants. They do it, not just in obedience, but cheerfully and ardently, and gather round her in ever greater numbers for the privilege of doing it.

Accompanying Mother Teresa, as we did, to these different activities for the purpose of filming them — to the Home for the Dying, to the lepers and unwanted children, I found I went through three phases. The first was horror mixed with pity, the second compassion pure and simple, and the third, reaching far beyond compassion, something I had never experienced before — an awareness that these dying and derelict men and women, these lepers with stumps instead of hands, these unwanted children, were not pitiable, repulsive or forlorn, but rather dear and delightful; as it might be, friends of long standing, brothers and sisters. How is it to be explained — the very heart and mystery of the Christian faith? To soothe those battered old heads, to grasp those poor stumps, to take in one's arms those children consigned to dustbins, because it is his head, as they are his stumps and his children, of whom he said that whosoever received one such child in his name received him.

Malcolm Muggeridge

Action

Sunday

My brothers, what use is it for a man to say he has faith when he does nothing to show it? Can that faith save him? Suppose a brother or a sister is in rags with not enough food for the day, and one of you says, 'Good luck to you, keep yourselves warm, and have plenty to eat,' but does nothing to supply their bodily needs, what is the good of that? So with faith; if it does not lead to action, it is in itself a lifeless thing.

James II 14-17 (N.E.B.)

Action is always superior to speech in the Gospels which is why the Word became flesh and not newsprint. Jesus did not harangue men on the dignity of labour: he worked at a carpenter's bench. He didn't talk much about immortality: he raised the dead. He didn't give a course of lectures on the value of human personality: he made friends with publicans and sinners. He didn't write a thesis on the primacy of the spiritual over the material: he walked on water. He didn't construct theologies of Heaven and Hell: he put a glass of water at the focal point. He didn't tell them: he showed them.

The world is surfeited with words, and false prophets are producing more than their share. But we fight them on their own ground and merely add to the din when we match them speech for speech and argument for argument. The words of the false prophet can only be confounded by the actions of the true prophet. Much of the wrangling about race relations in Britain, for example, is so much wasted time. If every time false prophets made speeches warning of the dangers of close contact between the races, true prophets went out and made friends with another coloured family, the perfect answer to a false case would have been made.

Maybe the world is saying to the Church: don't tell us: show us!

Colin Morris

Action

Monday

I expect to pass through this world but once; any good thing therefore that I can do, or any kindness that I can show to any fellow-creature, let me do it now; let me not defer or neglect it, for I shall not pass this way again.

Attributed to Stephen Grellet (1773-1855)

Isn't it strange that princes and kings
And clowns that caper in sawdust rings
And ordinary folk like you and me
Are builders for eternity
And each is given a bag of tools
An hour-glass and a book of rules
And each must build
Ere his time has flown
A stumbling block or a stepping stone.

Anon.

Two Men

Two old men died recently. The one, a man of war, had been instrumental in the murder of millions of men, and caused thousands of homes to be plunged into sorrow. And when he died the people sang his praises and the newspaper headlines took up the song and screamed it in headlines and front pages. The world remembered.

The other, a man of peace, went to a dark continent and brought light and healing to an ignorant people. He was instrumental in turning a dead nation into one of radiant life and brought happiness and kindness into thousands of homes. And when he died the newspapers squeezed his death notice grudgingly into an obscure column. The world forgot.

Alexander West

Action

"When the mood of faith is on you, then," says the Master, "make the most of it. Do not hesitate. Obey the intuitions of kindness. Have the faith to do the unexpected, the original, the daring thing while the mood lasts. Break your alabaster boxes. Minister to those who lie wounded by life's highway. Make some new venture in friendship or forgiveness. Go to the last furlong of the second mile. Take the high, hopeful view of your fellow-men. Give them of your best and expect from them their best in return."

G. Johnstone Jeffrey (1881-1961)

To do and dare — not what you would, but what is right. Never to hesitate over what is within your power, but boldly to grasp what lies before you. Not in the flight of fancy, but only in the deed there is freedom. Away with timidity and reluctance! Out into the storm of event, sustained only by the commandment of God and your faith, and freedom will receive your spirit with exultation.

Dietrich Bonhoeffer (1906-1945)

(Dietrich Bonhoeffer was arrested in April 1943
for his opposition to Hitler and, after imprisonment
in Buchenwald, was hanged by the Nazis at Flossenburg
on 9th April 1945.)

Action

Life seldom gives to any man so barren a day that chances to help somebody are not plentiful. To be cheerful under difficulties, by fortitude and patience making even sick rooms holy lands; to appreciate some fine unadvertised endeavour of an unnoticed man; to display that rare virtue, magnanimity to an unfriendly person; to speak a stout word for a good cause; to be kind to the humiliated and gracious to the hurt; to touch some youth with new confidence in human goodness and with fresh resolve to live life for noble ends — such opportunities are as free as air to breathe. . . . It is not lack of opportunity or of endowment that makes us useless. It is lack of insight, thoughtfulness, sympathy, imagination, and love.

To all folk discouraged about crippled lives, this then is the message: The world is in trouble and none can help more than hearts by trouble touched to understanding. Where millions are in adversity, serviceable men taught by hardship are deeply needed.

Harry Emerson Fosdick (1878-1969)

Heavenly Father, may our abiding with Him who came into our midst take us after Him into the centre of life's problems. Grant us the freedom from self that keeps sight clear enough to recognise need wherever it exists and, having seen, to accept our responsibility for Christly action.

The Soldier's Armoury,
28th September 1969

Action

Thursday

He that loveth not his brother whom he hath seen, how can he love God whom he hath not seen?

1 John IV 20

The Christian sees the need and he has the wherewithal to meet it. He sees sickness, and he has medicine and medical training. He sees ignorance, and he has knowledge. He sees hunger and he has food. He sees poverty and he has money. He sees lack of technical know-how, and he has technical skills. The simple question is, whether we will relate what we have to what we see.

John Stott

Christ has no hands but our hands
To do His work today;
Christ has no feet but our feet
To lead men in His way;
Christ has no tongue but our tongue
To tell men how He died;
Christ has no help but our help
To bring them to His side.

Action

Christianity is not simply a message to be heard; it is a deed to be done. . . . The real way to get things done is not to care who gets the credit for doing them.

Harry Emerson Fosdick (1878-1969)

There is no limit to what a man can do, so long as he does not care a straw who gets the credit for it.

C. E. Montague (1867-1928)

While women weep as they do now, I'll fight;
while little children go hungry as they do now, I'll fight;
while men go to prison, in and out, in and out, I'll fight;
while there yet remains one dark soul without the light of God, I'll
fight — I'll fight to the very end!

Said by General William Booth in his 82nd year
at a public meeting on 9th May, 1912 at the
Albert Hall, London — his last speech.

Action

Saturday

How dull it is to make a pause, to make an end,
To rust unburnished, not to shine in use!
As though to breathe were life. Life piled on life
Were all too little, and of one to me
Little remains. . . .
Death closes all; but something ere the end,
Some work of noble note, may yet be done,
Not unbecoming men that strove with gods. . . .
Though much is taken, much abides; and though
We are not now that strength which in old days
Moved earth and heaven; that which we are, we are;
One equal temper of heroic hearts,
Made weak by time and fate, but strong in will
To strive, to seek, to find, and not to yield.

Alfred, Lord Tennyson (1809-1892)

Come, let us lay a lance in rest,
And tilt at windmills under a wild sky!
For who would live so petty and unblest
That dare not tilt at something ere he die;
Rather than, screened by safe majority,
Preserve his little life to little ends,
And never raise a rebel cry!

John Galsworthy (1867-1933)

322

Giving

Beware that thou forget not the Lord thy God, in not keeping his commandments, and his judgments, and his statutes, which I command thee this day: lest when thou hast eaten and art full, and hast built goodly houses, and dwelt therein; then thine heart be lifted up, and thou forget the Lord thy God: for it is he that giveth thee power to get wealth.

Deuteronomy VIII:11, 12, 14, 18

There is a very old Gospel called the Gospel according to the Hebrews. That Gospel may well be as old as some of our own Gospels. It never got into the New Testament; it is largely lost and only fragments remain. One of these fragments is in Origen's commentary on Matthew, and it is another version of the story of the rich young ruler. In it two rich men come to Jesus. The story runs:

> The second of the rich men said to Jesus: 'Master, what good thing must I do to have life?' 'Fulfil the commandments of the Law and the Prophets,' Jesus said to him. 'I have done so,' the rich man answered. Jesus said to him: 'Go and sell everything you have, and distribute the proceeds to the poor, and come, follow me.' The rich man began to scratch his head, for he did not like this advice at all. The Lord said to him: 'How can you say, "I have kept the Law and the Prophets"? It is written in the Law that you must love your neighbour as yourself. And in point of fact many of your brothers, sons of Abraham, are clothed in filth and are dying of hunger, and your house is packed with good things, and not a single thing goes out of it to them.'

What was wrong with the rich young man was not his possessions, but his possessiveness. He was in fact possessed by his possessions. And the only cure for him was a radical change in his approach to the whole matter of possessions, a surgical eradication of the passion of possessiveness from his life. It is not wealth that is condemned; it is a certain attitude to wealth, the attitude in which a man has become so dominated by the desire to make and to have, to hold more and more, that a Christian use of possessions has become impossible for him.

William Barclay (1907-1978)

Giving

Monday

A part of a service . . .

Leader: Let us confess our indifference to the world's need, and ask God's forgiveness.

First Voice: Forgive us, O Father, that we are so content to live comfortably while our brothers suffer poverty and hunger. Forgive us for assuming that crumbs from our table will suffice to answer their cry for justice. Forgive us,

All: and help us to turn from our selfishness.

Leader: Let us pray for the poor of the earth.

Second Voice: You have awakened us, Lord God, to the hunger of millions of our fellows while many of us eat well. Help us to see clearly what you require of us, in giving aid and in renouncing privilege; and help us not to shrink from sacrifices. Help us to help them to do what they can for themselves:

All: and enable them not to give up hope.

Leader: Let us pray for a right use of the world's resources.

Third Voice: We rejoice, Lord, that you have made the earth so rich in natural resources. We pray that we may use them considerately: not wasting them on what we do not need; not polluting soil and air and seas; not wantonly destroying the life of animals and plants.

All: Help us to hand on to others an earth as fair as we received.

Leader: Let us pray for simplicity of life.

Fourth Voice: Grant, Lord, that we may live simply, as your children should. May we enjoy your gifts, and share them gladly. Help us not to worry, but to trust you for all things:

All: through Jesus Christ our Lord. Amen.

Giving

Nothing offers so practical a test of our love for Christ or for others as does our attitude to money and possessions. Nor does anything so test our claim to be delivered from this present evil world. The attitude of the unconverted man to money is too widespread to be other than well-known. The world asks how much we own; Christ asks how we use it. The world thinks more of getting; Christ thinks more of giving. The world asks what we give, Christ asks how we give; the former thinks of the amount, the latter of the motive. Men ask how much we give; the Bible how much we keep. To the unconverted, money is a means of gratification: to the converted, a means of grace; to the one an opportunity of comfort, to the other an opportunity of consecration.

Fred Mitchell

Some of us tremble lest we are always the takers and only too rarely the givers. Somehow we don't think, or take thought, until it is too late. We fail to take thought for others in the household, because we are so very busy with our own personal concerns. And some don't wish to be givers or takers: 'We don't want to be indebted to anybody, and we don't want them to bother with us and we don't want to have to bother with them.' The money lies in the bank unused, except when we want a larger car. The drawers remain full of goods for which we have little use, the beautiful guest-rooms lie clean and spotless, the furniture retains its lovely polish, for no energetic children are ever allowed to disturb the placid beauty of the home! How useless is unused money, how pointless are unpossessed possessions! God give us grace to be proper stewards.

Michael Griffiths

Giving

Wednesday

No man is so poor as to have nothing worth giving: as well might the mountain streamlets say they have nothing to give the sea because they are not rivers. Give what you have: to some one it may be better than you dare to think.

Henry Wadsworth Longfellow (1807-1882)

A Parable of Giving

I had gone a-begging from door to door in the village path when a golden chariot appeared in the distance, and I wondered who was this King of Kings! The chariot stopped where I stood. The Master's glance fell on me. Suddenly the Master held out His hand and said "What have you got to give to me?" I was stunned. A King opening His hand to a beggar. I was confused but slowly from my wallet I took out the least little grain of corn and gave it to Him. How great my surprise when at the day's end I emptied my bag on the floor, and there I found a little grain of gold among the poor heap. I wept bitterly and wished I had the heart to have given all I had to Him.

Rabindranath Tagore (1861-1941)

Giving

Give abundantly. Feel that you are rich. Have no mean thought in your heart. Of love, of thought, of all you have, give, give, give. You are followers of the World's Greatest Giver. Give of time, of personal ease and comfort, of rest, of fame, of healing, of power, of sympathy, of all these and many more. Learn this lesson, and you will become a great power to help others and to do mighty things.

Give to all you meet, or whose lives touch yours, of your prayers, your time, yourselves, your love, your thought. You must practise *this* giving first. Then give of this world's goods and money, as you have them given to you. To give money and material things, without having first made the habit daily, hourly, ever increasingly, of giving on the higher plane, is wrong.

Give, give, give all your best to all who need it. Be great givers — great givers. Give as I said My Father in Heaven gives. He who makes His sun to shine on the evil and on the good, and sendeth rain on the just and on the unjust. Remember, as I have told you before, give according to need, never according to desert. In giving, with the thought of supplying a real need you most closely resemble that Father in Heaven, the Great Giver.

As you receive, you must supply the needs of those I bring to you. Not questioning, not limiting. Their nearness to you, their relationship, must never count. Only their need is to guide you. Pray to become great givers.

"God Calling" (A Devotional Diary)
Ed. A. J. Russell

Giving

Friday

Say, what saw you, Man?
And say, what heard?
I saw while Angels sang,
Jesus the Word.

Saw you aught else, Man?
Aught else heard you?
I saw the Son of Man,
And the wind blew.

Saw you beside, Man?
Or heard beside?
I saw, while murderers mocked,
The Crucified.

Nay! what is this, Man?
And who is He?
The Holy Child must die
For you and me.

Oh! say, Brother! Oh! say, Brother!
What then shall be?
Home in His Sacred Heart
For you and me.

Oh! what can we give, Brother!
For such a thing?
Body and soul, Brother!
To Christ the King.

Lionel Johnson (1867-1902)

Giving

There are times when to give money is not enough. To give money may be at times an evasion of a still greater responsibility. I am not one of these people who play down the generosity in giving of people with money by saying: 'It's easy to write a cheque.' It may be — but there are many who can write cheques, and who do not. Nevertheless it must be said that there is need for something beyond impersonal giving. It was said of a man who was generous with money but who stopped there: 'With all his giving, he never gave himself.' And there are times when the giving of oneself is the greatest gift of all — for that is the gift that Jesus gave to men.

William Barclay (1907-1978)

O God, who in thy Son Jesus Christ has shown to us the true meaning of life, grant that we may know that only in giving and spending ourselves do we truly live.

Anon.

Take and receive, O Lord, my entire liberty,
My memory, my understanding, my whole will;
All that I am or possess is from Thee;
To Thee do I give them back, to do with according to Thy pleasure.
Give me only love of Thee, and Thy grace, and I am rich enough,
Nor do I ask for anything beside.

St. Ignatius (799-878)

Discipleship

Sunday

But if, when ye do well, and suffer for it, ye take it patiently, this is acceptable with God. For even hereunto were ye called: because Christ also suffered for us, leaving us an example, that ye should follow his steps.

I Peter II 20-21

It is now plain to see what a man ought to mean when he calls Jesus Lord, or when he speaks of the Lord Jesus, or the Lord Jesus Christ.

When I call Jesus Lord, I ought to mean that he is the absolute and undisputed owner and possessor of my life, and that he is the Master, whose servant and slave I must be all life long.

When I call Jesus Lord, it ought to mean that I think of him as the head of that great family in heaven and in earth of which God is the Father, and of which I through him have become a member.

When I call Jesus Lord, it ought to mean that I think of him as the help of the helpless and the guardian of those who have no other to protect them.

When I call Jesus Lord, it ought to mean that I look on him as having absolute authority over all my life, all my thoughts, all my actions.

When I call Jesus Lord, it ought to mean that he is the King and Emperor to whom I owe and give my constant homage, allegiance and loyalty.

When I call Jesus Lord, it ought to mean that for me he is the Divine One whom I must for ever worship and adore.

William Barclay (1907-1978)

Discipleship

Monday

He comes to us as One unknown, without a name, as of old by the lake-side He came to those men who knew Him not. He speaks to us the same word: "Follow thou me!" and sets us to the tasks which He has to fulfil for our time. He commands. And to those who obey Him, whether they be wise or simple, He will reveal Himself in the toils, the conflicts, the sufferings which they shall pass through in His fellowship, and, as an ineffable mystery, they shall learn in their own experience Who He is.

Albert Schweitzer (1875-1965)

I said: Let me walk in the fields.
He said: Nay, walk in the town.
I said: There are no flowers there.
He said: No flowers, but a crown.

I said: But the sky is black;
There is nothing but noise and din.
But He wept as He sent me back:
There is more, He said, there is sin.

I said: But the air is thick
And fogs are veiling the sun.
He answered: Yet hearts are sick
And souls in the dark undone.

I said: I shall miss the light
And friends will want me, they say.
He answered: Choose to-night,
If I am to miss you or they.

I cast one look at the fields,
Then set my face to the town.
He said: My child, do you yield?
Will you leave the fields for a crown?

Then into His hand went mine
And into my heart came He,
And I walk in a light divine,
The path that I feared to see.

George MacDonald (1824-1905)

Discipleship

Tuesday

True discipleship to Jesus is the opposite of spasmodic conventionality. We are even wrong when we call our public worship on Sunday "church service". Church service really begins on Monday morning at seven o'clock and lasts all the week. Church service is helpfulness to people; public worship is preparation for it. For the church service which the Master illustrated and approved is a life of ministry amid the dust and din of daily business in a sacrificial conflict for a Christian world. The inevitable expression of real Christianity is a life of sacrificial service.

Harry Emerson Fosdick (1878-1969)

'Take up thy cross,' the Saviour said,
'If thou wouldst My disciple be;
Take up thy cross, with willing heart,
And humbly follow after Me.'

Take up thy cross; let not its weight
Fill thy weak soul with vain alarm;
His strength shall bear thy spirit up,
And brace thy heart, and nerve thine arm.

Take up thy cross, nor heed the shame,
And let thy foolish pride be still;
Thy Lord refused not e'en to die
Upon a Cross, on Calvary's hill.

Take up thy cross, then, in His strength,
And calmly every danger brave;
'Twill guide thee to a better home,
And lead to victory o'er the grave.

Take up thy cross, and follow Christ,
Nor think till death to lay it down;
For only he who bears the cross
May hope to wear the glorious crown.

Charles William Everest (1814-1877)

Discipleship

Thursday

To attempt to free Jesus' sayings from their relativity to the particular situation is often to blunt their edge rather than to bring out their universality.

To take an example: there is a saying reported several times in the Gospels, about "bearing the cross." Luke, intent on applying it directly to the situation of his readers, represents Jesus as saying that His follower must "take up his cross *daily* and follow me." That rendering of the saying has largely influenced its application. It has been taken to refer to habitual forms of self-sacrifice or self-denial. The ascetic voluntarily undergoing austerities felt himself to be bearing his daily cross. We shallower folk have often reduced it to a metaphor for casual unpleasantnesses which we have to bear. A neuralgia or a defaulting servant is our "cross", and we make a virtue of necessity. What Jesus actually said, according to our earliest evidence, was, quite bluntly, "Whoever wants to follow me must shoulder his gallows-beam" — for such is perhaps the most significant rendering of the word for "cross". It means a beam which a condemned criminal carried to the place of execution, to which he was then nailed until he died. Jesus was not using the term metaphorically. Under Rome, crucifixion was the likeliest fate for those who defied the established powers. Nor did those who heard understand that He was asking for "daily" habits of austerity. He was enrolling volunteers for a desperate venture, and He wished them to understand that in joining it they must hold their lives forfeit. To march behind Him on that journey was as good as to tie a halter round one's neck. It was a saying for an emergency. A similar emergency may arise for some Christians in any age. In such a situation it is immediately applicable, in its original form and meaning. For most of us, in normal situations, it is not so applicable. But it is surely good for us to go back and understand that this is what Christ stood for in His day. We shall then at least not suppose that we are meeting His demands in our day by bearing a toothache bravely or fasting during Lent.

C. H. Dodd (1884-1973)

334

Discipleship

Another group of people talks about martyrdom and persecution on an ultra-personal level. When things don't go right for them in their personal lives they tend to identify themselves with the suffering of Jesus Christ. If there is financial failure or some deep anxiety over their domestic affairs they quickly invoke the name of the Lord for self-protection.

Christ had none of these things in mind when he spoke of knowing the hatred of the world.

The words of Jesus about 'being hated' can only be fully understood when there is an involvement for humanity's sake in a specific situation. The very qualification for martyrdom rests on the purity of our motives. Our motives must be absolutely devoid of all self-seeking. Our love for the world must be an absolute love based on our Christ-like compassion. Jesus is warning us as he speaks of persecution that the world will misunderstand and misconstrue and deliberately misinterpret our motives. This is because most men and women impute to others their own standards of values. The spiritual concepts of Jesus Christ are so far beyond them that they find it impossible to believe that human beings can be unconditionally committed for others. As a result, many people become infuriated at the sight of the folly of Christians. Christians are accused of being 'naive', 'puppets' and 'too idealistic'. When phrases like these fail to weaken the Christian position, then the hatred of men may take a physical form. It should not be imagined that the German martyrs who died in Nazi prison camps will be the only Christians in this century to know the deadliness of the attack from people who repudiate Christianity because it is dangerously offensive.

The Christian today must walk the razor's edge between acceptance on the one hand and rejection on the other. Because of his association with the world he will earn the abuse of those who call themselves religious. But by virtue of the fact that whatever the Christian does in the name of religion, he will also earn the condemnation of the world. Contrary to what most people think, involvement with the world and its travail does not lead to back-slapping pleasantries. It leads to 'hell'.

Ted Noffs

Discipleship

Saturday

Doctrines, however venerable, which cannot be put into action in the work-a-day world can safely be left in the care of the technical theologians who will preserve them in an atmosphere as cold as a refrigerator.

The worship of men and women spending themselves in compassionate action would have an air more of desperation than formality. They would stagger into church utterly drained of goodness, unable to face another day unless their numbed spirits were re-sensitized and their strength renewed. They would be too hoarse to sing, too stiff to kneel and too dog-tired to take in any long exhortations from the pulpit. They would await the reading of the Lesson with something akin to dread as God presented them with yet more impossible demands. Every false word in the service would stick out like a sore thumb and pretentiously ornate language would be heard no more. Instead, they would gasp out a simple litany exposing the horror and pain and misery they had shared, asking God to show them Jesus in it.

In this context, the most familiar truth would scorch. They would gulp the bread of Communion like starving men and reach out for the wine with the trembling hand of an alcoholic. What they knew about Crucifixion they would learn from the back streets of their town rather than the hymns of Charles Wesley. And they would not casually go through the motions of a ritual expectation of Resurrection on that first day of the week. There would be a heart-stopping suspense as the service progressed. Would they really find a Risen Lord at work in the heart of the tragic mess to which they would have to return? But would He accept a concrete deed as His due in place of a spiritualized devotion they could not affect?

Colin Morris

Self-giving

O Lord, let me not henceforth desire health or life, except to spend them for Thee, with Thee, and in Thee. Thou alone knowest what is good for me; do, therefore, what seemeth Thee best. Give to me, or take from me; conform my will to Thine; and grant that, with humble and perfect submission, and in holy confidence, I may receive the orders of Thine eternal Providence; and may equally adore all that comes to me from Thee; through Jesus Christ our Lord. Amen.

Blaise Pascal (1623-1662)

An Address
Presented by a Hundred and Sixty-Four Friends
to the House of Commons in 1659:

Friends, who are called a Parliament of these Nations:

We in love to our brethren that lie in prisons, and houses of correction, and dungeons, and many in fetters and irons, and have been cruelly beat by the cruel gaolers, and many have been persecuted to death, and have died in prison, and many lie sick and weak in prison, and on straw: so we in love to our brethren do offer up our bodies and selves to you, for to put us as lambs into the same dungeons, and houses of correction, and their straw, and nasty holes, and prisons; and do stand ready a sacrifice for to go into their places in love to our brethren, that they may go forth, and that they may not die in prison, as many of the brethren are dead already; for we are willing to lay down our lives for our brethren, and to take their sufferings upon us, which you would inflict upon them. For if our brethren suffer, we cannot but feel it. This is our love towards God and Christ, and our brethren, that we owe to them and our enemies, who are lovers of all your souls and your eternal good.

(The appeal did not succeed. Shortly afterwards, however, the House appointed a committee "to consider of the imprisonment of such persons who continue committed for conscience sake, and how and in what manner they are and continue committed, together with the whole cause thereof, and how they may be discharged; and to report the same to Parliament.")

Self-giving

Monday
Paul Schneider — German Pastor

From the very beginning Paul Schneider opposed National Socialism. Pastor of the two small parishes of Dickenschied and Womrath, he could not preach the Word without living it; he could not countenance the use of the lie as a political force — he called it by its name, and as a result he forfeited his life. Although he foresaw the only possible outcome, and although his love for wife and children went to the very depths of his being, he could not shirk denouncing openly the evil which he saw. The path he chose to follow led, in October 1937, to Buchenwald.

A fellow prisoner, Alfred Leikam, a lawyer, wrote in retrospect: 'In the spring of 1938 there was an order that all prisoners passing by the Nazi flag on their march to work should greet it by taking off their caps. Schneider declared that this saluting of the Nazi flag was idolatry and he refused to obey the order. One who envied him, or perhaps had a grudge against him, informed the authorities and he was charged with refusal to obey a command. Then began Paul Schneider's lone path of suffering. He was called to the SS and freely confessed his attitude. At first he received twenty-five lashes and was then put into the dark cell. This meant solitary confinement and he remained in this cell till his death. There he told the SS exactly what the Christian attitude to Nazism was. He spoke freely and without fear. There was probably no other man in Germany who denounced the regime so fearlessly. All the ingenuity of Nazi sadism was used against him. . . . The worst time for him was in the early summer of 1939. For several days he was hung up, with his hands behind him and his body permanently bent. This devilish device caused him continuous pain. His suffering was borne nobly and he was greatly honoured in the camp. We saw in him the meaning of the words: "My bonds in Christ are manifest in all the palace".'

Despite the terrible torment and the breakdown of his physical strength, Pastor Schneider brought consolation to his fellow prisoners and, as many of them acknowledged later, rescue from despair. Finally a camp doctor murdered him with an overdose of strophantin. He died on July 18, 1939.

The story of Paul Schneider is the record of a man who fought Nazism for no other reason than that he could not disobey Christ.

Self-giving

Mother Teresa's Way of Love

On Kindness

Be kind and merciful. Let no one ever come to you without coming away better and happier. Be the living expression of God's kindness: kindness in your face, kindness in your eyes, kindness in your smile, kindness in your warm greeting. In the slums we are the light of God's kindness to the poor. To children, to the poor, to all who suffer and are lonely, give always a happy smile. Give them not only your care, but also your heart.

Apostle of the Unwanted

The biggest disease today is not leprosy or tuberculosis, but rather the feeling of being unwanted, uncared for and deserted by everybody. The greatest evil is the lack of love and charity, the terrible indifference towards one's neighbour who lives at the roadside assaulted by exploitation, corruption, poverty and disease.

As each one of this Society is to become a Co-worker of Christ in the slums, each ought to understand what God and the Society expect from her. Let Christ radiate and live his life in her and through her in the slums. Let the poor seeing her be drawn to Christ and invite him to enter their homes and their lives. Let the sick and suffering find in her a real angel of comfort and consolation, let the little ones of the streets cling to her because she reminds them of him, the friend of the little ones.

Our life of poverty is as necessary as the work itself.

Only in heaven we will see how much we owe to the poor for helping us to love God better because of them.

Malcolm Muggeridge

Self-giving

Wednesday

The Japanese wounded were in a shocking state; I have never seen men filthier. Their uniforms were encrusted with mud, blood and excrement. Their wounds, sorely inflamed and full of pus, crawled with maggots.

Without a word, most of the officers in my section unbuckled their packs, took out part of their ration and a rag or two, and, with water canteens in their hands, went over to the Japanese train to help them. Our guards tried to prevent us, bawling, "No goodka! No goodka!" But we ignored them and knelt by the side of the enemy to give them food and water, to clean and bind up their wounds, to smile and say a kind word. Grateful cries of "Aragatto!" ("Thank you!") followed us when we left.

An Allied officer from another section of the train had been taking it all in. "What bloody fools you all are!" he said to me. "Don't you realise that those are the enemy?" . . . He gave me a scornful glance and, turning his back, left me to my thoughts.

I regarded my comrades with wonder. Eighteen months ago they would have joined readily in the destruction of our captors had they fallen into their hands. Now these same men were dressing the enemy's wounds. We had experienced a moment of grace, there in those blood-stained railway cars. God had broken through the barriers of our prejudice and had given us the will to obey His command, "Thou shalt love." . . .

Our experience of life in death had taught us that the way to life leads through death. To see Jesus was to see in Him that love which is the very highest form of life, that love which has sacrifice as the logical end of its action. To hang on to life, to guard it jealously, to preserve it, is to end up by burying it. . . .

We were beginning to understand that as there were no easy ways for God, so there were no easy ways for us. God, we saw, was honouring us by allowing us to share in His labours, aye, in His agony — for the world He loves. God, in finding us, had enabled us to find our brother.

Ernest Gordon

Self-giving

The Rev. David Wilkerson, leader of "Teen Challenge", an organisation concerned with helping teenage gang members and drug addicts in New York, tells of his search for a suitable girl for the staff of his Centre — to work with the female gang members or "Debs", themselves accustomed to carrying knives and frequently narcotics addicts and prostitutes. "What we needed was a girl who was attractive enough to gain the Debs' respect and yet who was solid enough in her own faith not to be shaken by their taunting or laughter. And we finally found her."

After Linda Meisner had had her first introduction to her future "clients", she turned in despair to Wilkerson. 'It's hopeless, David. I don't see how I can ever work with kids as hard as these.' His answer: 'Wait till you see what the Holy Spirit can do.'

From then on Linda's life was in constant danger. "Our young students," writes Wilkerson, "are walking into areas where armed officers of the law travel in pairs for protection. If a boy is high on heroin he might easily lash out with his knife, just for kicks. But a much more serious problem is the jealousy that is aroused when our workers threaten to break up relationships." Linda learned to face these dangers in the strength of the Holy Spirit, rewarded when occasionally some of the most hardened and depraved Debs were won for Christ. Once when she and her partner, Kay Ware, were talking to some of the girls in the street, two boys walked up and accused them of trying to take the girls away from them. Menacingly they were pushed and taunted.

"From nowhere something glistened in the dark. Linda looked. One of the boys held a crescent-shaped knife in his hand that shone in the night like the moon. Without warning he lunged at Linda. Linda slipped her body sideways. The knife ripped out a chunk of her dress but it did not touch her body. She turned to the boy while he was still off balance and spoke the words that had helped her before, putting all the meaning she could into them: 'God bless you.' Then she took Kay by the arm. 'Come over to the Centre tomorrow: 416 Clinton Avenue,' she said. 'We'll be expecting you.' Then she and Kay sauntered off across the street."

Much later she could write home to her parents in Iowa: 'You can actually feel the presence of evil. I know that my life is in danger, I have only one desire — to burn out for God.'

David Wilkerson

Self-giving

Friday

Real Christian ethics are not based on doing to others as you wish to be done by, handy as that rule may be. Christian ethics are powered by the love of Christ and are built on this one foundation — loving as He loved. He loved in such a way that He came into this world in total humanity and total vulnerability. This is what the word incarnation means, and this is how Christ loves. He is part and parcel of a working class family in a small village although being king of the universe. That is how Christ loves. He identifies Himself with men and women, who are the off-scourings of the city of Jerusalem and the region round about, in the scandal of public baptism, although being the one person in all the world who did not need to confess any sin. As John the Baptist noticed, that is how Christ loves. He is thronged day and night, men beg and beseech Him for His help, He has not enough time to eat nor even to pray. He saw the multitude and had compassion on them for they were as sheep without a shepherd and He gave Himself to them in total self-giving. That is how Christ loves. He endures the disgrace of arrest and crooked trial. He suffers the arrogance of men's tongues and the horseplay of crude soldiers' games; He undergoes the torture of a lash that bit to the bone and left the prisoner's back a wet lump of bleeding flesh. That is how Christ loves. He stretches out His hands and feet and through them are driven great nails; the cross is lifted up and dropped into the socket dug for it, He dies in agony. That is how Christ loves. He experiences the separation which only sinners can know, goes out into the darkness forsaken and derelict. That is how Christ loves. He surrenders Himself completely into the Father's hands and yields up His spirit, His remains to be laid in a borrowed grave. That is how Christ loves. He is dead and buried, He rises before the awestruck gaze of the angels and all of heaven's hosts and comes to a woman in her grief, to a man in his guilty conscience, to a group of men ashamed of their cowardice. That is how Christ loves.

Frank Cooke

Self-giving

This evening, Lord, I am afraid.
I am afraid, for your Gospel is terrible.
It is easy to hear it preached,
It is relatively easy not to be shocked by it,
But it is very difficult to live it.
I am afraid of deluding myself, Lord;
I am afraid of being satisfied with my decent little life;
I am afraid of my good habits, for I take them for virtues;
I am afraid of my little efforts, for I take them for progress;
I am afraid of my activities; they make me think I am giving myself;
I am afraid of my clever planning; I take it for success;
I am afraid of my influence; I imagine that it will transform lives;
I am afraid of what I give; it hides what I withhold;
I am afraid, Lord; there are people who are poorer than I;
Not so well educated,
         housed,
         heated,
         fed,
         cared for,
         loved.
I am afraid, Lord, for I do not do enough for them,
I do not do everything for them.

I should give everything,
I should give everything till there is not a single pain,
  a single misery, a single sin in the world.
I should then give all, Lord, all the time.
I should give my life.

Lord, it is not true, is it?
It is not true for everyone,
I am exaggerating, I must be sensible!

Son, there is only **one** commandment,
For **everyone:**
You shall love with **all** your heart,
        with **all** your soul,
        with **all** your strength.

Michel Quoist

Dedication

Sunday

In the year that King Uzziah died I saw also the Lord sitting upon a throne, high and lifted up, and his train filled the temple.

Above it stood the seraphims: each one had six wings; with twain he covered his face, and with twain he covered his feet, and with twain he did fly.

And one cried unto another, and said, Holy, holy, holy, is the Lord of hosts: the whole earth is full of his glory.

And the posts of the door moved at the voice of him that cried, and the house was filled with smoke.

Then said I, Woe is me! for I am undone; because I am a man of unclean lips, and I dwell in the midst of a people of unclean lips: for mine eyes have seen the King, the Lord of hosts.

Then flew one of the seraphims unto me, having a live coal in his hand, which he had taken with the tongs from off the altar:

And he laid it upon my mouth, and said, Lo, this hath touched thy lips; and thine iniquity is taken away, and thy sin purged.

Also I heard the voice of the Lord saying, Whom shall I send, and who will go for us? Then said I, Here am I; send me.

Isaiah VI 1-8

Dedication

The Unutterable Beauty

God, give me speech, in mercy touch my lips,
I cannot bear Thy Beauty and be still,
Watching the red-gold majesty that tips
The crest of yonder hill,
And out to sea smites on the sails of ships,

That flame like drifting stars across the deep,
Calling their silver comrades from the sky,
As long and ever longer shadows creep,
To sing their lullaby,
And hush the tired eyes of earth to sleep.

Thy radiancy of glory strikes me dumb,
Yet cries within my soul for power to raise
Such miracles of music as would sum
Thy splendour in a phrase,
Storing it safe for all the years to come.

O God, Who givest songs too sweet to sing,
Have mercy on Thy servant's feeble tongue,
In sacrificial silence sorrowing,
And grant that songs unsung,
Accepted at Thy mercy-seat, may bring

New light into the darkness of sad eyes,
New tenderness to stay the stream of tears,
New rainbows from the sunshine of surpise,
To guide men down the years,
Until they cross the last long bridge of sighs.

G. A. Studdert Kennedy (1883-1929)

You must live a life of communion and prayer if you are to save others.
Take My words as a command to you. "By prayer and fasting.".
Pray and deny yourself, and you will be used marvellously to save and help
others.

"God Calling" August 31
Ed. A. J. Russell

345

Dedication

Tuesday

Lord, make me an instrument of Thy peace. Where there is hatred, let me sow love. Where there is injury, pardon. Where there is doubt, faith. Where there is despair, hope. Where there is darkness, light. Where there is sadness, joy. O Divine Master, grant that I may not so much seek to be consoled as to console; to be understood, as to understand; to be loved, as to love; for it is in giving that we receive, it is in pardoning that we are pardoned, and it is in dying that we are born to Eternal Life. Amen.

St. Francis of Assisi (1182-1226)

May the mind of Christ my Saviour
Live in me from day to day,
By his love and power controlling
All I do or say.

May the word of God dwell richly
In my heart from hour to hour,
So that all may see I triumph
Only through his power.

May the peace of God my Father
Rule my life in everything,
That I may be calm to comfort
Sick and sorrowing.

May the love of Jesus fill me,
As the waters fill the sea;
Him exalting, self abasing,
This is victory.

May I run the race before me,
Strong and brave to face the foe,
Looking only unto Jesus
As I onward go.

Kate Barclay Wilkinson (1859-1928)

346

Dedication

This is my prayer to thee, my Lord — strike, strike at the root of penury in my heart.

Give me the strength lightly to bear my joys and sorrows.

Give me the strength to make my love fruitful in service.

Give me the strength never to disown the poor or bend my knees before insolent might.

Give me the strength to raise my mind high above daily trifles.

And give me the strength to surrender my strength to thy will with love.

Rabindranath Tagore (1861-1941)

Spirit of God, descend upon my heart;
Wean it from earth; through all its pulses move;
Stoop to my weakness, mighty as Thou art,
And make me love Thee as I ought to love.

I ask no dream, no prophet-ecstasies,
No sudden rending of the veil of clay,
No angel-visitant, no opening skies;
But take the dimness of my soul away.

Hast Thou not bid me love Thee, God and King —
All, all Thine own, soul, heart, and strength, and mind?
I see Thy Cross — there teach my heart to cling;
O let me seek Thee, and O let me find!

Teach me to feel that Thou art always nigh;
Teach me the struggles of the soul to bear,
To check the rising doubt, the rebel sigh;
Teach me the patience of unanswered prayer.

Teach me to love Thee as Thine angels love,
One holy passion filling all my frame —
The baptism of the heaven-descended Dove,
My heart an altar, and Thy love the flame.

George Croly (1780-1860)

Dedication

Thursday

Whose service is perfect freedom.

The Book of Common Prayer.

Make me a captive, Lord,
And then I shall be free;
Force me to render up my sword,
And I shall conqueror be.
I sink in life's alarms
When by myself I stand;
Imprison me within Thine arms,
And strong shall be my hand.

My heart is weak and poor
Until it master find;
It has no spring of action sure —
It varies with the wind.
It cannot freely move,
Till Thou hast wrought its chain;
Enslave it with Thy matchless love,
And deathless it shall reign.

My power is faint and low
Till I have learned to serve;
It wants the needed fire to glow,
It wants the breeze to nerve;
It cannot drive the world,
Until itself be driven;
Its flag can only be unfurled
When Thou shalt breathe from heaven.

My will is not my own
Till Thou hast made it Thine;
If it would reach a monarch's throne
It must its crown resign;
It only stands unbent,
Amid the clashing strife,
When on Thy bosom it has leant
And found in Thee its life.

George Matheson (1842-1906)

Dedication

God be in my head, and in my understanding;
God be in mine eyes, and in my looking;
God be in my mouth, and in my speaking;
God be in my heart, and in my thinking;
God be at mine end, and at my departing

Book of Hours (London, 1514)

Be Thou my vision, O Lord of my heart;
Naught be all else to me, save that Thou art —
Thou my best thought, by day or by night,
Waking or sleeping, Thy presence my light.

Be Thou my wisdom, Thou my true Word;
I ever with Thee, Thou with me, Lord;
Thou my great Father, I Thy true son;
Thou in me dwelling, and I with Thee one.

Be Thou my battle-shield, sword for the fight,
Be Thou my dignity, Thou my delight.
Thou my soul's shelter, Thou my high tower;
Raise Thou me heavnward, O Power of my power.

Riches I heed not, nor man's empty praise,
Thou mine inheritance, now and always;
Thou and Thou only, first in my heart,
High King of Heaven, my treasure Thou art.

High King of Heaven, after victory won,
May I reach heaven's joys, O bright heaven's Sun!
Heart of my own heart, whatever befall,
Still be my Vision, O Ruler of all.

Ancient Irish tr. by Mary Byrne (1880-1931);
versified by Eleanor Hull (1860-1935)

349

Dedication

Saturday

I have learned, in whatsoever state I am, therewith to be content. I know both how to be abased, and I know how to abound. . . . I can do all things through Christ which strengtheneth me.

Philippians IV 11-13

The Methodist Covenant with God:

I am no longer my own, but Thine. Put me to what Thou wilt, rank me with whom Thou wilt; put me to doing, put me to suffering; let me be employed for Thee or laid aside for Thee, exalted for Thee or brought low for Thee; Let me be full, let me be empty; let me have all things, let me have nothing; I freely and heartily yield all things to Thy pleasure and disposal.

And now, O glorious and blessed God, Father, Son and Holy Spirit, Thou art mine, and I am Thine. So be it. And the Covenant which I have made on earth, let it be ratified in heaven. Amen.

Communion

It was before the Passover festival. Jesus knew that his hour had come and he must leave this world and go to the Father. He had always loved his own who were in the world, and now he was to show the full extent of his love.

The devil had already put it into the mind of Judas son of Simon Iscariot to betray him. During supper, Jesus, well aware that the Father had entrusted everything to him, and that he had come from God and was going back to God, rose from table, laid aside his garments, and taking a towel, tied it round him. Then he poured water into a basin, and began to wash his disciples' feet and to wipe them with the towel.

When it was Simon Peter's turn, Peter said to him, 'You, Lord, washing my feet?' Jesus replied, 'You do not understand now what I am doing, but one day you will.' Peter said, 'I will never let you wash my feet.' 'If I do not wash you,' Jesus replied, 'you are not in fellowship with me.' 'Then, Lord,' said Simon Peter, 'not my feet only; wash my hands and head as well!'

Jesus said, 'A man who has bathed needs no further washing; he is altogether clean; and you are clean, though not every one of you.' He added the words 'not every one of you' because he knew who was going to betray him.

After washing their feet and taking his garments again, he sat down. 'Do you understand,' he asked, 'what I have done for you? You call me "Master" and "Lord", and rightly so, for that is what I am. Then if I, your Lord and Master, have washed your feet, you also ought to wash one another's feet. I have set you an example: you are to do as I have done for you.'

John XIII 1-15
(New English Bible)

Communion

Monday

Who shall ascend into the hill of the Lord? Or who shall stand in his holy place?

He that hath clean hands, and a pure heart; who hath not lifted up his soul unto vanity, nor sworn deceitfully.

He shall receive the blessing from the Lord, and righteousness from the God of his salvation.

Ye gates, lift up your heads on high;
ye doors that last for aye,
Be lifted up, that so the King
of glory enter may.
But who of glory is the King?
The mighty Lord is this;
Ev'n that same Lord, that great in might
and strong in battle is.

Ye gates, lift up your heads; ye doors,
doors that do last for aye,
Be lifted up, that so the King
of glory enter may.
But who is he that is the King
of glory? who is this?
The Lord of hosts, and none but he,
the King of glory is.

Psalm XXIV 3-5 and 7-10

Come in weakness; find strength.
Come in sickness; find health.
Come in chains; find freedom.
Come in confusion; find peace.
Come in sorrow; find joy.
Come in doubt; find faith.
Come in despair; find courage.

Come unready,
Come alone;
Find Christ.

From 'More Contemporary Prayers'
edited by Caryl Micklem

Communion

The Saviour of the world took bread.

Here, O my Lord, I see thee face to face;
Here would I touch and handle things unseen,
Here grasp with firmer hand the eternal grace,
And all my weariness upon thee lean.

Mine is the sin, but thine the righteousness;
Mine is the guilt, but thine the cleansing blood;
Here is my robe, my refuge, and my peace —
Thy blood, thy righteousness, O Lord my God.

Here would I feed upon the bread of God,
Here drink with thee the royal wine of heaven;
Here would I lay aside each earthly load,
Here taste afresh the calm of sin forgiven.

Horatius Bonar (1808-1889)

Jesus, Thou Joy of loving hearts,
Thou Fount of life, Thou Light of men,
From the best bliss that earth imparts
We turn unfilled to Thee again.

Thy truth unchanged hath ever stood;
Thou savest those that on Thee call;
To them that seek Thee Thou art good,
To them that find Thee, all in all.

We taste Thee, O Thou living Bread,
And long to feast upon Thee still;
We drink of Thee, the Fountain-head,
And thirst our souls from Thee to fill.

Our restless spirits yearn for Thee,
Where'er our changeful lot is cast —
Glad when Thy gracious smile we see,
Blest when our faith can hold Thee fast.

O Jesus, ever with us stay;
Make all our moments calm and bright;
Chase the dark night of sin away;
Shed o'er the World Thy holy light.

Attributed to St. Bernard of Clairvaux (1091-1153)
Tr. by Ray Palmer (1808-1887)

Communion

Wednesday

O taste and see that the Lord is good:
blessed is the man that trusteth in him.

Psalm XXXIV 8

According to Thy gracious word,
In meek humility,
This will I do, my dying Lord,
I will remember Thee.

Thy body, broken for my sake,
My bread from heaven shall be;
Thy testamental cup I take,
And thus remember Thee.

Gethsemane can I forget?
Or there Thy conflict see,
Thine agony and bloody sweat,
And not remember Thee?

When to the Cross I turn mine eyes,
And rest on Calvary,
O Lamb of God, my sacrifice,
I must remember Thee —

Remember Thee, and all Thy pains,
And all Thy love to me;
Yea, while a breath, a pulse remains,
Will I remember Thee.

And when these failing lips grow dumb,
And mind and memory flee,
When Thou shalt in Thy Kingdom come,
Jesus, remember me.

James Montgomery (1771-1854)

Communion

O Thou whose eternal love for our weak and struggling race was most perfectly shown forth in the blessed life and death of Jesus Christ our Lord, enable me now so to meditate upon my Lord's passion that, having fellowship with Him in His sorrow, I may also learn the secret of His strength and peace.

I remember Gethsemane:
I remember how Judas betrayed Him:
I remember how Peter denied Him:
I remember how they all forsook Him and fled:
I remember the scourging:
I remember the crown of thorns:
I remember how they spat upon Him:
I remember how they smote Him on the head with a reed:
I remember His pierced hands and feet:
I remember His agony on the Cross:
I remember His thirst:
I remember how He cried, My God, My God, why hast Thou forsaken me?

We may not know, we cannot tell,
What pains He had to bear;
But we believe it was for us
He hung and suffered there.

Grant, O most gracious God, that I who now kneel before Thee may be embraced in the great company of those to whom life and salvation have come through the Cross of Christ. Let the redeeming power that has flowed from His sufferings through so many generations flow now into my soul. Here let me find forgiveness of sin. Here let me learn to share with Christ the burden of the suffering of the world. Amen.

John Baillie (1886-1961)

Communion

Friday

Come down, O Love Divine,
Seek Thou this soul of mine,
And visit it with Thine own ardour glowing;
O Comforter, draw near,
Within my heart appear,
And kindle it, Thy holy flame bestowing.

O let it freely burn,
Till earthly passions turn
To dust and ashes, in its heat consuming;
And let Thy glorious light
Shine ever on my sight,
And clothe me round, the while my path illuming.

Let holy charity
Mine outward vesture be,
And lowliness become mine inner clothing;
True lowliness of heart,
Which takes the humbler part,
And o'er its own shortcomings weeps with loathing.

And so the yearning strong,
With which the soul will long,
Shall far outpass the power of human telling;
For none can guess its grace,
Till he become the place
Wherein the Holy Spirit makes His dwelling.

Bianco da Siena (? -1434)
tr. by Richard Frederick Littledale (1833-1890)

Communion

Feast after feast thus comes and passes by,
Yet, passing, points to the glad feast above,
Giving sweet foretaste of the festal joy,
The Lamb's great bridal feast of bliss and love.

Horatius Bonar (1808-1889)

Come in, O come! The door stands open now;
I knew Thy voice; Lord Jesus, it was Thou.
The sun has set long since; the storms begin:
'Tis time for Thee, my Saviour; O come in!

I seek no more to alter things, or mend,
Before the coming of so great a Friend:
All were at best unseemly; and 'twere ill,
Beyond all else, to keep Thee waiting still.

Then, as Thou art, all holiness and bliss,
Come in, and see my dwelling as it is;
I bid Thee welcome boldly, in the name
Of Thy great glory and my want and shame.

Come, not to find, but make, this troubled heart
A dwelling worthy of Thee as Thou art;
To chase the gloom, the terror, and the sin,
Come, all Thyself, yea come, Lord Jesus, in!

Handley C. G. Moule (1841-1920)

Thou hast given so much to us, give one thing more,
a grateful heart; for Christ's sake. Amen.

George Herbert (1593-1632)

Blessing

Sunday

Iona

O ye angels of the Lord, bless ye the Lord, praise Him and
  magnify Him for ever.
O ye Saints of the Isles, bless ye the Lord.
O ye Servants of Christ who here sang God's praises and hence
  went forth to preach, bless ye the Lord.
O ye souls of the faithful, who rest in Jesus,
O ye kindly folk of the Island,
O ye pilgrims who seek joy and health in this beloved Isle, bless
  ye the Lord.
O ye sheep and hornèd cattle,
O ye lambs that gambol on the sward,
O ye seals that glisten in the waters, bless ye the Lord.
O ye ravens and hoodies,
O ye rooks that caw from the sycamores,
O ye buzzards that float on the wind-currents, bless ye the Lord.
O ye gulls that fill the beaches with your clamour,
O ye terns and gannets that dive headlong for your prey,
O ye curlews and corncrakes,
O ye pied shelduck and Bride's ghillies,
O ye dunlins that wheel in unison over the waves, bless ye the
  Lord.
O ye larks that carol in the heavens,
O ye blackbirds that pipe at the dawning,
O ye pipits and wheatears,
O ye warblers and wrens that make the glens joyful with song,
O ye bees that love the heather, bless ye the Lord.
O ye primroses and bluebells,
O ye flowers that gem the marsh with colour,
O ye golden flags that deck Columba's Bay with glory, bless ye
  the Lord.
O ye piled rocks fashioned by Nature's might thro' myriad ages,
O ye majestic Bens of Mull,
O ye white sands and emerald shallows,
O ye blue and purple deeps of ocean,
O ye winds and clouds, bless ye the Lord.
O all ye works of the Lord, bless ye the Lord, praise Him and
  magnify Him for ever.

E. D. Sedding, Ascension Day, 1947

Blessing

Let him walk in the gloom whoso will:
peace be with him, but whence is his right
To declare that the world is in darkness,
because he has turned from the light,
Or to seek to o'ershadow my day with the pall
of his self-chosen night?

"Yea, I know!" cried the true man of old;
and whosoe'er wills it, may know,
"My Redeemer — He liveth!" I seek for a sign
of His presence, and lo,
As He spake to the light and it was,
so He speaks to my soul — and I know!

Solomon Solis-Cohen

Bless the Lord, O my soul: and all that is within me, bless his holy name.
Bless the Lord, O my soul, and forget not all his benefits.

Psalm 103 1-2

Blessing

Tuesday

O God, save us from offering unto Thee any prayer which we are not prepared that Thou shouldest answer. Save us from praying to know Thy will unless we are prepared to do it. Save us from praying to see Thy face unless we are prepared that the vision should burn all the self out of us and make us let go our hateful little sins. Save us from asking for world vision, till we are ready to face world responsibilities. Save us from asking that we may follow Christ, without counting His lonely way, His utter sacrifice, His broken heart.

Take us very quietly each one and shut us in with Thyself. It may be Thou art going to ask one of us to step right out to world adventure. It may be Thou art going to ask a harder thing; that we should see all the need of the world and long to serve it in far-off lands, and yet stay just where we are. Only show us Thy will, and make us want to do it more than anything else in the world, and in that doing, find life. We ask it for the honour of Jesus Christ our Lord. Amen.

Leslie D. Weatherhead (1893-1976)

Teach us, good Lord, to serve Thee as Thou deservest; to give and not to count the cost; to fight and not to heed the wounds; to toil and not to seek for rest; to labour and not to ask for any reward, save that of knowing that we do Thy will; through Jesus Christ our Lord. Amen.

Ignatius Loyola (1491-1556)

Blessing

Almighty and merciful God, to Whom the light and the darkness are both alike, and without Whom nothing befalls Thy children, strengthen us to meet all the experiences of life with a steadfast and undaunted heart, help us to go on our way bravely whether it be rough or smooth, and when the mists hide Thy face, to continue patiently till they are dispersed by the Sun of Thy unchanging love, through Jesus Christ our Lord. Amen.

Of Thy goodness, give us;
with Thy love, inspire us;
by Thy spirit, guide us;
by Thy power, protect us;
in Thy mercy, receive us now and always.
Amen.

An Ancient Collect

Expect great things from God,
attempt great things for God.

Blessing

Thursday

O Lord Jesus Christ, Who art the Way, the Truth, and the Life, we pray Thee suffer us not to stray from Thee, Who art the Way, nor to distrust Thee, Who art the Truth, nor to rest in any other thing than Thee, Who art the Life. Teach us by Thy Holy Spirit what to believe, what to do, and wherein to take our rest. For Thine own name's sake we ask it. Amen.

Desiderius Erasmus (1467-1536)

Go forth into the world in peace; be of good courage; hold fast that which is good; render to no man evil for evil; strengthen the faint-hearted; support the weak; help the afflicted; honour all men; love and serve the Lord; rejoicing in the power of the Holy Spirit. Amen.

Revised Prayer Book, 1928

Blessing

O Christ, our only Saviour, so dwell within us that we may go forth with the light of hope in our eyes, and the fire of inspiration on our lips, Thy Word on our tongue, and Thy love in our hearts. Amen.

Source unknown

Finally, brethren, whatsoever things are true, whatsoever things are honest, whatsoever things are just, whatsoever things are pure, whatsoever things are lovely, whatsoever things are of good report; if there be any virtue, and if there be any praise, think on these things. . . . and the God of peace shall be with you.

Philippians IV 8-9

Blessing

The Lord shall keep thy soul; he shall
preserve thee from all ill.
Henceforth thy going out and in
God keep for ever will.

Psalm 121 7-8

*All shall be well, and all shall be well
and all manner of thing shall be well.*

Lady Julian of Norwich (1342-1443)

Now unto him that is able to keep you from falling, and to present you
faultless before the presence of his glory with exceeding joy,
To the only wise God our Saviour, be glory and majesty, dominion and
power, both now and ever. Amen.

Jude vv 24-25

Acknowledgements

The author has made every effort to ensure that no copyright has been infringed in the use of the passages quoted, and grateful thanks are due to those in the following list who have readily granted permission. Unfortunately it has not been possible to trace the sources of some of the poems and prose passages; for these omissions pardon is sought and sincere apology made.

Messrs. George Allen & Unwin Ltd. for quotation from *Barnardo of Stepney* by A. E. Williams and poem *Is It Nothing to You* by May Probyn.

Messrs. W. H. Allen & Co. Plc. for quotation from *In God's Underworld* by Richard Wurmbrand.

Quotations excerpted from *The Power to Heal* by Francis MacNutt, copyright © 1977, and from *Healing Prayer* by Barbara Leahy Shlemon, copyright © 1976, both by Ave Maria Press, Notre Dame, Indiana 46556, USA. All rights reserved. Used with permission of the publisher.

Passages from Ecclesiastes from the *Good News Bible,* published by the Bible Societies and Collins, © American Bible Society 1976, and reproduced by permission.

Dlia pol'zy Dela, world copyright © 1970 Alexander Solzhenitsyn. Reprinted by permission of The Bodley Head from *Stories and Prose Poems.*

Astronaut Frank Borman, Apollo 8 commander, for inclusion of his prayer, broadcast as his spacecraft orbited the moon on Christmas Eve, 1968.

The Publishing Manager of the British Medical Journal and Mrs. Jean Kent for article by the late Dr. Philip Kent.

Sir Laurens van der Post and Messrs. Chatto & Windus Ltd. for extract from the former's *A Far Off Place.*

Messrs. T. & T. Clark Ltd. for extracts from *No Uncertain Sound* by R. Leonard Small; also from *The Strong Name* and *The Gates of New Life* by James Stewart.

Messrs. James Clarke & Co. Ltd. and Lutterworth Press for quotations from *This Desirable Property* by Stuart Jackman, from *By Searching* by Isobel Kuhn, and from *Christian Resources* by G. Johnstone Jeffrey.

Messrs. William Collins, Sons & Co. Ltd. for extracts from *Dying We Live* and *Naught for Your Comfort* by Trevor Huddleston; from *Jesus Rediscovered, Muggeridge through the Microphone* and *Something Beautiful for God* by Malcolm Muggeridge; from *Miracle on the River Kwai* by Ernest Gordon; from *Letters and Papers from Prison* by Dietrich Bonhoeffer; from *Prayers for Young People* and *Ethics in a Permissive Society* by William Barclay; from *The Lost Footsteps* by Silviu Craciunas; from *The Wayside Chapel* by Ted Noffs; from *The Authority of the Bible* by C. H. Dodd; from *The Need to Believe* by Murdo Ewen Macdonald; from *Breakthrough* by Alan Walker; from *Mere Christianity, Surprised by Joy* and *Miracles* by C. S. Lewis; from *Making Men Whole* by J. B. Phillips; from *The New Testament in Modern English* translated by J. B. Phillips; from *God's Frozen People* by Mark Gibbs and T. Ralph Morton.

365

Acknowledgements

Rev. Frank Cooke, Purley and Andover Christian Trust, for extract from his book *Jesus Rules OK* (published by Henry E. Walter Ltd.).

For quotations taken from *Enfolded in Love* edited by Robert Llewellyn, published and copyright 1980 by Messrs. Darton, Longman & Todd Ltd., London, and used by permission of the publishers.

The Billy Graham Evangelistic Association for poem by William Alfred Pratney and for extract from article *Night of Nights* by Dr. Billy Graham, taken from Decision Magazine (February 1970 and December 1971 respectively). All rights reserved; used by permission.

Messrs. Andre Deutsch Ltd. for permission to use the poem *Twelfth Night* from *My Many Coated Man* (1955) by Laurie Lee.

The former Drummond Press for sermon quotation from *The Word for All Seasons* by William Yule (edited by Rev. John Birkbeck, M.C.).

The Epworth Press for quotation from *The Pattern of Prayer* by W. E. Sangster and Leslie Davison, and, together with Rev. Dr. Colin Morris, for quotations from the latter's book *Include Me Out.*

Messrs. Faber & Faber Ltd. for quotations from *Markings* by Dag Hammarskjöld, translated by W. H. Auden and Leif Sjöberg, also the poem *Journey of the Magi* from the Collected Poems of T. S. Eliot, 1909-1962.

Messrs. Gill & Macmillan Ltd. for extracts from *Prayers of Life* and *The Christian Response* by Michel Quoist.

Messrs. Victor Gollancz Ltd. for quotation by Rabbi Yaakov Yitzhak of Lublin, mentioned in *The New Year of Grace* by Victor Gollancz, and for extract from *The Man Born to be King* by Dorothy L. Sayers.

Rev. A. M. Gunn, Aberfeldy, for prayer from his notes on *Thinking and Praying.*

Extracts from *Beyond Our Selves* by Catherine Marshall reprinted by permission of Messrs. William Heinemann Ltd.

Edward England Books (Highland Books Division) for quotations by Reginald East and Bert Jordan in *We Believe in Healing.*

Messrs. Hodder & Stoughton Ltd. for extracts from *God's Smuggler* by Brother Andrew; *You Must Be Joking* by Michael Green; *The Helper* by Catherine Marshall; *Rich Christians in an Age of Hunger* by Ronald J. Sider; *A Faith to Proclaim* and *The Wind of the Spirit* by James S. Stewart; *We the Crucifiers* by G. W. Target; *Robert the Bruce: Price of the King's Peace* by Nigel Tranter; *Faith for the Future* by Colin Urquhart; *A Severe Mercy* by Sheldon Vanauken; *Modern Miracles* by Jack Winslow; also, together with the Salvation Army, for quotations from *The Soldier's Armoury;* also as

Acknowledgements

publishers of the works of G. A. Studdert Kennedy for quotations from *The Best of G. A. Studdert Kennedy* and for the poem *The Unutterable Beauty* from the book of that name; also, together with Rev. Dr. Colin Morris, for quotation from Dr. Morris's *Mankind My Church*.

Rev. David Howell, warden, The Church's Ministry of Healing, Crowhurst, Sussex, for permission to include the poem *The Sentry* by F. A. Jenkins in the latter's booklet *Rough Hewn*.

Inter-Varsity Press for extracts from *Take My Life, Consistent Christianity* and *Cinderella with Amnesia* by Michael Griffiths; also from *The Stewardship of Money* by Fred Mitchell.

Messrs. Arthur James Ltd. for quotations from *God Calling*, edited by A. J. Russell, and *Coping with Life* by Hugh O. Douglas.

Excerpts from *Midstream* by Helen Keller. Copyright © 1929 by Helen Keller and Crowell Publishing Company. Reprinted by permission of Doubleday, a division of Bantam, Doubleday, Dell Publishing Group Inc.

The estate of Martin Luther King Jr. for quotation from *Strength to Love* (publishers Messrs. Hodder & Stoughton Ltd.)

Kingsway Publications Ltd. for extracts from *At Break of Day* by Fred Mitchell and (as British publishers) from *Moving on in the Spirit* by Dennis Bennett.

The Editor of *Leadership Today* magazine for anonymous poem quoted in article by Clive Calver, August 1987.

The Leprosy Mission, 50 Portland Place, London W1, for quotations *Without the Camp* by W. R. McKeown, Secretary for Australia, in the Mission's Quarterly Magazine, summer 1970, and by Eddie Askew, International Director, from meditations and prayers, *Disguises of Love*.

The Editor of the Church of Scotland's monthly magazine *Life and Work* for the poem *Days* by Doris G. Cox, also, along with him, Rev. Dr. Horace Walker and Rev. Norman M. Bowman for contributions of theirs to the magazine.

Longman Group UK Ltd. for quotation from *Personal Religion and the Life of Fellowship* by William Temple.

Messrs. Macmillan Ltd., London and Basingstoke, for quotations from *Gitanjali* and *Sadhana* by Rabindranath Tagore and from *Readings from St. John's Gospel* by William Temple.

Messrs. Marshall Pickering for extracts from *A Step Further* by Joni Eareckson and Steve Estes; also from *Selected to Live* by Johanna-Ruth Dobschiner and *The Cross and the Switchblade* by David Wilkerson.

Acknowledgements

The Methodist Church, Division of Education and Youth, for prayer by Godfrey S. Pain from his book *Youth at Worship.*

Mrs. Rhena Schweitzer Miller for quotation from *The Quest for the Historical Jesus* by her father Albert Schweitzer.

Mrs. Esther Russell and Rev. Hubert Mitchell for poem *Has God Been Here?* by their father Andrew E. Mitchell.

Messrs. John Murray (Publishers) Ltd. for quotations from *The Faith of Edward Wilson* by George Seaver.

The National Adult School Organisation for verse of the hymn *I feel the winds of God today* by Jessie Adams.

Messrs. James Nisbet & Co. Ltd. for extract from *The Healing Cross* by H. H. Farmer.

The poem *Cancer Ward* by Mary Dickinson, reproduced by kind permission of Nursing Times. This poem first appeared in Nursing Mirror on 7th February, 1964.

The following, reprinted by permission of Oxford University Press: poem *Dark and Cold We May Be* from *A Sleep of Prisoners* by Christopher Fry; two extracts from *Invitation to Pilgrimage* and three prayers from *A Diary of Private Prayer* by John Baillie; for the hymn *Father eternal, ruler of creation* by Laurence Housman (1865-1957).

Extracts from *New English Bible,* second edition © 1970, by permission of Oxford & Cambridge University Presses.

Extracts from the introduction to *The Four Gospels,* translated by E. V. Rieu (Harmondsworth, 1952) reproduced by permission of Penguin Books Ltd.

Mrs. Vera M. Phillips for quotations from *God Our Contemporary, Ring of Truth* and *New Testament Christianity* by J. B. Phillips.

Messrs. Routledge & Kegan Paul Ltd. for extract from *The Family Life of Old People* by Peter Townsend.

Extracts from *Holy Common Sense* by David H. C. Read, from *What I Believe* by R. Leonard Small, and from *Suffering Man, Loving God* by James Martin, reproduced by kind permission of The Saint Andrew Press, Edinburgh.

Rev. P. T. Bisset, warden, St. Ninian's Training and Resource Centre, Crieff, for quotations from the booklets *Why I Believe* and *When Christ Calls* by D. P. Thomson.

Mrs. Mary Sammon for quotation from the sermons of her father-in-law, John H. Sammon.

Acknowledgements

For the poem *When I'm Alone* by Siegfried Sassoon by permission of George Sassoon.

SCM Press Ltd. for quotations from the following: *More Contemporary Prayers* edited by Caryl Micklem; *The Meaning of Prayer* by H. E. Fosdick; *Paul Schneider* by E. H. Robertson; *Crucified and Crowned* by William Barclay; *Discipleship* by Leslie D. Weatherhead; *The Church and the New Order* by William Paton; *The Adventure of Living* by Paul Tournier.

Messrs. Anthony Sheil Associates Ltd. for quotations from *A Labrador Doctor* by Wilfred T. Grenfell.

The Society of Authors as the literary representative of the estate of John Masefield; also of the estate of Richard Le Gallienne; on behalf of the Bernard Shaw estate, and, with Mrs Nicolete Gray, on behalf of the Laurence Binyon estate.

The Society for Promoting Christian Knowledge for extracts from *Whispers of His Power* by Amy Carmichael and from *Amy Carmichael of Dohnavur* by Frank Houghton.

The Father Superior of The Society of St. John the Evangelist for inclusion of the Ascension Day poem on Iona by Father E. D. Sedding, SSJE.

Tear Fund for extracts from *Tear Times* and from a Tear Fund leaflet.

Messrs. Unwin Hyman Ltd. for quotation from *The Small Woman* by Alan Burgess.

Dr. A. D. Weatherhead, Professor A. K. Weatherhead and Mrs L. M. Caunt for extracts from *It Happened in Palestine, His Life and Ours, How Can I Find God? A Shepherd Remembers* and *A Private House of Prayer* by Leslie D. Weatherhead.

Mrs. Mary Whitehouse, CBE, for quotations from her book *Who Does She Think She Is?*

Work (UK) Ltd. for quotations from *World Aflame* by Billy Graham and from *The Taste of New Wine* by Keith Miller, revised and expanded edition, published 1986 by Word Books.